Space and the Postmodern Fantastic in Contemporary Literatu~

C000149446

"This impressive study of the postmodern Fantastic makes a fresh foray into the terrain through its sustained emphasis upon the paradigms of space and place. Its genuinely global reach is especially exciting and, for those readers whose access to literary texts is too often restricted to works written or translated into English, García's insights into the Hispanic writings of José María Merino, Patricia Esteban Erlés, José B. Adolph and others, opens up a particularly rich literary landscape."
—Lucie Armitt, University of Lincoln, UK

Arising from the philosophical conviction that our sense of space plays a direct role in our apprehension and construction of reality (both factual and fictional), this book investigates how conceptions of postmodern space have transformed the history of the impossible in literature. Deeply influenced by the work of Jorge Luis Borges and Julio Cortázar, there has been an unprecedented rise in the number of fantastic texts in which the impossible is bound to space—space not as a scene of action but as an impossible element performing a fantastic transgression within the storyworld. This book conceptualizes and contextualizes this postmodern, fantastic use of space that disrupts the reader's comfortable notion of space as objective reality in favor of the concept of space as socially mediated, constructed and conventional. In an illustration of the transnational nature of this phenomenon, García analyses a varied corpus of the Fantastic in the past four decades from different cultures and languages, merging literary analysis with classical questions of space related to the fields of philosophy, urban studies and anthropology. Texts include authors such as Julio Cortázar (Argentina), John Barth (USA), J. G. Ballard (UK), Jacques Sternberg (Belgium), Fernando Iwasaki (Perú), Juan José Millás (Spain) and Éric Faye (France). This book contributes to Literary Theory and Comparative Literature in the areas of the Fantastic, narratology and Geocriticism and informs the continuing interdisciplinary debate on how human beings make sense of space.

Patricia García is Assistant Professor in the School of Cultures, Languages and Area Studies at the University of Nottingham, UK.

Routledge Interdisciplinary Perspectives on Literature

Space and the Postmodern Fantastic in Contemporary Literature

The Architectural Void

Patricia García

LONDON AND NEW YORK

First published 2015
by Routledge

2 Park Square, Milton Park, Abingdon, Oxfordshire OX14 4RN
711 Third Avenue, New York, NY 10017

Routledge is an imprint of the Taylor & Francis Group, an informa business

First issued in paperback 2018

Library of Congress Cataloging in Publication Data

García, Patricia, 1983-
Space and the postmodern fantastic in contemporary literature : the architectural void / Patricia García.
    pages cm. — (Routledge interdisciplinary perspectives on literature ; 44)
Includes bibliographical references and index.
    1. Space (Architecture) in literature. 2. Postmodernism (Literature)
    3. Fantastic, The, in literature. 4. Geographical perception in literature.
    I. Title.
PN56.S667G37 2015
809'.93384—dc23   2014047684

ISBN: 978-1-138-82422-5 (hbk)
ISBN: 978-1-138-54776-6 (pbk)

Typeset in Sabon
by codeMantra

"A mis padres, por su casa feliz"

Contents

List of Figures

Acknowledgments

There are many people I would like to thank for making this book possible.

First of all, my kindest acknowledgments are for Dr. David Roas (Universidad Autónoma de Barcelona) for his generosity and rigorous academic insight, and for Jean-Philippe Imbert (Dublin City University) for his creative drive and patience during all these years. Without their professional and personal support, this book would certainly have been a much less creative and enriching experience. I also very much value the assistance of Prof. Dale Knickerbocker (East Carolina University) for his helpful feedback regarding this subject of research.

I am also indebted to Dublin City University and the Irish Research Council for trusting this project with funding.

Furthermore, I want to thank all those authors with whom I have been in contact throughout these years, who sometimes even provided me with their original works by email and post. Among these are Jean-Paul Beaumier, David Roas, Cristina Fernández Cubas and Claude-Emmanuelle Yance. In addition, I deeply appreciate the support of authors Ángel Olgoso, Fernando Iwasaki and Jean-Pol Sternberg (as a representative of Jacques Sternberg), film maker Jeremy Clapin and production company Dark Prince for allowing the partial reproduction of the short stories "Los palafitos", "La casa de muñecas", "La Brume" and "La Banlieue", and of captions from the wonderful short film "Skhizein" to illustrate my argument.

I am immensely grateful to all those friends who made research a much less lonely activity. Special thanks go to Adrián Unger for his ability to draw bridges between quantum physics and the everyday world, to Míde Ní Shúilleabháin for being a model reader of my work and to Antonio de Linares for envisaging a light at the end of the tunnel. I also very much appreciate the support of all those friends and family who provided me with a change of scenery, generously offering me their houses in different countries during times of study and writing.

Finally, my most personal thanks go to my parents for their invaluable practical help as private secretaries every time I was in urgent need of references, books or documents (which was very often) and, most importantly, for not expecting anything from this book other than it making me happy.

"Le nid de l'homme, le monde de l'homme, n'est jamais fini. Et l'imagination nous aide à le continuer."

(Gaston Bachelard, *La Poétique de l'espace*)

"En el palacio que imperfectamente exploré, la arquitectura carecía de fin. Abundaban el corredor sin salida, la alta ventana inalcanzable, la aparatosa puerta que daba a una celda o a un pozo, las increíbles escaleras inversas, con los peldaños y la balaustrada hacia abajo."

(Jorge Luis Borges, "El inmortal")

Introduction
The *Arkhitekton*

"No being exists or can exist which is not related to space in some way".
(Isaac Newton)

Jorge Luis Borges once remarked in a conversation with Alifano (1983) that reality needs a centre, a map, a structure; without architecture, there is no universal coherence. Thus, even the labyrinth—a construction designed to confuse man but with a logical architectural form—is nevertheless an image of hope. "Somehow we are saved", said Borges (in Mualem 2012:74), as long as the real can claim 'an architecture'.

With this statement, Borges emphasised the necessity of believing in a constructed (or *constructible*) reality for this reality to be manageable: only then does cosmos escape chaos. This philosophy of reality as potentially constructed by the subjects who inhabit it—a vision far removed from the objective, immutable, positivistic 'real'—sums up the relativist postmodern *Zeitgeist* of which Borges' fictions and essays have been precursors. What is even more interesting is that this idea of a constructed real is not so recent after all: in fact, it can be traced back to the Greek root of the word 'architect' (*arkhitekton*). From the Greek words *arkhe* ("the beginning" or "origin"), *arkhon* ("the ruler") and *tekton* ("builder", "creator of artifice"), one of the multiple meanings of this term represents the origin transformed by the architect into a defined, and thus habitable, space for the human being. By setting boundaries to the world, the architect constructed a space in which man could dwell. The architect in Western civilisation had the power and skill (*tekton*) to manipulate the origin (*arché*) into 'liveable' space. Moreover, the etymology suggests that the action of 'building' can be understood not only as giving material shape to physical space but also as 'raising' reality from the origin, hence the origin of architecture as a divine activity in Western mythology (cf. Azara 2005). This not only advances the foundational idea of reality as a human construction but also asserts the importance of spatiality in human experience: architecture is a structuring principle of reality. John Ruskin captured this beautifully at the opening of *The Poetry of Architecture* with the statement: "no man can be an architect, who is not a metaphysician" (1905:1).

Space—in particular in the ways we articulate it—is a means by which we organise the world. This, in turn, introduces the category of space as a man-made construction. Such an understanding of space represents a radical departure from the tradition that has predominated in Western culture for centuries, whereby space was regarded as a simple container in which the human being dwells: a given, objective and measurable entity, perceptible only in its mathematical dimensions. Space, according to the previous etymological reading of the word 'architect' (and architecture), is constructed by the human for the human.

This book, anchored as it is in a parallel between architecture and literature as arts of building an artificial reality, is born from both an observation and a hypothesis. The observation is that the literary Fantastic—understood here as the incursion of an impossible element into a realistic frame shared by narrator and reader—is not found only in the haunted houses, remote castles and further Gothic enclaves of the late eighteenth and early nineteenth century; neither is it limited to its migration into the city, as occurred at the turn of the nineteenth century with the acceleration of Modernity, nor restricted to appearances in such contemporary spaces as metro stations or airports. There is a modality of the Fantastic which, while first envisaged in a few short stories of the nineteenth century such as "The Fall of the House of Usher" (E. A. Poe 1839) and greatly influenced by the metaphysical Fantastic of Jorge Luis Borges and the everyday Fantastic of Julio Cortázar, is consolidated within the corpus of the last decades. In the texts belonging to this modality, physical space does not provide the frame in which the Fantastic will appear; instead space *is* the Fantastic. Holes that render invisible those who happen upon them, structures that entrap and devour the individual, elastic constructions separated by fluctuating distances, intermittent buildings that disappear and reappear as they please, tunnels that compress distances, compartments that invert the logical order of the big in the small and spaces that suddenly multiply—these are some of the examples of this textual phenomenon. In this modality, the impossible supernatural element *does not take place in space* but is rather *an event of space*, bound to some architectural element or to the (normal, logical) physical laws governing this dimension. Without a doubt, this phenomenon has textual precedents. However, it is only from the late seventies onwards that its presence has been observed within a multitude of cultural and literary traditions. Furthermore, it is in this postmodern context, when the dimension of space has been reevaluated from sociohistorical, scientific, philosophical and literary angles, that this literary phenomenon is most in need of investigation.

The hypothesis, on the other hand, stems from a philosophical concern, one relevant to the linkage between physical space and the weakening experience of reality in the postmodern context. In the following paragraphs, the relevant aspects of this context are outlined in order to illustrate how this assumption took shape.

THE 'SPATIAL TURN' IN POSTMODERNITY

Over the past few decades, a large number of literary scholars (e.g., McHale 1987; Ryan 1991; Álvarez Méndez 2002; Aínsa 2006; Westphal 2007, 2011a) have demonstrated how the reconfiguration in our way of understanding space in the late twentieth century has not only accentuated the significance of narrative space but has also prompted a reconfiguration of the category of the real, which inevitably affects its counterpart, the fictional. This has given birth to a form of literature bearing the label of 'the postmodern'.

The terms 'Postmodernism' and 'Postmodernity' have been the centre of polemic discussion in literary and cultural theories, the first term tending to being employed as an aesthetic movement while the latter is often associated instead with the cultural and historical aspects. For the purpose of this book, this conceptual distinction will be ignored since both aspects are not easily separated one from the other, in particular with interdisciplinary studies. While it is not my intention to contribute to this debate, it may be useful to specify what is to be understood by 'postmodern' in this book and then to apply this definition to the more constricted and relevant frame of the postmodern Fantastic. I will briefly discuss two well-established approaches. McHale in *Postmodernist Fiction* (1987) defines Postmodernism as a shift from the epistemological concern shaping Modernism (How can knowledge be attained?) toward a characteristic ontological one (What is 'real'? What is not 'real'? What is a world? How does a world come into being?). This change of dominant is particularly present within cultural and aesthetic productions from the late sixties until the present day. Lyotard's perspective on the postmodern (1979), in contrast, concentrates on epistemological doubt. His theory of the end of Grand Narratives calls into question the 'truth' of any official and universal discourse. Lyotard's understanding of reality as narrative suggests that subjectivity is inherent in any discourse aimed at legitimising history and other fundamental epistemological constructions of Western culture. Narrative, then, is always an incomplete testimony of reality, and since our means of expressing the real is narrative, all views on reality are necessarily incomplete. The epistemological and ontological dominants are in many cases not easily abstracted from each other, in particular in the case of the postmodern Fantastic; a preoccupation with both *the nature of reality* (leading to a reexamination of the real/fictional) as well as with *our limited means of gaining truth* about reality dominates the themes and plots of the postmodern Fantastic, as the following chapters will show.

Positivist claims of an objective reality that is external to the individual are today tenuous, given that even scientific research has now been proven to be vulnerable to the subject carrying out the research. The major breakthrough originated with Albert Einstein's Theory of Relativity (1905 and

1915), when Einstein demonstrated that time and space were inextricably bound up with one another, redefining the structure of physical reality into a four-dimensional space-time continuum. Space was found to be affected not only by time but also by mass, in particular by the presence of high density mass, causing it to wrap. This was the end of the Newtonian certainty of time and space as absolute, uniform categories, independent of the physical contents of the universe. Newton's perspective, which had dominated the scientific scene for over three hundred years, yielded to the relativist model. Even more influential, from a philosophical point of view, were the later discoveries of quantum mechanics, in particular Heisenberg's Principle of Indeterminacy (1925). As is well known, this principle establishes that at a subatomic level the behaviour of the object being monitored is necessarily impacted by the presence of the observer. This was a definite shift away from positivistic idealism of the nineteenth century, with science now forced to recognise its own limitations and paradoxes.

In consequence, the idea of an attainable, absolute model of knowledge vanished, to be replaced by a view of the real as inevitably deriving from how the subjects in it perceive it. Once more, as in the figure of the *arkhitekton*, the subject regained the ability and responsibility of being the author of his/her own reality.

Relativism was, however, to propagate beyond the realm of physics. Einstein's Nobel Prize formula concerning the equivalence mass-energy was to be a crucial step toward the atomic and digital age. In just a few decades, its repercussions infiltrated everyday life in the form of a technological revolution that deeply affected conceptions of distance and location by, for example, facilitating the transmission of large amounts of information across long distances in a matter of seconds. Parallel to this, phenomena of wide-reaching impact like the atomic bomb accelerated a global consciousness and prompted a redefinition of human geography. The Second World War triggered large volumes of immigration across geopolitical borders, while the Cold War was to see the rapid emergence of a succession of states as well as further geopolitical restructuring, boosted by the fall of the Iron Curtain and the enlargement of the European Union. In the socio-urban domain, the reconstruction of the postwar urban landscape originated a new model of contemporary city (cf. "Postmetropolis", Soja 2000). Simultaneously, in the historical domain, the process of de-colonisation encouraged advocacy for the end of a single centre of reference in favour of a multiplicity of points of view. This concurrence of events was to render it increasingly evident that notions of identity and culture could not be ascribed to a single stable territory. Geography no longer referred only to the physical place in which the human being was located; it also encompassed a variety of dimensions intertwined.

Not only have advances in physics and a series of historical confluences reconfigured our vision and experience of space, they have also given rise to an unprecedented interest in the dimension of space within academic discourses. While never ignoring the fact that we are temporally bound beings, during the past few decades, the so-called Spatial Turn in the Humanities and Social Sciences has increasingly emphasised the importance of spatiality in understanding the history of the human being and of its artistic products. In a famous conference in 1967 entitled "Des Espaces Autres", Michel Foucault predicted that we were entering an era in which thinking in spatial terms would be key to understanding the increasing prominence of the simultaneous and the juxtaposed. The Spatial Turn has ensured that space—a physical and architectonic dimension, but also an intimate (Bachelard 1958), social (Lefebvre 1974; De Certeau 1980; Augé 1992), political (Foucault 1967), urban (Soja 1989), sexual (Massey 1994), cultural (Jameson 1990) and economic (Harvey 1990) category—is no longer a neutral concept and cannot be considered independent from that which it contains, and therefore neither can it be considered as immune to historical, political and aesthetic changes. Whereas from a mathematical perspective space is a relatively stable category, from a humanist angle space is a category with a history. Proof of this lies in the diverse ways in which space was conceived of throughout Antiquity, the Middle Ages, the Renaissance, Modernity or Postmodernity, as well as in the different paradigms of space in philosophy (e.g., the approximations by Aristotle, Leibniz, Kant or Heidegger) and in the history of physics (e.g., the theories of Newton and Einstein). What is more, as Jammer (1954) and Disalle (2006) have shown, even the objective concept of space in physics has evolved in tandem with these diverse philosophical propositions; and as such the study of space has been reasserted in human science as a scholarly field requiring and creating connections across disciplines.

In the domain of literature, the relatively recent interest in the spatial dimension in Literary Theory breaks from a tradition that prioritised time over space. This primacy of the temporal was to a large extent due to the generic distinction between spatial and temporal arts. Lessing's influential essay "Laocoon: or the Limits of Poetry and Painting" (1766) was one of the pioneer essays in positioning literature within the temporal. From this perspective, the literary text is conceived of as a succession of words, sounds and events while, for example, sculpture or painting instead offers objects juxtaposed in space and simultaneously apprehended. Space in narratives often seemed to have no further function than to supply a general background for the action.

This restriction has been challenged since the middle of the twentieth century as manifold contributions have convincingly argued that the selected, described, represented and symbolised spaces are of central value to literary analysis (e.g., Mikhail Bakthin's chronotope [1975], Franco Moretti's literary cartographies [1998, 2005], Marie-Laure Ryan's cognitive approach to narrative [1991, 1993], Bertrand Westphal's geocritical method [2007] and Robert Tally's interdisciplinary summary on human spatiality [2013]).

However, it appears that this Spatial Turn in Literary Theory is not yet consolidated in the scholarship of the Fantastic. On the one hand, existing methodologies on space in narrative (Hamon 1972; Ronen 1986; Soubey-roux 1993; Pimentel 2001; Álvarez Méndez 2002) traditionally centre their approaches on realist literatures. The Fantastic, if mentioned at all, appears as an ambiguous category and very often refers to any form of supernatural intervention. The result is that there is no comprehensive model for analys-ing space in relation to the Fantastic ('Fantastic' considered as a particular narrative form and not as a meta-category for the imaginary or supernatu-ral; see Chapter 1).

On the other hand, while there are plenty of studies in which 'fantastic space' acts as a metaphor for a large variety of aspects—such as the trans-gression of literary genres, the unconscious or the confrontation with the domain of the other—the list of studies focusing on space as physical dimen-sion recreated in the fantastic text is extremely limited. Campra (2001) and Roas (2011) remind us of the central function that the dimension of space occupies within the literature of the Fantastic: spatial references and detailed descriptions of places are key devices that enable the reader to identify with the space that is presented as realistic. That allows for the generation of the impression of verisimilitude required prior to the fantastic transgression. As regards space as theme, the spatial category is present from the foundational studies by Castex (1951), Caillois (1975) and Todorov (1975). However, even in these works, space appears bound to time in one interdependent category, forming the cluster of "space-time distortions". Following on from this intellectual move toward exploring the intersection between time and space, some more recent studies (Aguirre 1990; Fournier Kiss 2007) have identified the thematic potential of settings. Such studies emphasise the chronotopic nature of certain settings and analyse the evolution of the Fan-tastic according to the function and symbolism of these settings. However, is narrative space to be limited to those referential or chronotopic values? What new perspectives can be obtained by foregrounding spatiality in the fantastic text? This book, dedicated to exploring the linkage between the Fantastic and space in the postmodern context, has been inspired by these questions.

THE POSTMODERN FANTASTIC AS A PHENOMENON OF SPACE

The production of a large volume of texts questioning the objective nature of reality has given rise to a specific form that has been labelled as 'postmod-ern Fantastic' (Grossman 2000; Horstkotte 2004; Roas 2011). With Jorge Luis Borges and, subsequently, Julio Cortázar as founding fathers, the post-modern Fantastic was to consolidate across different literary traditions from the 1970s onward. What gives coherence to the texts that fall under this category is the following: although the impossible element still operates in a presumed 'reality' shared by both narrator and reader, this reality is revealed as chronically unstable and weak, as a construction marked by codes of routine and social conventions. This ontological weakening materialises in the form of specific, recurrent traits. While the next chapters will explore the question in more detail, it is useful here to consider a few examples that illustrate these traits. A very clear example is the reaction of the protagonists toward the supernatural. The postmodern protagonist often reacts with very little surprise or consternation, in sharp contrast to the terrified characters found in the Fantastic of Hoffmann, Poe or Maupassant. In the postmodern Fantastic, more often than not, the character confronted with the supernatural event accepts the Impossible with resignation, in a natural manner, as just one of the many oddities of this eccentric world in which he/she lives.

It is important to emphasise that the postmodern Fantastic, just as is the case with the Postmodern more generally, is not a radical break from the tradition of the Fantastic founded in the eighteenth and nineteenth centuries. I am therefore inclined to avoid the term 'neofantastic' (Alazraki 1983), which appears to have left an imprint within the current academic scene, as it does not seem to reflect this continuity. As the analysis offered by this book will show, the postmodern Fantastic not only incorporates new motifs but also integrates traditional motifs, though with a distinct renovating impulse.

The banalisation of the fantastic event is often accompanied in the Fantastic by another typically postmodern literary technique: that of metafiction. The prevalence of this technique can be explained in relation to the Language Turn, which saw a growing distrust of the ability of language to refer to reality. Once again, a fundamental precursor of this model of the Fantastic can be found in the fiction of Borges, for example in his use of intertextuality to question the notions of originality, authenticity, truth and of reality, a paradigmatic example being "Tlön, Uqbar, Orbis Tertius" (1961).

The critical attention paid by scholars of the Fantastic to the Linguistic Turn and the contrast with the lack of attention given to the Spatial Turn led me to formulate the following questions:

Just as the Linguistic Turn profoundly affected the Fantastic in terms of themes, motifs and plot structures ("the Fantastic of Language", Erdal Jordan 1998; Campra 2001; Casas 2010; Rodríguez 2010), could a similar role not be attributed to the Spatial Turn? Does space—shown to be a fundamental category of human experience of reality as well as a tool for conveying the impression of textual realism—not act as a vehicle to reflect this turn in an aesthetic form? And if so, in what way?

These questions are as yet unexplored within the critical corpus of the Fantastic. Over the last few decades, there has been an unprecedented rise in the number of short stories in which the impossible element is bound to space: space not as the scene of actions but as the impossible element in the story. This transgression of space disrupts the comforting notion of space as objective entity in favour of the idea of space as constructed and conventional. Conceptualising and contextualising this phenomenon is the main aim of this book.

THE POSTMODERN FANTASTIC AS A COMPARATIVE FANTASTIC

A fundamental factor in deciding on a comparative angle was the realisation that the phenomenon of spatial transgression relegated the cultural markers of each literary tradition to a secondary position. Paradoxically, it was of little importance whether a text belonged to the French, Spanish, Peruvian or Belgium Fantastic, as many texts showed thematic and structural parallels beyond their national origin. This demonstrated a shift from the interest in 'place' (understood as a sociocultural location) toward a preoccupation with 'space' (understood as a global physical dimension). In contrast, however, very few studies are dedicated to the Fantastic across national and disciplinary borders. Furthermore, studies on the contemporary fantastic are scant, with a few exceptions (Horstkotte 2004; Grossman 2004). What could the reasons be? Perhaps the lack of available translations or the uneven quality of many of the literary works published in the past few decades might have discouraged scholars from embracing a more diverse corpus focused on a literary phenomenon and not limited by geographical borders.

The primary methodological principle when writing this book was to overcome these limitations and examine texts from diverse sociocultural traditions. The works chosen here encompass foundational traditions of the Fantastic, such as the French and British, as well as those of the more modern emergence, as seen in the Quebecois and Spanish texts. The analysis seeks to strike a balance between canonical French, Spanish or English-speaking authors—such as H. P. Lovecraft, J. L. Borges, Julio Cortázar, J. G. Ballard, John Barth, José B. Adolph, Jacques Sternberg, José María Merino, Juan José Millás and Cristina Fernández Cubas—and emerging voices of this narrative form, such as Peruvian Fernando Iwasaki, French writer Éric Faye, Quebecois Claude-Emmanuelle Yance, Jean-Paul Beaumier and Spanish authors Ángel Olgoso, José-Ferrer Bermejo, David Roas and Patricia Esteban Erlés. All these authors are well-established writers of the Fantastic in their own countries but less well-known internationally (very often due to the lack of translations). My goal has been to bring these different traditions of the Fantastic together under the lens of spatiality. Each chapter concentrates on three or four texts taken as paradigmatic for the phenomenon I am seeking to conceptualise. In this manner, and in order to emphasise the thematic convergences within the specific frame of the postmodern Fantastic, national divergences have not been prioritised in the analysis.

***

The first chapter is of a theoretical-conceptual nature. It examines different approaches to the Fantastic, from the foundational (e.g., Todorov 1975) to more recent approaches (e.g., Roas 2012). It also offers a conceptual distinction between what I label 'the Fantastic of Place' (where the impossible happens in space) and 'the Fantastic of Space' (where the impossible element is spatial). This latter concept is the leitmotif of the next four chapters.

Returning to the initial metaphor of reality as 'an architecture', fictional reality is conceived here as an architectural object. In this 'architext' (expropriating Genette's play on words, 1979), the author founds a reality and erects a world with rhetorical tools, and the reader recreates this world in the act of reading. Paralleling narrative with an architectural creation, the following categories are four basic spatial 'stages' in the architectural configuration of any literary world and coincide with the basic philosophical and architectural categories of human space:

To start with, the writer—like the *arkhitekton*—creates a space for the characters and other objects. Each occupies a position, a place where every material object of this storyworld 'is'. The dimension of space is inextricably related to that of body and subject for the very simple reason that subjects need a physical space in which to be. When transferred to the fictional world, this means that characters need narrative space in which to exist. Therefore, Chapter 2 [*BODY: (Not) Being in Space*] is dedicated to exploring the relationship between body and space, since the body is the referential axis through which the subject establishes distances between himself and his surroundings. This principle is central to the phenomenology of perception proposed by Maurice Merleau-Ponty (1945), which inspired an entire current of architectural thought. By also drawing from the spatial philosophy of Martin Heidegger (1951), this chapter combines the notion of physical position—in the textual world, corresponding to the emplacement of the character's body—with its existential dimension. To analyse how this relationship is transgressed, I refer to Frederic Jameson's (1991) and Anthony Vidler's (1991) analyses of postmodern architectural space as a weakening of the corporeal and existential experience. The resulting textual transgressions of bodies in space are therefore literal 'dis-locations' that lead to diverse modalities of subjects forced to redefine themselves in relation to their exceptional—fantastic—position in space.

Second, the architect-writer also needs to furnish the world; or to erect 'paper monuments', to use Philippe Hamon's expression (1992). To differentiate, partition and distribute these elements, a system of defining spatial frames is established. The notion of 'boundary' is a fundamental referential element in constructing an articulated, realistic environment. As anthropology of space reminds us, the *limes* was one of the first principles through which primitive civilisations identified their space as their world. Chapter 3 (*BOUNDARY: Liquid Constructions*) is dedicated to transgressions of physical boundaries that define objects and buildings and the distances between them. In the context of the postmodern, this phenomenon ties in with what the architects Paul Virilio (1991) and Bernard Tschumi (1996) refer to as the 'liquefaction' of the postmodern built-environment. Several analogies will be noted between this notion of architectural 'liquefaction' and the examined textual spaces.

Third, the elements in this textual world also need to be distributed into hierarchical levels. Just as the principle of hierarchy in architecture defines interlocking components, so too do the writer's architectural skills establish how the different spaces relate to each other as container and contained, part and whole: an object into a room; a room into a house; a house on a street, etc. The disruption of this apparently simple hierarchical logic is the subject of Chapter 4 (*HIERARCHY: Spaces Inside-Out*). Since they have been widely analysed in postmodern literary criticism, the strategies of metafiction and metalepsis (disruption of fictional levels) are left aside here in order to focus on how transgressions of architectural hierarchies, including the interplay between referent and replica, bring the notion of referentiality to the fore.

Fourth space as configured by the architect-writer encompasses a set of rules establishing how the components relate to each other. In its fullest sense, this space is a textual world conceived by characters as their reality. Drawing critically from Possible Worlds Theory, Chapter 5 (*WORLD: Ontological Plurality*) is centered on the transgression of the scheme of the one single, referential 'world' typically found in realistic texts.

Chapter 1 is a revised and extended version of earlier efforts published separately in *Revista Letras&Letras* (2012) and *Brumal: Research Journal on the Fantastic* (2013b). The concept of the 'threshold sentence' in Chapter 4 initially appeared in the volume *Visiones de lo fantástico: aproximaciones teóricas* (2013a). Finally, the study on "Los palafitos" in Chapter 5 is a revised and extended version of the essay "El espacio como sujeto fantástico: el ejemplo de 'Los palafitos'" published in *Pasavento: Revista de Estudios Hispánicos* (2013c).

The challenge when writing this book was to avoid lists of isolated spatial metaphors and recurrent settings within the postmodern Fantastic. Neither did I want to provide a catalogue of impossible topologies. Instead, this work started as an exercise of abstraction to determine forms in which reality and space (factual and fictional) are codependent. In this way, the reverse task could also be carried out: identifying how space could transgress the impression of realism. As a result, these four suggested themes not only affect large numbers of narratives—thus broadening their applicability beyond the texts quoted—but, more importantly, they also embrace and provide a structure for derivative transgressions such as physical disappearance in space or of spaces, animations of buildings or alterations of distances, volumes and dimensions.

These chapters are neither mutually exclusive nor do they present a complete and finalised model for the topic at stake. Claiming that this structure covers the composition of human spatiality entirely would be a philosophical imposture; a limited number of abstract categories cannot resolve the complex nature of human space and its relationship with textual models of reality. Nevertheless, conscious of these limitations, I have wanted in this book to create a comprehensive systematisation of the relevance of literary space in order to construct and thus to transgress narrative realism. By being distinct and yet complementary, 'body', 'boundary', 'hierarchy' and 'word' provide coherence and multiple points of connection.

What role do fictional spaces have in our construction of experience and understanding of the world? What is our conception of postmodern space? How does literature mediate in this conception? How have different ideas of space nurtured different fantastic traditions, and how is this present in the postmodern Fantastic? What perspective on human spatiality does the literary Fantastic provide that is not provided by any other artistic form? These are the questions that haunt this book and, in order to explore them, I delve into literary analysis as well as into classical questions of space as appertaining to the fields of philosophy, urban studies and anthropology. Consequently, those anthropologists, sociologists and philosophers concerned with the dialogue between space and transgression, and between space and reality, might find some inspiration in the following chapters. It might also appeal to those interested in how we understand, perceive and artistically interpret human spatiality in the postmodern context.

Finally, a small note on the chosen title. If architecture in the etymological sense is a foundation, a construction of a reality, 'the Architectural Void' seemed an appropriate metaphor for the phenomenon that this book seeks to systematise. The dimension of space in the following fantastic texts fails to provide reference, structure and meaning. On the contrary, space becomes a-referential, a-structural, illogical and disorienting: it weakens the impression of a consistent reality. Therefore, by transgressing the constructed realism within the text, all the examined spatial transgressions have one aspect in common: they attempt to unmask the frail foundations that we humans, precarious architects of our world, have laid to find orientation in our so-called reality.

1 The Fantastic of Place and the Fantastic of Space

"Le normal a des limites, l'anormal n'en a pas"

(Michel de Ghelderode)

1. DEFINING THE FANTASTIC

What exactly is the Fantastic? A much-disputed term, in literary criticism as well as in popular culture, the Fantastic has acquired a number of connotations and is used both loosely and restrictively. The lack of consensus as to what it implies requires a brief outline of its diverse definitions in order to define the boundaries of this book. From the large list of studies seeking to define the Fantastic, two lines of thought can be distinguished:

Fantastic = The Supernatural

The first line of thought is promoted by a group of scholars (Rabkin 1977, 1979; Hume 1984; Cornwell 1990; Attebery 1992; Armitt 1996; Gomel 2014 and in general the International Association of the Fantastic in the Arts in the US) who do not regard the Fantastic to be a specific narrative form distinct from other literary manifestations of the supernatural. Instead, in this approach, the term is often employed interchangeably with that of 'fantasy literature' to refer to any texts that "deviate from [that which is considered] consensus reality" (Hume 1984:21). From this perspective, fantastic literature is considered as contrasting with realistic or 'mimetic' literature. Their label embraces a variety of forms including fantasy, horror, the Gothic, fables, the Marvellous, science fiction, fairy tales and myths.

This approach to the Fantastic as an umbrella term for the supernatural presents various problems. First, if the presence of the supernatural is sufficient qualification for a text to belong to the Fantastic—the supernatural being a synonym in such case for the Fantastic—then the result would be a corpus so large in extent and wide in scope that the component works would bear very little in common at the level of structures, themes and effect. The Fantastic by this definition would embrace such diverse texts as *The Odyssey*, *Hamlet*, Hans Christian Andersen's fairy tales, *Dracula* or

One Hundred Years of Solitude. This aspect was already remarked on by Todorov, who argued for a more precise understanding of the Fantastic in his work *The Fantastic: a Structural Approach to a Literary Genre* (1970):

> We cannot conceive a genre which would regroup all works in which the supernatural intervenes and which would thereby have to accommodate Homer as well as Shakespeare, Cervantes as well as Goethe. The supernatural does not characterise works closely enough, its extension is much too great. (1975:34)

Second, the opposition between realist/non-realist, or mimetic/non-mimetic, is not sufficient to distinguish different forms of literature. All fiction could be regarded as mimetic; this does not imply that a literary text is a faithful imitation of the factual world but rather that a literary world is never completely disengaged from our extratextual world (thus, it is never non-mimetic). Even the fantasy worlds of *Lord of the Rings* (J. R. Tolkien 1949) are mimetic in the sense that they derive from the factual world of the author and reader. At the same time, all literary texts could also be regarded as 'non-mimetic' in the sense that a literary text is always imaginary: no matter how loyal a literary world is to the extratextual referent, all—even realistic texts—are a fictional invention. In literature, there is always, as Doležel puts it, "a bidirectional exchange, [with a textual world] with 'material' drawn from actuality, [while] in the opposite direction, fictional constructs deeply influence our imaging and understanding of reality" (2008: prologue, x). Therefore, the mimetic/non-mimetic opposition is not an infallible tool to employ when aiming for a definition of the Fantastic. Every literary text generates a fictional world, with a basis both in factual reality and in invented elements.

Third, this umbrella definition seems to take for granted that the idea of 'reality' is a stable and thus context-independent entity. However, is 'reality' really an objective category? The very idea of 'reality' is a paradigm with a shifting history; so much ink has been spent exploring how 'reality' has changed over successive historical periods under the guise of different aesthetic, scientific, philosophical paradigms. To mention just one example, over the past few decades, research has highlighted the fact that we have shifted from the certainties of reality as being a stable and objective category toward an understanding of the concept as a negotiated social construction:

> [...] a kind of collective fiction, constructed and sustained by the processes of socialisation, institutionalisation, and everyday social interaction, especially through the medium of language. [...] an arbitrary convention given the appearance of permanence and validity through time and habit.
>
> (Berger & Luckman 1967:37–40)

This point, central to postmodern thought and argued by sociologists Peter L. Berger and Thomas Luckmann among others, is a key inspiration of this book. Any theorisation of the Fantastic forces a reflection on what is considered to be 'real' in a particular time period. "Presenting that which cannot be but *is*", proclaims Jackson, the Fantastic "exposes a culture's definition of that which can be: it traces the limits of its epistemological and ontological frame" (1981:23). This important consideration opens up a second angle on the Fantastic, which in turn has, for the reasons detailed below, informed the perspective endorsed here.

The Fantastic as *One* of the Supernatural Modes

A more focused perspective of the Fantastic enables a more precise examination of the genesis and evolution of its narrative form. As a large number of scholars of the Fantastic have reiterated (e.g., Castex 1951; Campra 2001; Roas 2001, 2011), the categories of realism and fantastic have a history. Our modern understanding of 'real' and 'impossible' began to be forged in the Enlightenment. The Impossible as an ontological (and literary) category appears in a rationalistic context where miracles and prodigies are largely eliminated as possible explanations of reality. In contrast, in the mid-eighteenth century a substantial body of literary work was produced "as a compensation of an excess of rationalism" (Caillois 1975:23). It is this sociohistorical moment that marks the genesis of the Fantastic, which initially shared roots with the Gothic English novel, for example as in Horace Walpole's *The Castle of Otranto* (1764) and Jan Potocki's *Manuscrit trouvé à Saragosse* (1794–1810). In an increasingly secularised and rational society, the entry of the Fantastic into the literary sphere served to interrogate those aspects that science and reason could not answer. Using the same techniques as employed in realistic literature (e.g., realistic settings and devices to enhance the verisimilitude of the narration), the narratives of the Fantastic sought to destabilise the presuppositions of positivism (see Roas 2003:10–15). E. T. A. Hoffmann's *Fantasiestücke* and *Nachtstücke* (1814–1816), Mary Shelley's *Frankenstein* (1818), Edgar Allan Poe's *Tales of the Grotesque and Arabesque* (1840), Guy de Maupassant's short stories and Bram Stoker's *Dracula* (1897) are among some of the most well-known works that played a fundamental role in the consolidation of this narrative form.

Based on this historical angle, and in contrast to the all-inclusive perspective, a more restrictive approach to the Fantastic—with specific features and a determined historical starting point—has been to the fore in Europe as well as in South America. The key role that the French critical school played in this grounding of the Fantastic is notable; with the publication of the French translation of Hoffmann's *Fantasiestücke* (*Fantasy Pieces*) as *Contes fantastiques* ("Fantastic Tales", Loeve-Veimras 1829), the term *fantastique* entered the French critical scene. The term later became systematised in French literary theory through its use by various scholars, who concentrated

on its history (Castex 1951), themes (Vax 1960, 1965; Caillois 1975), structures (Todorov 1975) and sociocultural context (Bessière 1974). All of them
have proportioned theories reclaiming the specificity of the Fantastic in relation to the supernatural—this specificity, on the other hand, has been rather
ignored in English-speaking countries, one of the major examples being the
International Association of the Fantastic in the Arts. Vax gives the example
of the multiple shapes of the revenant: is Christ's resurrection perceived with
the same astonishment and fear as a vampire?, he wonders. This distinction
leads him to establish that the supernatural motif in itself is not enough to
define the Fantastic: "It is not the motif which makes the Fantastic, it is the
Fantastic that which develops from the motif" (Vax 1965:61).[1]

One of the crucial defenders of a restrictive approach to the Fantastic
was Tzvetan Todorov. His theory is based on the premise that the Fantastic
is different to other modes of the supernatural: it creates a moment of hesitation on the part of the reader, a moment between the acceptance of the
supernatural as possible within the fictional universe and the denial of this
possibility:

> The person who experiences the event must opt for one of two pos-
> sible solutions: either he is a victim of an illusion of the senses, of a
> product of the imagination—and laws of the world remain what they
> are; or else the event has indeed taken place, it is an integral part of
> reality—but then this reality is controlled by forces unknown to us.
> The [F]antastic occupies the duration of this uncertainty.
>
> (Todorov 1975:25)

In this respect, the Fantastic occupies a space between a realistic and a
marvellous text while being neither one nor the other. The problem, as
later considered by literary criticism of the Fantastic, lies in the fact that
this definition of the Fantastic as a 'moment of suspension' is of very little use in understanding the functioning of the form: the Fantastic seems
to be a genre defined by its neighbouring genres. Furthermore, while the
premise of the Fantastic as hesitation is applicable to a particular type
of the Fantastic that is based on an ambiguous denouement (Henry
James's *The Turn of the Screw*, for example), it does not encompass other
canonical works in which the supernatural is perceived and presented as
impossible. The characters of Count Dracula and Dr. Frankenstein's monster are neither rationalised with a logical explanation nor do they fall
within a magical universe.

Todorov's theory, however, is still applicable to one of the many forms of
the Fantastic, namely the 'ambiguous Fantastic'. After Todorov's study, a large
and varied number of theoreticians of the Fantastic have provided revised
theories on the Fantastic, but they all coincide in one aspect: Bessière (1974),
Jackson (1981), Erdal Jordan (1998), Campra (2001), Roas (2001, 2011)
or Bozzetto (2005), to name but a few, regard the Fantastic as a *conflictive*

opposition between the natural and the supernatural: the Fantastic arises in a realistic world in which the supernatural itself is not integrated as a natural law but is instead a disruption of this realistic environment. There first needs to be a textual reality similar to ours in order for it to be transgressed by the Fantastic; only then can the supernatural be conceived as impossible. The Fantastic is thus the only literary form in which the supernatural element is presented as impossible within the text. It provokes a disruptive effect in the implied reader, forcing him or her to revise (metaphorically speaking) his assumptions on empirical reality.

Following this train of thought, the Fantastic is understood in this book to be a transgression of the realistic environment of the story. Verisimilitude is thus a premise of the Fantastic. The Fantastic is fundamentally a transgression of what Roland Barthes calls the "effect of realism" (1968). This has led some scholars to refer to this transgression as an effect (the "fantastic effect", see Roas 2001; 2011). The fantastic text must rely on the assumption of a 'real' world, on what we understand as 'reality', codified by our laws of reason and social conventions. Several literary devices are employed to convey this impression of veracity or authenticity, one of these being the use of spatial markers in descriptions and of real spatial referents. Because it is presented as an exception within the textual reality and thus disrupts the logic that rules that storyworld, the fantastic element or event always generates a conflict. This contrasts with other literary forms in which the supernatural is an accepted part of the codes ruling the storyworld. Therefore, this approach to the Fantastic makes it possible to exclude utopic, dystopic or fantasy architecture like the Land of Oz, Narnia or Middle-Earth from its scope and many of the examples mentioned by Elana Gomel in her study on space and literatures of the supernatural (2014).

As an exception within a realistic frame, the Fantastic's questioning of the 'real' operates negatively. As Campra puts it: "while for the 'real' an autonomy is postulated, the concept of 'fantastic' is uniquely defined in negative: it is that which is not" (2001:154). This coincides with Jackson's "negative rationality", where the Fantastic is conceptualised only "by negative terms according to the categories of realism: im-possible, un-real, name-less, form-less, un-known, in-visible" (1981:21), and with Reisz's observation that "when confronting the fantastic events within the parameters provided by factual reality, the reader states its incompatibility" (2001:7).

2. GEOCRITICISM AND THE FANTASTIC: A METHOD

When establishing a typology of transgressions of space in the Fantastic, the method of textual analysis will need to embrace narrative space in all its complexity. Existing methodologies on space in narrative offer limited means of carrying out such a study. They tend to centre their approaches on realist literatures (e.g., Hamon 1972, Ronen 1986, Soubeyroux 1993,

Pimentel 2001, Álvarez Méndez 2002 and Tally 2013). Nevertheless, they have inspired the method of text analysis I propose in this book, which is anchored on two premises:

(a) Narrative space is a sign (Álvarez Méndez 2002). No matter how faithful it is to its referent, narrative space is always fictional, created through various textual strategies and recreated by the reader when presented with it. A place, once it enters a narrative universe of a book, too becomes a sign. Space is an element of the many in a fictional structure based on four dimensions of what Álvarez Méndez calls the 'spatial sign': the situational (space as referent), the rhetorical (space as signifier), the semantic-actant (space as signified, with agency to influence events narrated in the plot) and the pragmatic (the space of the act of reading).

(b) The representation and function of narrative space should not be examined only at the textual level; the extratextual context also plays a fundamental role. As will be shown, the four examined transgressions of space in the Fantastic (Chapters 2 to 4) are tropes of particular recurrence and significance in the postmodern context. These can be regarded as 'symptoms' of this sociocultural era. It is evident, therefore, that interdisciplinary approaches are necessary for dealing with narrative spaces in general but more so with postmodern spatiality.

Returning to the idea of a socially and historically constructed 'reality', evolutions of the notion of 'reality' will materialise in the literary text as the next chapters will show. Literature can be a powerful element in revealing the fissures of the thought system (or world-view construction) that predominates in any given era (cf. Iser 1978a/b). Since it reveals the artificiality of this constructed model of reality through the irruption of the Impossible, the Fantastic is a particularly excellent means by which to examine this sociocultural construction of 'the real'. This book will contend that different sociocultural paradigms of the real generate different textual forms. The very difference of them is at the heart of how the dimension of space functions in them. Taking into account the previous considerations, my analysis encompasses the following dimensions:

Situational Dimension: Location

The first dimension focuses on the selection, disposition and organisation of locations. This can be regarded as a sort of mapping exercise or inventory that contrasts fictional space with its extratextual referent. In the case of the Fantastic, this is the simplest level of analysis since a realistic setting is always a precondition for the fantastic transgression. Nevertheless, on some occasions, the setting will be of more relevance to the fantastic transgression than may seem the case at first sight. As shown in short stories such as "La casa" (José B. Adolph 1975) or "Dejen salir" (José Ferrer-Bermejo 1982), a location as seemingly unremarkable as an ordinary house or metro station can in fact be quite exceptional and thus significant in the history of this narrative form.

Rhetorical Dimension: Discourse

Once transferred to the page, space is always an invention, a fictional entity. The dimension of discourse focuses on devices used to recreate a three-dimensional space within the two-dimensional medium of the line. This can comprise aspects such as the inherent selectivity of narrative (Zoran 1984), which is in contrast to other arts such as sculpture, where space can be displayed from several angles simultaneously. Devices that construct space, not only through the visual but also through the other senses (the geocritical 'polysensoriality', Westphal 2011a:132–136), are also important, as will be best seen in the Fantastic in short stories like "Los palafitos" (Ángel Olgoso 2007).

The linguistic dimension also considers the distribution of words on the page (Ryan's "spatial extension of the text" 2014:12–13; Álzarez Mendez's "textual space" 2002). This will be of relevance when confronted with topologies such as the Möbius strip of "Lost in the Funhouse" (John Barth 1969) or the calligraphy found in the protagonist's diary of "Rien n'a de sens sinon intérieur" (Claude-Emmanuelle Yance 1987).

Semantic-Actant Dimension: Story

Just as a character affects the course of a narrative, so too can space play a role in the evolution of the events within the story. Often ignored in classical narratology (e.g., Ricoeur 1983), space can also be an important element in the plot. This is the case of space-centred genres, such as travel narratives, treasure hunts and detective fictions, where the plot is directly intertwined with the setting.

The semantic-actant dimension examines the way in which the Fantastic is presented within the structure of the story and the way in which it might influence the plot. A representative example of this can be found in the short story "Trastornos de carácter" (Juan José Millás 1989). In a scenario frequently encountered in detective fiction, the plot is fuelled by a specific place: the so-called 'locked-room situation'.

At the same time, spaces—as signs—have a semantic charge. They can have multiple layers of meanings carved over time. In order to unpack these layers of meaning, the semantic-actant dimension draws from studies on spatial imagery from phenomenological, anthropological and symbolic perspectives.

Focusing on the semantic-actant dimension will also allow for the examination of how fantastic transgression functions in the story. Is it with horror, bewilderment and surprise that it is received within the storyworld? This dimension will reveal important differences between classical forms of the Fantastic and the postmodern Fantastic.

Pragmatic Dimension: The Reading Time

Geocritical approaches to literature (e.g., Westphal 2007; Tally 2013) have emphasised that the study of space in literature is also the study of literature in space. Neither Westphal nor Tally focuses on the representation of space in the Fantastic, although the latter recognizes the need for further study of what he calls "otherworldly literature" (2013:146–154). But both critics demonstrate that different paradigms of space in factual reality generate different textual representations. Conversely, textual space also influences our perception of real spaces. This dual influence is of extreme importance. Spaces play a central role in our construction of experience and understanding of the world. Changes in the way space is perceived by the human being affect the very construction of reality, both factual and aesthetic, and its re-creation. Therefore, any analysis of narrative space necessitates a good understanding of the sociohistorical frames that determine the spatiality of a particular era.

While the previous dimensions of analysis were centred on the intraliterary sphere, this one explores the linkage between text and reality. What transgression of space is taking place, and how is it supposedly going to be received by the implied or model reader? Why is this transgression relevant for the postmodern context? This inquiry involves two aspects: first, what does this type of spatial transgression mean in the history of the Fantastic? Second, it requires a conceptualisation, a label: unlike the zombie, the vampire and other famous supernatural creatures, these transgressions of space do not have any referent in current criticism of the Fantastic yet. For this purpose, anthropological, architectural, philosophical, phenomenological, sociological and cultural analyses on postmodern human spatiality help conceptualise these spatial tropes and inform how these spatial transgressions relate to their context.

Before proceeding to the textual analysis, a final conceptual distinction needs to be established, this one concerning the role of space in the story: how do space and transgression interact? Does space play the same role in each text of the Fantastic? Should the role of space be reduced to a tool used to construct the realistic environment of the story?

3. PLACE VERSUS SPACE

In the history of the Fantastic, a large variety of examples exists where space plays a fundamental role. Among early works, we find the haunted Venta Quemada inn from *The Manuscript Found in Saragossa* (1804), E. T. A. Hoffmann's "The Deserted House" (1817), Usher's mansion ("The Fall of the House of Usher", E. A. Poe 1839), the reappearing door of "The Door in the Wall" (H. G. Wells 1911) and many Lovecraftian enclaves such as Innsmouth, Arkham, Dunwich and Kinsgport. With regard to early postmodern texts, we find Jorge Luis Borges' microcosmic point ("The Aleph", 1949), Julio Cortazar's condemned door at the hotel Cervantes ("The Condemned Door", 1956) the haunted mansion from "House Taken Over" (Julio Cortázar 1946) and Shirley Jackson's Hill House (*The Haunting of Hill House*, 1959). More recent examples of fantastic narratives in which space is a thematic protagonist include John Barth's entrapping maze (*Lost in the Funhouse*, 1968), the devouring house of José B. Adolph ("La casa", 1975), the stairs which only go upwards ("La escalera de Sarto", Ricardo Doménech 1980) and the Möbius-shaped metro station of "Dejen salir" ("Exit", José Ferrer-Bermejo 1982).

In order to establish a clear differentiation between the ways in which space intervenes in the fantastic transgression, I propose two theoretical models: the Fantastic of Place and the Fantastic of Space. While there exists a wide range of critical analysis from a multitude of academic perspectives on the binary of space/place (cf. Jammer 1954; Bollnow 1963; Lefebvre 1974; Carter *et. al.* 1993; Casey 1997; Westphal 2007), a brief—and perhaps oversimplified—conceptualisation drawing from Yi-Fu Tuan (1977) and Marc Augé (1992) will suit our aim here, which is to transfer this binary to the study of fantastic transgressions.

Related to the Greek *topos* and the Latin word *locus*, designating the locality 'where something is placed', the notion of 'place' is fundamentally tied to the articulation, or materialisation, of 'space'. Anthropologist Marc Augé (2008:36–43) argues that 'place' has three characteristics: identity, relations (to each other, to what frames it, to the human being) and history. Therefore, from an anthropological perspective, the idea of 'place' is a human invention, constricted by ritual markings that invest it with meaning and attach to it functions and values. Philosopher and geographer Yi-Fu Tuan has dealt extensively with this distinction in *Space and Place: The Perspective of Experience* (1977):

> Open space has no trodden paths and signposts. It has no fixed pattern of established human meaning; it is like a blank sheet on which meaning is imposed. Enclosed and humanised space is place. Compared to space, place is a calm centre of established values. Human beings require both space and place.
>
> (Tuan 1977:54)

This quote sums up the central distinction between space and place, a conceptualisation that served as the starting point of Bertrand Westphal's geocritical method for Comparative Literature studies (2007:5). 'Place' is understood as framed space and 'space' as a wider entity constituted by the physical properties of its places and by the way in which these places relate to each other. Space is thus articulated and divided into places and, conversely, places are located in space.

The same view to the binary place/space is found in Westphal's second geocritical book *Le Monde plausible* (2011b). Influenced by Deleuze's and Guattari's geophilosophy (1980), Westphal conceives 'space' as smooth and open, while 'place' is striated and closed. Applying this to classic travel narratives, he states that the greatest explorers—Ulysses, Columbus, etc.—have always aimed at "transforming an unspeakable space into a common place"

(2011b:171). In his analysis of the *Odyssey*, Westphal relates this binary of place/space to a metaphor for the Penelope/Ulysses relationship. Penelope, while tending the hearth, is "the sedentary of Ithaca [...]. Immobile in her island, immobilised by her pretendants who besiege her palace" (2011b:68), she remains (*demeurer, demur*, from the Latin *mora*: 'to remain', 'to linger') the static and stable element. In contrast, Ulysses' journeys are metaphorical expansions of the boundaries that constrict the 'place'. While Penelope symbolises the "closed place" (2011b:70), Ulysses is "the open space" (2011b:68–71).

A similar example is provided by Vernant (1983:126–174), who explains this binary in terms of the Greek deities Hestia and Hermes. Hestia represents the centre of the domestic sphere; she is the keeper of the circular hearth that denotes the navel tying the house to the earth. Hermes is her antagonist. God of the liminal, the wall-piercer, he is the centrifugal element, the messenger who can cross boundaries and displaces freely across them. Hestia is the central point, the place; Hermes is the messenger who represents 'space' with no constricting boundaries.

In contrast to the relatively precise idea of place, space in this book will be conceived of as an abstract physical category composed of a set of relations and dimensions. Places, on the other hand, are constricted by a set of frames that define their physical shape, render them mathematically measurable and allow them to be mapped or localised within a coordinate system.

In the passage quoted above, Tuan also remarks that 'place' and 'space' are not necessarily mutually exclusive concepts and I am aware that its distinction is, in many ways, artificial. Nonetheless, a differentiation can be of particular relevance to the two models of the Fantastic I develop in this chapter. Since narrative space consists of both places and spaces, the crucial difference concerns *where* the dramatic effect of the Fantastic is directed. In a nutshell, place-centred fantastic stories focus on a particular site (or a group of sites) and on what occurs *in* it (or them). Therefore, in the model I have denominated, the Fantastic of Place (a site) acts as a receptacle of the supernatural. This contrasts with the Fantastic of Space, which, since it affects the laws of space, deals with a more complex phenomenon. Space here is what *causes*—and not what *hosts*—the fantastic transgression. The next sections show some examples of this distinction.

Place as Host versus Agent of Transgression

The first characteristic of place-oriented transgressions can be traced back to the philosophical and aesthetic importance ascribed to a setting within the Gothic-Romantic tradition. This tradition was highly influenced by Edmund Burke's aesthetics of the Sublime in *A Philosophical Enquiry into the Origin of Our Ideas of the Sublime and Beautiful* (1757). The Sublime, as Burke understood it, appeals to primal passions, anticipates our reasoning, and, since it is never fully graspable, terrifies. This theory is embodied in the Gothic enclave, which is primarily devoted to conveying an uncanny atmosphere by being typically isolated, hard to access and in decay, between life and death: "silent, lonely, and sublime" is how Emily described her first glimpse of Montoni's castle in *The Mysteries of Udolpho* (Radcliffe 1992:227). Central features of the Gothic enclave—high intensity and physical threat, symbolic projection of the character and catalyst of supreme sensitivity—influenced a long tradition of the Fantastic in relation to spatiality, particularly prominent during the late eighteenth and early nineteenth centuries. A particular space acts as the ideal *medium* for the exceptional to be experienced. The (architectural, geographical) characteristics of certain places are considered as facilitating the apparition and perception of events beyond human reason. This principle inherent to the Fantastic of Place is found in Charles Grivel's study on the Fantastic (1983). He dedicates an entire section to describe what he calls the "places of the Fantastic" (1983:26–32) and elaborates a list of places that quality for the Fantastic ("apte à produire le fantastique", 1983:26–30). The house, the ruin, the hotel and the laboratory are examples of this and their characteristics are the same outlined in this paragraph (remote, unknown, in ruins and dimly lighted).

> Le fantastique détaille particulièrement les lieux d'apparition des phé-nomènes grâce auxquels il entend porter le trouble au cœur du spec-tateur. [...] Une tour, un souterrain, une forêt sombre engendrent la pénombre nécessaire au surgissement de l'objet inquiétant. Un bon lieu est doc, par définition, pénombreux, propre à faire embrayer l'apparition. (26)

Grivel's definition of the Fantastic in relation to spatiality is an excellent example of the Fantastic of Place, applied to the traditional forms of the Fantastic. However, as the following chapters will show, Grivel's theory is radically contradicted in postmodern forms of the Fantastic. If, according to him, "Le lieu qui fait peur est, bien entendu, lié à la connaissance restreinte qu'on en possède" (26), the newer modes of the Fantastic show precisely a terror of that which is known, of our most ordinary spaces.

Returning to the issue of place, there are a few good examples that clearly show the relation between place and fantastic events characteristic to the Fantastic of Place. One is "The Suitable Surroundings" (1891) by American author Ambrose Bierce. Consider the following excerpts:

> [...] Let me ask you how you would enjoy your breakfast if you took it in this street car. Suppose the phonograph so perfected as to be able to give you an entire opera,—singing, orchestration, and all; do you think you would get much pleasure out of it if you turned it on at your office during business hours? Do you really care for a serenade by Schubert when you hear it fiddled by an untimely Italian on a morning ferryboat? [...]

My stuff in this morning's *Messenger* is plainly sub-headed 'A Ghost Story.' That is ample notice to all. Every honorable reader will understand it as prescribing by implication the conditions under which the work is to be read.

(Bierce 2004:100–101)

In this short story, Mr Coulson, a writer, challenges his friend Marsh to read his recently published ghost story (which I will refer to as 'the manuscript'). However, in order to achieve the desired effect, he asks Marsh to read it in what Coulson considers "the suitable surroundings": "You are brave enough to read me in a street car, but—in a deserted house—alone—in the forest—at night!" (2004:101). For that purpose, the writer suggests the abandoned Breede's House, the locus where Mr Breede committed suicide and which now has the reputation of being haunted. Marsh spends the night, but the next morning his corpse is found in the house, the manuscript by his side. It turns out that this manuscript is not a ghost story at all: instead it recounts the suicide of Breede on that same night, the 15th of July, many years before and details the reasons that drove him to this act.

The circumstances of Marsh's death are not clarified, and this opens up the ground for rational or supernatural interpretations. While he might have been killed by old Breede's ghost, it is also suggested that he might simply have died during the night, scared by what he was reading and, most importantly, terrified because of *where* he was reading it. This has led some scholars to state that "the significance of the location" was enough to generate Marsh's mortal panic attack (T. Blume 2004:183). His death at the 'haunted' house could be attributed to the psychological fear connected with those 'suitable surroundings', as indicated by the story's title: namely, to the associations triggered in his mind by the place in which he is reading the manuscript.[2]

Bierce, through Mr Coulson's voice, condenses in an explicit manner the spatial conventions of the ghost story setting: a silent night broken by the screech owl, a dilapidated house reputedly haunted, in a remote part of the woods and entered alone in the dark with only the help of the dim light of a candle. By so doing, Bierce is playing with the idea that certain events need a specific frame, or place, to generate a desired effect.

A more humorous example is provided by Marcel Schwob in his short story "Un Squelette" (1889). The protagonist spends the night at an 'atypical' haunted hotel. The first paragraph is a long list of clichés associated to the ghost story genre, which this story will subvert:

Ce n'était pas un château vermoulu perché sur une colline boisée au bord d'un précipice ténébreux. Elle n'avait pas été abandonnée depuis plusieurs siècles. Son dernier propriétaire n'était pas mort d'une manière mystérieuse. Les paysans ne se signaient pas avec effroi en passant devant. Aucune lumière blafarde ne se montrait à ses fenêtres en ruines quand le beffroi du village sonnait minuit. Les arbres du parc n'étaient pas des ifs, et les enfants peureux ne venaient pas guetter à travers les haies des formes blanches à la nuit tombante. Je n'arrivai pas dans une hôtellerie où toutes les chambres étaient retenues. L'aubergiste ne se gratta pas longtemps la tête, une chandelle à la main, et ne finit pas par me proposer en hésitant de me dresser un lit dans la salle basse du donjon. Il n'ajouta pas d'une mine effarée que de tous les voyageurs qui y avaient couché aucun n'était revenu pour raconter sa fin terrible. Il ne me parla pas des bruits diaboliques qu'on entendait la nuit dans le vieux manoir.

(Schwob 2008:114–115)

The ghost of the narrator's friend, Tom Bobbins, appears during the night, and the humour of this story is precisely constructed upon the fact that it is not a true 'ghost' because it is out of place; that is not where you meet a ghost ("Peut-être reviendra-t-il aux véritables moeurs des fantômes, en secouant ses chaînes et en hurlant des imprécations sataniques", 2008:120).

In relation to the Gothic topos, Bierce's short story also foregrounds that which, after decades of literary tradition, the reader may associate with a particular 'place'. As the writer character expresses, referring to the story's subtitle of 'Ghost Story': "Every honourable reader will understand it as prescribing by implication the conditions under which the work is to be read" (2004:100). The author is thus ironically capturing a long tradition of the Fantastic that is based on the conviction that the aim of the literary text, in particular of the short text, is to provoke a specific effect—generally of fear—in the reader. The atmosphere generated by the place of the action is equally or even more important in achieving this effect than the actual events narrated. As proclaimed by H. P. Lovecraft, "Atmosphere is the all-important thing" (2008:19).

Many of Lovecraft's fictions exemplify this. Consider this paragraph from *Through the Gates of the Silver Key* (1932), its opening anticipating the strange case of Randolph Carter, who disappears by transcending the human tridimensional perception of space and time:

> [...] in a deep niche on one side there ticked a curious coffin-shaped clock whose dial bore baffling hieroglyphs and whose four hands did not move in consonance with any time system known on this planet. *It was a singular and disturbing room, but well fitted to the business now at hand.*

(Lovecraft 2005:264, emphasis added)

Note how the use of the atmospheric and the premonitory bears parallels with Bierce's story. In particular, the last sentence captures the way in which the environment is used to generate a sense of the extraordinary in the room where the events will unfold. The use of 'place' to generate a particular effect is present in Edgar Allan Poe's influential essay "The Philosophy of Composition" (1846). Poe's approach to the short story is strongly conditioned by his belief in the unity of form and effect: every element is directed toward the production of a single effect, which will culminate in the final resolution. Therefore, the effectiveness of that which is told will depend on how 'suitable' the elements of the story, including the location and the atmosphere, are. The best literary example of this theory is the narrator's arrival at the Usher mansion, where the duality of house/family and its imminent downfall are already metaphorically anticipated by the "barely perceptible fissure" (cf. "anticipatory metaphorical image", Casas 2010:12):

> Beyond this indication of extensive decay, however, the fabric gave little token of instability. Perhaps the eye of a scrutinizing observer might have discovered a barely perceptible fissure, which extending from the roof of the building in front, made its way down the wall in a zigzag direction, until it became lost in the sullen waters of the tarn.
> (Poe 2004:201–202)

In contrast to this tradition of the uncanny literary topos, a large variety of short stories take place in completely ordinary settings (e.g., "The Tale-Tell Heart", Poe 1843; "Who knows?", Maupassant 1890). In the second half of the nineteenth century in particular, the fantastic setting began to distance itself progressively from this Gothic horror enclave that 'calls for' the supernatural. The location of the action was to become the least important aspect in the generation of the Fantastic. Instead of being in the foreground, location now acted only as a backdrop against which the supernatural surprisingly arose. This 'ordinariness' of the setting was to be significant in the evolution of the Fantastic (cf. Roas 2011:15–20).

However, this does not imply that the place of action is no longer important to the plot. Its situational function is still central but is, to some extent, reversed: instead of acting as the site that evokes this premonitory sensation, it is now a place that the reader does not directly associate with the supernatural.

In the corpus of the Fantastic of Place, the place of action plays a central role in the narrative, particularly due to the attributes attached to this enclave. However, it has to be born in mind that no matter how relevant its atmospheric function is in the story—whether terror-inducing or ordinary—the place itself is physically normal and not impossible in accordance with our extraliterary laws. Although the place of action might initially be presented as exceptional—as is the case of "The Nameless City" (Lovecraft 1921) and of Borges' city of "The Immortal" (1949)—it is later revealed that this anomaly is due to the exceptional phenomenon it hosts and not to its own physical impossibility. Instead, as with the classic motif of the haunted house, it is another element (the ghost, for example) that breaches the realistic laws.

The role of 'place' as outlined above contrasts with the Fantastic of Space. A clear example of this distinction can be found in "La casa" (1975; see Chapter II) by Peruvian José B. Adolph. The action is set in a seemingly normal house in an ordinary city. As the story unfolds, we are told how this building devours its occupant, a random man who, on his way to work, had been inexplicably drawn to it. This house is portrayed as being literally the supernatural subject. It becomes a fantastic space because it causes—and not just evokes—the events. With regard to the transgression, what needs to be addressed is: what is of more importance, the house as 'place' or the house as 'space'? To the fore is not the fact that the action is happening in this particular place but rather that the fantastic transgression resides in the physical impossibility of a space literally devouring a man: a cannibal space. Thus, this short story works as an example of the Fantastic of Space: a literary phenomenon where the normal laws of physical space that rule our extratextual experience are not respected.

While in literary theory, agency has been a function traditionally attributed to human characters or to 'humanised' entities, such as talking animals and animated objects (cf. Prince 1982:71; Margolin 2005:52; Bal 2006:12), many short stories of the Fantastic remind us that a space can also be an entity capable of provoking action and causing events. Such spaces are the subject of analysis in Chapters 2, 3, 4 and 5.

Thresholds: Stable versus Fantastic Boundaries

In the textual world, physical boundaries are amongst the most fundamental elements of narrative space in order to create and define "the physically existing environment in which characters live and move" (Ryan 2014:5). The drawing of a distinction between two types of boundaries might serve to show how this principle functions differently in both the Fantastic of Place and the Fantastic of Space. The difference lies in that which will be denominated a 'stable' versus a 'fantastic' boundary. The clearest example of a stable boundary is the motif of the threshold in the Fantastic.

Thresholds are liminal motifs par excellence in the fantastic. Holes ("Mi hermana Elba", Cristina Fernández Cubas 1980), doors ("The Condemned Door", Julio Cortázar 1951), doorsteps ("The Thing on the Doorstep", H. P. Lovecraft 1937, "The Fall of the House of Usher", E. A. Poe 1939), courtyards ("El hombre en el umbral", Jorge Luis Borges 1949) and mirrors and stairs (*The Turn of the Screw*, Henry James 1898) work as borders between the realistic domain and the supernatural.[3]

The threshold is often a site in which a high emotional intensity is concentrated, indicating "a moment of crisis, at an unfinalisable—and unpredeterminable—turning point" (Bakhtin 2003:61). In the vast majority of cases, the primary function of the threshold is to frame the access into the supernatural: the function of this form of boundary is to provide a stable spatial frame that separates the realistic and the fantastic domains but in itself there is nothing physically impossible about it. This is true in the case of the mysterious entrance to "The Deserted House" (E. T. A. Hoffmann 1817), H. P. Lovecraft's doorstep at "The Thing on the Doorstep" (1937), the court-yard's threshold in "The Man on the Threshold" (J. L. Borges 1949) and the door connecting the narrator to the Fantastic in "The Condemned Door" (Julio Cortázar 1951). Even so, the recurrence within the Fantastic of the threshold calls for a more detailed analysis as to the various functions that it may have within this narrative form.

Many elements of the heroic myth (Campbell 1948; Doležel 1998) appear alongside the fantastic threshold. An example is the excursion from the known towards the supernatural, when the character leaves his ordinary environment in order to discover something, answer a call or resolve a prob-lem. In a pattern found very frequently in Gothic tales of remote places and castles, the action begins with the physical displacement of the character in what Campbell calls "the crossing of the first threshold" (2008:64–80). For example, the narrator of *The Shadow over Innsmouth* (1931), intrigued by the rumours of the Arkham's villagers regarding the secrecy about Inns-mouth's origins and inhabitants, decides to travel to Innsmouth. The fol-lowing extracts show how there is an emphasis in these threshold crossings by means of the deictics specifying spatial location, which separate the character's ordinary environment from the unknown place:

> 3 May. Bistritz.—*Left* Munich at 8:35 p.m., on 1st May, arriving at Vienna early next morning; should have *arrived* at 6:46, but train was an hour late. Buda-Pesth seems a wonderful place, from the glimpse which I got of it from the train and the little I could walk through the streets. I feared to go very far from the station, as we had *arrived* late and would start as near the correct time as possible.
> (*Dracula*, Stoker 2003:5, emphasis added)

> I arrived *here* yesterday, and my first task is to assure my dear sister of my welfare and increasing confidence in the success of my undertak-ing. I am already *far north of London*, and as I walk in the streets of *Petersburgh*, I feel a cold northern breeze play upon my cheeks, which braces my nerves and fills me with delight.
> (*Frankenstein*, Shelley 2008:9, emphasis added)

> Nevertheless, in *this* mansion of gloom I now proposed to myself a sojourn of some weeks. [...] A letter, however, had lately *reached me in a distant part of the country*—a letter from him—which, in its wildly importunate nature, had admitted of no other than a personal reply.
> ("The Fall of the House of Usher", Poe 2004:200, emphasis added)

The threshold means as much a departure 'from' as an access 'into'. Crossing that limit symbolises going through or across what should be impenetrable, which is another characteristic the Fantastic inherits from the heroic mythical narrative schema. These thresholds reflect points of conflict: the entity crossing the threshold is preparing for a new code, as is the case with the crossing of the Rue d'Auseuil (from the French 'at/on the threshold'), which separates the city from the fantastic abyss ("The Music of Erich Zann", H. P. Lovecraft 1921).

In many texts, the separation between the 'here' and 'there' increases the tension of what lies behind and thus thresholds serve as both ontological and narrative frames that structure the discourse and the plot. "Listen now to what I am about to tell you" [...] ("The Deserted House", Hoffmann 1996:461), "And now, as if called into life by my entrance into the mysterious house, my adventures began" (1996:466).

The framing function of the threshold finds an analogy with the creative process in Poe's "The Philosophy of Composition" (1846): "A close circumscription of space is absolutely necessary to the effect of insulated incident: it has the force of a frame to a picture. It has an indisputable moral power in keeping concentrated the attention" (2004:681). As Carringer has suggested (1974:508), Poe's use of 'framing' to enhance a desired effect could explain his choice of enclosed spaces as well as his use of a concise narrative form— the short story—to concentrate the plot on a single effect.

The threshold, therefore, is an element used to focus the tension on the 'before' and 'after'. This is very clearly seen in the opening paragraphs of "The Boarded Window" (Ambrose Bierce 1891). In this short story, the window is the element around which are concentrated the various turning points of the narrative:

> [... a window that] was boarded up—nobody could remember a time when it was not. And none knew why it was so closed [...]. I fancy there are few persons living today who ever knew the secret of that window, but I am one, as you shall see. (2004:109)

As seen in this short story, the threshold—the boarded window—functions to enhance the suspense, directing attention toward the question of why it is boarded ("the secret of that window" [2004:109]).

In other texts, the threshold 'facilitates' the supernatural apparition. "Climax for a Ghost Story" (1919), by the English writer I. A. Ireland, may serve as an illustrative example. In this very brief story, which I reproduce here, a locked door holds a man and a girl inside a room. As it reads, after a brief exchange of words, the girl exits the room by traversing this door:

> "How eerie!" said the girl, advancing cautiously. "—And what a heavy door!" She touched it as she spoke and it suddenly swung to with a click.
> "Good Lord!" said the man. "I don't believe there's a handle inside. Why, you've locked us both in!"

"Not both of us. Only one of us," said the girl, and before his eyes
she passed straight through the door, and vanished.

(Ireland, in Manguel 1983:49)

This text clearly sets out how a physical border, impenetrable to humans,
is crossed by the ghost. What then is physically impossible, the door or the
girl? It is the girl who is attributed with the supernatural characteristics
necessary to cross through this door; the door itself is not endowed with
such supernatural power. Thus, the threshold in this case is not the element
that transgresses the physical laws of reality. This is the case of the large
majority of traditional stories of the Fantastic, either the threshold facilitates the access into another domain or, as in "Climax for a Ghost Story",
the physical boundary is transgressed by a character. In all these cases, the
importance lies in the threshold remaining a stable frame of the realistic
environment: it is a referential architectural element.

In contrast, some narratives call into question the role of the boundary
in constructing relations of distance, reference and location. David Roas'
"Excepciones" (2010) is a good example: this story concerns a man who
'fails' (Roas 2010:135) to cross the threshold into his house. Each time he
tries to cross the threshold, he finds himself outside again. The spatial dichotomy of in/out becomes obsolete: since 'inside' does not exist anymore for
the character 'outside' loses its meaning as an opposition to it. Roas' story
shows how in transgressing the stable notion of boundary (the threshold
that should provide access to the house) spatial oppositions (here outside/
inside) are invalidated. Similarly, Jacques Sternberg's "L'Étage" (1974) represents the invalidation of the dichotomy of up/down. Every time the character
goes up these peculiar stairs, he finds himself back on the ground floor.

In summary, in the first group of texts, the threshold either separates
and connects the natural from and to the supernatural domain or acts as
the limit against which the transgression operates, as in the example of the
ghost that crosses the physical frontier of a door or wall. However, the fantastic threshold in fantastic narratives, often a place around which turning
points and dramatic tension are concentrated, may not be what causes the
fantastic effect. In contrast, in the stories mentioned in the previous paragraph, the architectural boundary serves not to create the effect of realism
but rather to transgress it. This spatial transgression destroys the notion of a
'reliable', 'objective' system of distances and references, an aspect which will
be analysed in more detail in Chapter 3.

Time-Condensing Place

Mexican writer Octavio Paz once said that architecture was the least cor-
ruptible witness of history ("Para mí, la arquitectura es el testigo insoborn-
able de una sociedad", Paz 1983:33). With these words, he captured an
essential mechanism by which 'space' is transformed into 'place': time. In

line with this emphasis on the temporal, Philippe Hamon mentions that "[If] the notion of *place* is only a function of memory, if even the most significant of buildings is always a monument, [...] then memory is only a function of architectural spaces" (1992:3).

Regarded as the architectural articulation of space, the notion of place is characterised by its relation to the temporal. As Westphal puts it, places are "stratigraphic", condensing a long history ("the stratigraphic vision", Westphal 2011a:137–143). A sense of the past and the imprint of history confer places with a sense of identity. This observation is what informs the theory of "non-places" formulated by sociologist Marc Augé (2008). These non-places are transitional and functional areas, such as airports, metro-stations and shopping centres, whose lack of collective history and social bond distinguishes them from the traditional 'anthropological place'.

The relationship between place and time is a recurrent characteristic of the Fantastic of Place. A common feature of the stories belonging to this model is that the central locus of the action functions as the site that frames a story through time, as seen, for example, in the motifs of the saga and family tragedy. The place of action, the house for example, is portrayed as a container of a story to be revealed, a story frequently connected to a traumatic episode from the past. A 'place' is at the disposal of 'time': it is the embodiment of history and memory.

This is particularly relevant to the traditional ghost story; Jameson even considers it "the architectural genre par excellence, wedded as it is to rooms and buildings ineradicably stained with the memory of gruesome events, material structures in which the past literally 'weighs like a nightmare on the brain of the living'" (1998:185). Berthin also identifies two literary strategies of the Gothic—anachronism and analepsis—as deriving from the themes of the question of origin and family secrets related to a place (2010:67–83).

A classic example of what I label time-condesing places can be found in E. T. A. Hoffmann's "The Deserted House" (1817). The significance of the house with which the narrator is obsessed relates to the history contained within. This setting serves as the thematic channel for a secret from the past to be discovered. Another classic text is Poe's "The Fall of the House of Usher" (1839). The mansion of Usher literally embodies a whole familial structure and history to the point where the end of the Usher descent line is paralleled by the downfall of this building.

M. R. James' "The Haunted Dolls' House" (1925) is a further classical example. In this text, the 'living' dolls' house preserves and reproduces the family history of Ilbridge's House. Only by digging into the past in the city archives does the narrator finally discover why it is that the house presents this supernatural animation. Following this same pattern, the narrator of "The Shunned House" (H. P. Lovecraft 1937) goes to the city archives to carry out detailed genealogical research on the history of the building, which will help solve the mystery. In another story from the same author, "The Unnamable" (1925), Carter tells his sceptical friend about a creature that haunts the dilapidated house in front of them. In order to convince his friend about the existence of the supernatural, Carter specifically appeals to this idea of place as containing many layers of lives across time: "[...] how can it be absurd to suppose that deserted houses are full of queer sentient things, or that told graveyards teem with the terrible, unbodied intelligence of generations" (2005:83).[4]

H. P. Lovecraft makes this time-condensing feature of place a central theme of his creative production, as captured in the stories of the Cthulhu Mythos, an extraterrestial race that once ruled the Earth and now can be found in places like Innsmouth and Arkham. The imprint of time is frequently the source of cosmic terror, with the temporal portrayed as an 'unspeakable' excess contained in a physical place, as this fragment from *The Shadow over Innsmouth* reflects:

> [...] the thought of such linked infinities of black, brooding compartments given over to cobwebs and memories and the conqueror worm, start up vestigial fears and aversions that not even the stoutest philosophy can disperse. (1993:231)

A similar pattern can be seen in this passage from "The Nameless City" (1921):

> Not even the physical horror of my position in that cramped corridor [...] could match the lethal dread I felt at the abysmal antiquity of the scene and its soul. (2005:39)

The stories that feature time-condensing places share very similar structures, which consist of: (a) the presentation of the fantastic mystery, (b) the carrying out of some research activity to find clues as to what happened and (c) the final discovery of the cause of the Fantastic. The revelation, which often restores the place to its normality, comes at the end, as happens in "The Shunned House" ("The next spring no more pale grass and strange weeds came up in the shunned house's terraced garden" 2005:115).

Furthermore, the supernatural is often confined not only to a particular place but also to a particular time; the place also dictates the 'when', as with the nocturnal music of Erich Zann that invoked the abyss at the Rue d'Auseuil ("The Music of Erich Zann", Lovecraft 1921). A traditional motif that best illustrates this symbiosis between space and time is 'the overnight stay', as, for example, in the Venta Quemada Inn, deserted during the day and diabolic at night, where Alfonso stops to rest in *The Manuscript Found in Saragossa* (1804). Similarly, in *The Shadow over Innsmouth* (1931), the narrator has to spend the night at the strange Gilman House, despite the fact that "[n]one of the non-natives ever stayed out late at night, there being a widespread impression that it was not wise to do so. Besides, the streets were loathsomely dark" (1993:230).

As observed, the place of action, by enhancing the temporal dimension, serves to activate the Fantastic. However, this place of action is not the supernatural element in itself. It is, nonetheless, central to the story, since the narrative tension is constructed through its attributes. Its physical frames and thresholds serve to direct attention toward that which the place contains. Lastly, suspense is very often concentrated on events that took place in that particular physical structure—that is, on the temporal.

Since time and space are two interrelated coordinates in our experience of reality, in the fantastic text, both are often disrupted simultaneously. However, it is important to note that this is not the case for every short story of the Fantastic. While this might seem an obvious fact, it has, surprisingly, not been embraced in classic thematic studies, where space and time appear as a single fantastic theme (Castex 1951; Caillois 1966; Todorov 1970).

(a) Disruptions of Time

When the temporal line is subverted, space is modified as a result. This can be clearly seen in the motif of the loop into the past or the future. The temporal displacement also implies a spatial displacement, which can result in a juxtaposition between a space in the past and its present or future version. However, should this be regarded as a transgression of time as well as space? Consider, for example, "La noche más larga" (José María Merino 1982), where a character tells of how he arrives at a house to seek shelter from the rain and spends the night there. When the character wakes up, it is to a house that presents symptoms of sudden decay: ruins, cobwebs, dust, rottenness and rust. What for the narrator was only a night's sleep has resulted in a time lapse of 20 years. The house he expects to find on awakening is the same house that he had entered but much later in time, so also much older. In this story, there is nothing fantastic about the two houses; they are two physically and logically possible spaces. The transgression is instead located in the chronological time line. Time has contracted or expanded— depending on how we regard it—and the change in space is a result of this. These types of temporal transgressions appertain to a hypothetical model of the Fantastic of Time, which has not yet been systematised (see Roas article "Cronologías alteradas", 2012).

(b) Disruptions of Space-Time

Another possible transgression affects the physical laws of space as well as the dimension of time. This is the case in "Los palafitos" (Ángel Olgoso 2007), which will be analysed later in Chapter 5. The character enters an impossible village, a setting that does not respect his (nor the reader's) dimensions of time and space. Getting to this village necessitates not just a leap in time but a journey to a completely different world, one very similar to ours but where the history of humanity has undergone a different fate.

The space-time continuum is also modified in Julio Cortázar's "The Highway of the South" (1966). Not only are the characters entrapped in an impossible, ever-expanding traffic jam but so too are the weather seasons accelerated. Similarly, "The Other Haven" (1966), by the same author, unifies two places at two different historical moments (Paris in the late nineteenth century during the Franco-Prussian war and Buenos Aires after the Second World War).

Although the segregation is artificial to some extent, nothing prevents the dimension of space from being isolated from that of time in the literary analysis. This will help us focus on functions and meanings of space in the Fantastic. Therefore, when confronted with texts that present this double transgression of time and space, my analysis will emphasise the representation and transgressive function of narrative space over that of time.

(c) Disruptions of Space

Narrative space is always dependant on narrative time, in the sense that the spatial distortion is progressively disclosed to the reader through the sequential unfolding of the text. However, not every transgression of the spatial dimension entails a transgression of the temporal. There is no temporal disruption when the house of "La casa" (José B. Adolph 1975, see Chapter II) devours its inhabitant, nor when the museum-house of "El museo" (José María Merino 1982, see Chapter II) prevents the tenant from leaving. In these two examples, our human sense of chronological time is undisturbed; it is rather the animation of space that provokes the breach of the laws of reality. Similarly, in another text, "La Banlieue" (Jacques Sternberg 1988), at every corner we encounter the same café in which the narrator is supposed to have a date. The many versions of the café coexist in the present and therefore the temporal line is not altered. This feature is at the core of the Fantastic of Space.

In summary, it can be concluded that the Fantastic of Place and the Fantastic of Space are two categories in which space functions as a protagonist and yet the function of space within the Fantastic is diametrically opposed in the two cases. In the Fantastic of Place, space is seen as the *host* of the fantastic agent, while in the Fantastic of Space, space is the *agent* of the transgression, provoking the breach of logical laws. In the first instance, space functions as a stable dimension reinforcing, or being 'part of', the effect of reality. The place of action, no matter how uncanny or how mundane, acts as the frame of reference of the real. Thus, the physical laws of this place (e.g., three-dimensionality, distance, hierarchy) are not altered. In the second model, space in itself is the transgressive element. Space is the fantastic monster, the element that questions the laws of reality established in the text and thus the tension is displaced from the particular place of action to the transgression undergone by this dimension.

4. "THE NAMELESS CITY" (H. P. LOVECRAFT 1921) AS PROTOTYPE OF THE FANTASTIC OF PLACE

"The Nameless City" was one of H. P. Lovecraft's favourite stories and is a striking example of the role of narrative space in the disclosure of the Fantastic. As this is the text in which Lovecraft introduces the figure of the mad Arab poet Abdul Alhzared for the first time, "The Nameless City" is often considered the first of Lovecraft's Mythos stories, a series that tells of an extraterrestrial civilisation discovered through a series of bas-reliefs and that is later developed in "The Call of Cthulhu" (1926) and *At the Mountains of Madness* (1931).

The story concerns an explorer who is relating his discovery of the "nameless city" in the Arabian desert, where he investigates the history of a lost human race. This ruined city had, until then, remained hidden to humans but was nonetheless kept alive in the folklore of the locals. While the narrator explores the architectural features of the city—in particular the disposition and size of chambers and their decorations—he discovers it to be the home of an ancient and immortal extraterrestial civilisation that lurks in its undergrounds. Lovecraft was inspired by an article on "Arabia" in the ninth edition of the *Encyclopaedia Britannica*. In particular, his attention was drawn to "Irem, the City of Pillars, invisible to ordinary eyes, but occasionally and at rare intervals, revealed to some heaven-favoured traveller" (Joshi 2005:407).

What is particularly well-constructed in this piece is that the supernatural is revealed through the explorers' movements in space. The city, the centre of the action, also plays a central role in the evolution of the plot. Consider the first paragraph:

> When I drew nigh the nameless city I knew it was accursed. I was travelling in a parched and terrible valley under the moon, and afar I saw it protruding uncannily above the sands as parts of a corpse may protrude from an ill-made grave. Fear spoke from the age-worn stones of this hoary survivor of the deluge, this great-grandmother of the eldest pyramid; and a viewless aura repelled me and bade me retreat from antique and sinister secrets that no man should see, and no man else had ever dared to see.
>
> ("The Nameless City", Lovecraft 2005:30)

With these opening lines, the presentation of the city prepares the reader for that which will be narrated. The three aforementioned characteristics of the Fantastic of Place are activated.

First, with regard to the atmospheric function, the very first line abruptly establishes the place as anomalous ("I knew it was accursed"). Second, with regard to the threshold as tension-concentrating motif, the silhouette is revealed through the sand, suggesting some mystery to which the explorer is drawn ("I saw it protruding uncannily above the sands as parts of a corpse may protrude from an ill-made grave"). Third, it is also a site that condenses time, an event belonging to a remote episode of human history ("antique and sinister secrets"). These three functions are further elaborated throughout the entire short story.

(a) Atmospheric Function of the Setting

The strange environment surrounding the city is signalled from the start through the descriptions of its remote location in space ("a parched and terrible valley", "afar") as well as in time ("age-worn stones", "this great-grandmother of the eldest pyramid"). To establish the uncanny atmosphere surrounding the city, two main discourses predominate: the liminal and the excessive, both dysfunctions of the notion of referential boundary.

The city is presented as a corpse, "protruding uncannily", through two reiterated natural elements—wind and sand—whose imprint is left on the city and its surroundings to convey the impression of forgetfulness. It is a "crumbling and inarticulate" (2005:30) place with "many secrets of ages too remote for calculation, though sandstorms had long effaced any carvings which may have been outside" (30). The expression of "a viewless aura" (30) suggests something that is only sensed but not physically present. Therefore, the image that the city evokes is that of a spectre, lurking between life and death, half hidden in the desert and half shapeless, half real and half legendary, "told of in strange tales but seen by no living man" (30).

From the moment the narrator enters the city, we discover that there are elements that exceed human spatial and temporal references. The city's roofs and ceilings are too low for a human and too old to be placed in our time line ("the antiquity of the spot was unwholesome" [31], "the abysmal antiquity" [39]) but also too developed to be prehistorical. It is a place located at the margins of human time ("There is no legend so old as to give it a name" [30]; "uncounted ages" [30]).

Lovecraft employs the technique of anamorphosis—the distorted sense of proportions and dimensions—to bring forth the indescribable confrontation with an unnatural place ("too regular to be natural" [33]). With its murals exceeding the human understanding of images, the city seems to have been erected and decorated by people other than humans and not designed for humans to inhabit.

(b) Framing Function of the Threshold

Thresholds are crucial throughout this text. Starting with the motif of the excursion, this first departure from the traveller's ordinary environment is immediately activated and repeated throughout the story ("I defied them and went into the untrodden waste with my camel" [30]). The displacement between chambers and corridors and the various levels of floors serve to reinforce the idea of an anamorphic physical structure: the overall proportions cannot be embraced due to the many "changes of direction and of steepness"

(34). Each door and tunnel and further spatial frames increase the tension and suspense as to what might be behind and mark the turning points in the action. The progressive revelation of the reptile race reflected through the different rooms, temples and thresholds the protagonist accesses is particularly effective in the text ("Very low and sand-choked were all of the dark apertures near me, but I cleared one with my spade and crawled through it, carrying a torch to reveal whatever mysteries it might hold" [32]). Since the narration is homodiegetic, the reader follows the protagonist through every new chamber and thus accompanies him in the slow discovery of the Fantastic.

The city, a place composed of a multitude of thresholds and rooms, regulates the pace at which the secret is discovered by the protagonist. Every step forward is a step further toward the final revelation. Although it has been progressively imprinted in the spaces that the explorer encounters, the fantastic effect occurs at the end, a structure that is similar to Todorov's formula of temporal arrangement in the Fantastic (1975:87). The increasing tension culminates in the discovery of the last chamber, which contains an aperture into a phosphorescent void.

Lovecraft's fiction is marked by the motif of the abyss at the very end of his stories, as in "The Shunned House" and "The Music of Erich Zann". This spatial form reflects Rosemary Jackson's idea of the Fantastic as a space of non-signification, as "a zero point of non-meaning" (1981:42) that "moves into, or opens up, a space without/outside cultural order" (42). The Lovecraftian abyss is the space of nothingness, the unspeakable, that area which finds no human referents because it is beyond language. In another of Lovecraft's short stories, the character who incarnates reason and logical intellect believes "that nothing can be really 'unnamable'" ("The Unnamable", 2005:83). In "The Nameless City", this aspect is present in the title. There can be no word for the city, "that unvocal place; that place which I alone of living men had seen" (31), "the nameless city that men dare not know" (34). This aspect is also reflected in the many expressions of vagueness and imprecision, for example when the narrator tries to describe the city: "vague stones and symbols" (32); "obscure and cryptical shrines" (32).

(c) The Time-Condensing Site

The Nameless City functions as a time-condensing site in that it hosts a lost civilisation outside of the historical frame of humanity. Its history is imprinted in the odd murals and architectural features and that which worries the protagonist is how to locate this city within human history. This appears even more clearly toward the end:

> My fears, indeed, concerned the past rather than the future. Not even the physical horror of my position in that cramped corridor of dead reptiles and antediluvian frescoes, miles below the world I knew and faced by another world of eerie light and mist, could match the

lethal dread I felt at the *abysmal antiquity* of the scene and its soul. (39, emphasis added)

It is important to note that the strange features initially attributed to the architecture of the city are projected onto its inhabitants as the story evolves. The last pages of the story are dedicated to describing the forgotten supernatural civilisation that lurks in the city. The same techniques that were applied to architectural form at the beginning are then employed in the characterisation of this extraterrestrial race. The excessive and liminal is present in their bodies ("their heads, which presented a contour violating all known biological principles" [36]), as is the indefinable ("the horns and the noselessness and the alligator-like jaw placed the things outside all established categories" [36]; "Monstrous, unnatural, colossal, was the thing—too far beyond all the ideas of man to be believed except in the silent damnable small hours when one cannot sleep" [41]). The encounter with the forgotten race is used to raise the issue of mankind's fear vis-à-vis the alien, indicative of the cosmic terror and leitmotif in Lovecraft's fiction.

In conclusion, the setting in "The Nameless City" is extremely important in relation to the disclosure of the fantastic element. 'Where' it happens is as important as 'what' happens. The supernatural is not only anticipated by the atmospheric description of the city but is also projected onto the city's physical structure. "Far, ancient and forbidden" (34), the city puts the reader "into the frame of mind appropriate to the sentiment of the piece" ("The Suitable Surroundings", Bierce 2004:100). The architectural features of the city intensify its exceptional aura. The city is the portal to the supernatural that is buried under its surface, waiting to be disclosed through infinity of framing walls, tunnels and other threshold motifs that regulate the pace at which the discovery takes place.

However, to what extent is the city supernatural? The impossible element of this story is not the city itself but rather that which it contains. There is in the end nothing impossible about the city as physical space, despite its strange proportions, location, multiple thresholds and excessive antiquity. This short story is a very good example of the features of the Fantastic of Place. As shown, this model gathers the sum of fantastic texts that foreground the atmospheric, delimiting and temporal use of a particular site as host of the supernatural intervention. Event is tightly conditioned by place and vice versa; the locus of the action advances that which will happen there.

5. THE FANTASTIC HOLE: "MI HERMANA ELBA" (CRISTINA FERNÁNDEZ CUBAS, 1980) AS PROTOTYPE OF THE FANTASTIC OF SPACE

Since the positivistic context of the late eighteenth century, the Fantastic has been seeking to give voice to that which the discourse of reason could not codify. The hole, a motif that recurs in the plots of the fantastic text from its origins to its postmodern versions, is a prototypical visualisation of this. This section is dedicated to explore this spatial image that very clearly illustrates the transgressive function of the Fantastic.

As Neus Rotger has suggested (2003), the form of the hole embodies the subversive essence of the Fantastic in that it perforates the rational discourse of the positivistic conception of reality that predominated during the eighteenth and nineteenth centuries. Note also the parallels with Grivel's conception of the Fantastic as "arising from the visual crumbling of a place previously conceived as full: the place does not hold, one knows, its substance dissipates, wilts, disintegrates" (Grivel in Founier Kiss 2007:143).

The hole embodies an ontological and epistemic uncertainty: it is a blank space, a domain that has not been codified yet. I will mention two very different and yet complementary examples that illustrate this. In his essay "Geography and Some Explorers" (1924), Joseph Conrad discusses the cartography of *terrae incognitae*. He writes about fabulous creatures that filled in the gaps of unknown territories before the discovery of the New World and about the huge blank spaces of Africa (an Imperialistic "white Africa", to be precise) during the Age of Reason:

> And it was Africa, the continent out of which the Romans used to say some new thing was always coming, that got cleared of the dull imaginary wonders of the Dark Ages, which were replaced by exciting spaces of white paper. Regions unknown! My imagination could depict to itself there worthy, adventurous, and devoted men nibbling at the edges, attacking from north and south and east and west, conquering a bit of truth here and a bit of truth there, and sometimes swallowed up by the mystery their hearts were so persistently set on unveiling.
>
> (Conrad 2010:12)

These non-cartographied blank spaces nurtured Conrad's literary imagination in a similar way to how they inspired Philippe Vasset's *Un livre blanc* (2007). In this book, Vasset recalls his exploration of blank spaces present in a modern map of Paris. These, he discovers, are areas belonging to that which society doesn't want to see: the poor, the immigrant, the neglected or abandoned. He ends his search with the following statement, discrediting the reliability of maps to represent reality: "Despite the permanent satellite coverage and the network of security cameras, we don't know the world at all" (2007:136).[5]

As these examples show, the fantastic hole reveals the inconsistencies of a (supposedly) coherent and solid structure. This metaphorical relation between the perforation and the Fantastic, as well as the image of an epistemological and ontological uncertainty, makes this motif an archetype of the Fantastic of Space.

The most common understanding of the word 'hole' relates to cavities in material structures. The first entry for the word in the *Collins English*

Dictionary gives "perforation of a solid surface" and similarly the *Oxford English Dictionary* gives "a hollow place, cavity, excavation". This definition can be extended to apply to biological structures; that is, an empty hollow space in an existent organ (*Oxford English Dictionary*). The issue of biological voids and psychoanalytical theory is extensively discussed in "The Uncanny" by Freud (1919), where he points to the symbolic potential of holes: their multiplicity of meanings can evoke anxiety, in particular because of their 'void' or lack of explicit reference. Leaving aside this psychoanalytical approach, Freud suggests that the figure of the hole recalls a presence through the ascertainment of its absence; it is precisely this oscillation between absence and presence, not as dichotomy but rather as coexisting principles, that renders the hole a transgressive form in the human imaginary.

Of use in elaborating on this aspect is Michel Foucault's concept of "heterotopia". In his essay "Des Espaces Autres" (1967), Foucault analyses the way different civilisations have dealt in spatial terms with the 'different' or 'extraordinary'. According to Foucault, this has been accomplished by situating the different and extraordinary in what he calls "heterotopias", these being physical containers (with or without clear geographical markers) where "individuals whose behaviour is deviant in relation to the required mean or norm are placed" (Foucault 1986:25). Heterotopias are places reserved by society for individuals in a state of crisis (death and cemeteries, madness and psychiatrics, etc.). However, Foucault's use of the heterotopia relates to the sociohistorical dimension and not to the literary, and his concept is sometimes loosely or overused in postmodern criticism. For this reason, the more restricted notion of 'fantastic hole' is as archetypical image of the Fantastic of Space, which nevertheless draws from the Foucauldian heterotopia.

The fantastic hole can be understood as a heterotopic form in that it is the physical form of the non-empirically perceptive or rationalised; that which does not fit within a given sociocultural frame. Furthermore, it is a liminal space that transgresses binaries, articulating absence and presence, oscillating between lack and excess of meaning.

There are various examples in history of how man has dealt with the supernatural in a 'heterotopic' way. In some Ancient cosmologies, the hole served as a symbolic projection of the unknown. That which could not be scientifically explained was assigned a space, both devoid of specific referents and below or beyond the visible confines of the territory while being at the same time a constituent part of this territory. For example, Anaximander's model of the universe consisted of a dark boundary (the sky) pierced through by holes (stars) that were seen as windows revealing a mysterious fire beyond. Another example is the Roman *Mundus* ('world' in Latin), a cavity in which the 'supernatural' was safely contained. The *Mundus* was a circular trench excavated for ghosts, spirits and other non-human creatures to be literally 'buried' there, with this receptacle of the supernatural ceremonially and exceptionally opened three times a year for the spirit of the dead to come among the living and to reconcile the two worlds (Rykwert 1988:59). The *Mundus* very clearly exemplifies the relationship between the notion of hole as boundary to distinguish and isolate the supernatural.

In the fictional text, the representation of this perforation of human reason often occurs in the metaphor of a physical structure that disappears, an unexpected hole in material space. An example is the house of "La casa feliz" (José María Merino 2004), a building that disappears just when it is about to be inhabited. This nomadic structure refuses to be bound to the physical laws that anchor it to the ground. This is also related to a recurrent motif which I call the 'pierced map': namely a certain place nowhere to be found in the maps. Take for example the cases of Castle Dracula (1847):

> I was not able to light on any map or work giving the exact locality of the Castle Dracula, as there are no maps of this country as yet to compare with our own Ordnance Survey Maps.
>
> (*Dracula*, Stoker 2003:6)

of Innsmouth,

> Any reference to a town not shewn on common maps or listed in recent guide-books would have interested me, and the agent's odd manner of allusion roused something like real curiosity.
>
> (*The Shadow over Innsmouth*, Lovecraft 1993:217)

and of the Rue d'Auseuil,

> I have examined maps of the city with the greatest care, yet have never again found the Rue d'Auseil. These maps have not been modern maps alone, for I know that names change. I have, on the contrary, delved deeply into all the antiquities of the place, and have personally explored every region, of whatever name, which could possibly answer to the street I know as the Rue d'Auseil.
>
> ("The Music of Erich Zann", Lovecraft 1984:56)

Elsewhere the fantastic hole works as an extension of reality by adding further dimensions. An example of this is Joe Hill's "Voluntary Committal" (2005). In a completely ordinary environment, a child builds a cardboard construction that leads to an unknown dimension from which no one has ever returned. Another variation of this motif takes a real extratextual space and perforates it, as is the case of the Naples in *La Porte des enfers* (Laurent Gaudé 2008). In this novel, which tells of a mother who mourns the tragic death of her lost child, various orifices arise in different areas of the city connecting it with the underworld.

Because the hole hides, it also evokes. This idea of a potential heightening through 'excess of meaning' can be interpreted in a Heideggerian sense: since they frame an absence (physical, ontological, epistemological), holes can be regarded as potential sources of anxiety. As the German philosopher suggested, "[a] boundary is not that at which something stops but, as the Greeks recognised, the boundary is that from which something begins its presencing" (1971:152).

This exact notion is the central theme of "La casa ciega" (David Roas 2010). The character becomes obsessed with the inside of a boarded house that he sees from the train during his regular journey to work. His anxiety increases when he realises, observing through his binoculars, that the boarded windows and doors of the house are fake, painted on the surface. The boarded house functions as some sort of Pandora's box. Even though the story cannot be said to belong strictly to the Fantastic, since nothing explicitly impossible occurs, the protagonist's fear is symptomatic of an ontological and epistemic uncertainty related to that which he cannot see: an empty and blind space that projects a multitude of possibilities. This recalls Westphal's statement that "to point at/to demarcate [*signaler*] emptiness, it is to start filling it" (2011b:77) and coincides with the doubt haunting Maupassant's work. His definition of the Fantastic as an unbearable uncertainty is captured with the following words in "Lettre d'un fou": "[…] cette terreur confuse du surnaturel qui hante l'homme depuis la naissance n'est autre chose que ce qui nous demeure voilé!" (2000:200). The eternal doubt, the compulsory question (Qui sait?), the anxiety of not-knowing why, how and what is at the heart of his Fantastic.

The hole can be considered as a paradigmatic form of fantastic transgressions of space because it captures in it the four thematic lines suggested in this book. First, the hole makes the *body* disappear from its exterior; it swallows it up (Chapter 2). Second, the hole challenges the ordinary framing function, the physical *boundary,* by perforating a solid space (Chapter 3). Third, it is an inversion of logical *spatial hierarchies*, since its inside could be unexpectedly larger than its external dimensions (Chapter 4). Finally, it can act as a whole *world*, extending what is presented as reality in the text into a further dimension (Chapter 5).

Among the various texts that could have been selected to illustrate how the fantastic hole works as paradigm of the Fantastic of Space, "Mi hermana Elba" (1980) by Cristina Fernández Cubas is the most suitable, since in this text the motif does not appear only in the referential dimension of space but also affects the syntactic, semantic and pragmatic dimensions outlined in my model of analysis (section 2). This allows for the connotations of the trope of the hole to be extended into a view of reality, as recurs in the postmodern Fantastic.

"Mi Hermana Elba" is the title given to Fernández Cubas' first volume of short stories (1980), a book that had a major impact on the growth of the Fantastic in Spain (Castro Díez 2000; Andres-Suárez and Casas [eds.] 2007; Roas and Casas [eds.] 2008). Fernández Cubas' use of narrative space and her skill in generating uncanny atmospheres are the most unique features of her prose.

In the story "Mi hermana Elba", the narrator, Elba's sister, finds her old diary after a long time. This diary contains a description of her childhood with Elba, who has since died. After their parents' divorce, the two girls were sent to an isolated boarding school. There, in the company of another student, Fátima, they discover certain places that are invisible to the rest of their companions and that make them invisible to others. After the summer, Fátima and the narrator begin to lose interest in these exceptional areas. Elba has meanwhile been moved to another school for special children and is increasingly ostracised by her sister. The story ends with Elba's sudden fall from a balcony, while the sister writes of how quickly she forgets this tragic event. The text closes with a perverse sentence in the diary ("TODAY IS THE HAPPIEST DAY OF MY LIFE" [2008:73], capitals in original), written by the narrator on the day of Elba's funeral, her happiness stemming from getting a kiss from the boy she fancied.[6]

Location: The Hideouts

The main location of the action is a boarding school run by an enclosed order of nuns. This convent is a rigidly structured space, constrained both by physical frontiers (e.g., the outside fence, the closed order's door, permitted and prohibited zones) and by disciplinary regulations. The narrator alludes to this isolation with the sentence "nothing could exist outside from those cold marbles, from the fruit-trees in the garden or the carob trees that flanked the entrance" (2008:59). Breaking with the constricted frame of the convent, the hideouts from external reality provide the means for the girls to extend their vital space and escape from the rules. In relation to this, note the recurrence of the microcosm topos in Fernández Cubas' fiction—for example, the closed nuns' order of "Mundo" (1994), the remote tower of *El columpio* (1995) and the house of "La ventana en el jardín" (1980).

It is important to note that a logical explanation for these fantastic spaces is not provided in the text; it is not specified, for example, even in retrospect, that these invisible and 'invisible-ing' spaces were invented by the young girls. On the contrary, there are various scenes that reaffirm the fact of the impossible nature of these spaces. From the start, these 'voids' exclude the girls from the logical rules of the real world.

Discourse: The Exception

These hideouts are referred to as an extension of confined space (they are "worlds without limits" [67]) and as an escape from monotony ("refuges" where they have "a strange immunity" [66]). Most importantly, these are spaces of alterity, in contrast to the norm. It is in this last aspect that the discourse on the Fantastic is located. From the start, the existence of these fantastic spaces is incomprehensible to the narrator, who does not view them as a natural part of her environment. These "mysterious conducts whose understanding escaped [them]" (66) challenge the discourse of reason:

> All sorts of images of the dangerous adventure I just lived were still spinning in my head but, above all, I had a large amount of questions for which, no matter how hard I tried, I couldn't find any satisfactory answer. (65)

Since these spaces constitute a referential void, there is no word in our compendium of signifiers that can adequately describe them. Their semantic construction is achieved through the technique of *catachresis*: they are assigned a term (and concept) of something existing in the actual real world which bears a physical and conceptual resemblance to them. In this respect, note the variety of *catachrestic* designations to refer to these spaces: "hideouts" (66), "conducts" (66), "paths" (67), "refuges" (69), etc.

Another rhetorical strategy used to designate these impossible spaces is that of 'semantic impertinence'. This strategy juxtaposes semantic fields that are if not incompatible, at least unconnected (Erdal Jordan 1998:115; Casas 2010:11–12). Some of these are "good" because they never "fail" (66), some of them are "ancient" (66), some are "small but safe" (66) and others are "spacious and cosy" (66).

As a consequence, their physical attributes create an initial cognitive dissonance in the reader. These spaces also cancel spatial dichotomies—in this case, the locational dichotomy of here-there—by representing both elements of the dichotomy simultaneously. The holes are neither here nor there. This is best captured in the sentence: "We were there but we weren't. Even if you thought we were there, we weren't there" (65).

The Perforated Story

One of the functions of the fantastic spaces in this story is to help trace the relationship and personal evolution of the protagonists. These spaces function as a leitmotif of the different stages in the lives of the protagonists and the interest in them ends with the arrival of adolescence. Considering this relation between fantastic hideouts and the characters, an allegoric reading of the story is very tempting. These spaces could be interpreted as projections of children's wishful thinking; these 'invented' areas allow them to extend their allowed zone of action and to transgress the mandatory boundaries imposed by adults. This is the interpretation favoured by Castro Díez (1992) and Beilin (2004), who regard these holes as symbols of children's need for protective and imaginary (sites as liminal moment between childhood and adolescence).

However, there are enough elements within the text to suggest that the fantastic element should not to be read as purely metaphorical. For instance, the discovery and existence of these spaces are explicitly described as surprising and ontologically problematic. This 'fantastic' reading reveals an insight into the issue of memory and time that has a lot in common with the postmodern context that this book deals with. It is necessary, in support of this point, to consider the fundamental role of the diary that provides the narration.

The diary is a discursive space that intensifies the verisimilitude of the event; it is an intimate testimony in first person. However, for the same reason, it enhances the subjectivity of the narrated facts. It is from the start a narration composed not only of memories but also of passages that cannot be remembered. This is clearly represented in the first page of the short story, in which the narrator juxtaposes the process of reconstruction with some impediments that her memory poses. Some passages and fragments in the written diary can be "illuminated by memory" (55) and others remain in the dark. Specially, what is missing is the thread that links the various elements concerning Elba's death and the narrator's reaction to it.

The adult character is about to access memories of her childhood and her sister Elba. However, in the process of reconstruction that memory necessarily implies, she just has her memories from the past, vulnerable to the modifications of time, and the diary, unaltered as an object but whose content is equally obscured by the passing of time.

Since we are dealing with a two-level framed narrative, the figure of the reader is a dual presence: the extratextual reader (us) and the intratextual reader (i.e., Elba's sister as an adult who is re-reading her old diary). We as readers might expect that the perspective the present offers of the past events will help clarify and, most importantly, connect the open questions in the story: for instance, the nature of the fantastic hideouts, Elba's mysterious powers and lethal fall from the balcony and the strange reaction of the main character, who quickly forgets both the hideouts as well as Elba's death. However, the story does not satisfy these expectations. The perspective of the present on what is told in the diary does not after all help to generate a tissue of logical connections between these open questions. On the contrary, part of the disturbing effect of the short story is that the adult narrator remains incapable, or unwilling, to fill in these blank areas with meaning. It is as if the very motif of the hideouts was transposed into the narrated events of the diary.

It is useful here to recall Wolfgang Iser's well-known concept of semantic gaps (1978a). According to Iser, narrative tissue is necessarily incomplete since it is based on selection of information. It is only through inevitable omissions that a story gains its dynamism. The act of reading, the reader's response to the text, helps weave connections between loose ends and also elaborates causal relationships silenced in the text. In Iser's view of literature as tissue, it is the figure of the reader that infers meaning and fills in these gaps. The active and creative reader gives the texts its consistency, not dissimilar to the illusion of consistency provided by physical space.

This is what Iser calls "consistency-building" (Iser 1978a:291). "[The reader] seek[s] continually for consistency, because only then can he close up situations and comprehend the unfamiliar".[7]

In "Mi hermana Elba", the reader's gap-filling exercise (establishing connections) is largely unsuccessful; neither the character nor the reader is capable of filling these crucial gaps in the narration, in particular those centred on an uncertain causation (What caused Elba's death? Why did the narrators forget Elba's death so quickly?), ontology (What is the nature of the hideouts?) and epistemology (What can we know about the past? How reliable is our memory?).

The Porous Reality

To draw an analogy between such invisible spaces and the act of remembrance, the text offers a view of memory as intrinsically composed by blind angles. These gaps, open cracks of an old diary, prevent a complete recuperation of the past and, in so doing, prevent a coherent means of understanding the present identity. The text thus evokes an image of memory as composed by a great deal of dead angles that prevent a *reconstruction* of the past. Memory is a faulty and perforated tissue precisely because every history is in itself a story, always entailing a subjective selection of information. By the very act of remembering, even one's own past becomes an incomplete testimony (cf. Lyotard 1984). This is perhaps the key idea underlying this text: the function of the fantastic holes in perforating physical solid space is paralleled with the role of narrative as a vehicle for referring to a (necessarily) incomplete reality. This approach to memory also promotes a view of the human mind as being composed of pores that prevent us from fully comprehending some phenomena that take place in factual reality.

The blank areas or holes inherent to the view of reality suggested in "Mi hermana Elba" are also found in other postmodern short fictions of the Fantastic.

Another illustrative example is "L'Érreur" (1974) by Jacques Sternberg, a short text that tells of a man who returns home only to realise that his building, number 64, has disappeared. On his street, number 62 is now adjacent to number 66. Even in the unlikely event that his house had been demolished during the day, an empty surface should have remained between 62 and 66, marking the space where his building once stood. The fantastic hole in this case is thus not only the absence of the building but also the impossible cancellation of space between the neighbouring buildings 62 and 66. What is remarkable is how the character tries to make sense of the fantastic event by attributing it to a trick played by his mind, "an error on his conscience, something forgotten" ("L'Érreur", Sternberng 1998:94), as if a loophole in the structure of his memory had been projected onto physical reality. The character of this story attributes the impossible disappearance of his house to some trick his mind plays on him.

This view of human psyche as mysterious, fragile and misleading was present in earlier works, for instance in Guy de Maupassant's fantastic short stories ("Who Knows?", 1890; "Le Horla", 1887). However, what confers Fernández Cubas' and Sternberg's texts with a postmodern aura is that in their stories the psyche is not viewed as a source of anguish and madness as is the case with the nineteenth century French author. Instead, the characters in these later stories accept this mental 'erosion' in a surprisingly natural manner. This feature, which will recur in the short stories analysed in the next chapters, presents the individual as someone who is certain that the mind is performing mental 'slippages'. The subject is aware that consciousness is as intermittent, porous and unreliable as the strange phenomena perceived in factual reality (such as a fantastic hole discovered in a boarding school or a building that vanishes unexpectedly). This becomes an interesting inversion of the traditional fantastic scheme, which had portrayed its characters as *victims* of the impossible occurrence. Now the subject is at least partially also an *agent causing* the Fantastic; in other words, an individual who is conscious of his/her own limitation when apprehending reality, which shows a distinct postmodern acceptance of insufficient reliable tools to explain the real (cf. Lyotard 1984).

* * *

I wanted to show in this chapter that an approach to the fantastic transgression as a phenomenon performed by space—the Fantastic of Space—opens up new angles of analysis and understanding. Just as the function of narrative space differs from the Fantastic of Place to the Fantastic of Space, so too is it true that not all transgressions of the Fantastic of Space are identical. A further analysis of this second model entails a more abstract reflection on how space intervenes in the human—and textual—construction of reality. To this end, the following four chapters are concerned with four central principles in the construction of human spatiality: 'body', 'boundary', 'hierarchy' and 'world'.

These four categories converge in the motif of the fantastic hole. While this motif is found throughout the history of the Fantastic, examining how it is treated in the specific case of the postmodern Fantastic reveals a paradigm that will recur in the following chapters. As in the short story of Cristina Fernández Cubas considered above, a world very similar to ours is built, but this world contains unpredictable holes that are constantly overlooked. Underlying this narrative is a view of reality as an inherently porous construction, containing a variety of gaps that our human inductive and deductive apparatus is incapable of deciphering. "Our minds are permeable to forgetfulness", says the protagonist of "The Aleph" (Borges 1999:286). Fernández Cubas herself captured this in her short story "Mi hermana Elba" and stated it even more explicitly in a later interview: "for me, the so-called reality is full of black holes" (interview by Paula Corroto, 2011, my own translation).

NOTES

1. This translation is mine.
2. Of importance is not only the physical place where the ghost story is read by Marsh. The time and date of the action were also carefully chosen by the author. The original publication in the newspaper *The Examiner* was timed to coincide with the date of the manuscript's central event, the 15th of July. Furthermore, Bierce changed Marsh's original "reading time" of the ghost story from 10 o'clock to a more 'ghostly' 12 o'clock. It has been suggested that this was done not only to respect the convention of this fateful time but also to evoke an atmosphere of complete darkness among the reader because it may not be totally dark at 10 o'clock in mid-July in northern countries (T. Blume 2004:181–183).
3. In scholarship of the Fantastic, the threshold is one of the spatial motifs that has received most attention. For studies on the threshold as setting, see Rust 1988; Castro 2002; May 2006; Gama-Khalil 2008, and for perspectives on the Fantastic as implicitly a liminal genre, see Todorov 1970; Jackson 1981; Ruthner 2012.
4. Stephen King also appeals to the history embedded in places in his story of the haunted hotel room "1408", which later became a feature film directed by Mikael Håfström (2007): "[...], every writer of shock/suspense tales should write at least one story about the Ghostly Room at the Inn. [...] hotel rooms are just naturally creepy places, don't you think? I mean, how many people have slept in that bed before you? How many of them were sick? How many were losing their minds? How many were perhaps thinking about reading a few final verses from the Bible in the drawer of the nightstand beside them and then hanging themselves in the closet beside the TV?" (King, Introduction to "1408" 2002:329).
5. This translation is mine. Philippe Vasset's book has given birth to the geo-sociological project *Zones Blanches: l'Atelier de géographie paralelle* (www.unsiteblanc.com), which aims to investigate and map all those blank spaces that "escape modelisation".
6. Since no official English translation of this short story could be found, all translations are mine.
7. "[...] the reader, in establishing these interrelations between past, present and future, actually causes the text to reveal its potential multiplicity of connections. These connections are the product of the reader's mind working on the raw material of the text, though they are not the text itself—for this consists just of sentences, statements, information, etc. [...] This interplay obviously does not take place in the text itself, but can only come into being through the process of reading [...] This process formulates something that is unformulated in the text and yet represents its intention" (Iser 1978b:278–287).

2 Body
(Not) Being in Space

"There would be no space at all for me if I had no body"
(Maurice Merleau-Ponty)

1. SUBJECT, SPACE, REALITY

Let us start our exploration of the linkage between space and transgression with the most simple, fundamental principle of human spatiality: we are in space. And this notion of being in space is as much physical and situational as it is existential. If something exists, it occurs, it *takes place*. As Robert T. Tally identifies in his introduction to *Spatiality* (2013), the reassuring arrow or dot of '*you are here*' in city maps is a relief (since it confirms orientation) and reveals a more transcendental dimension: our "cartographic anxiety" (2013:1), our spatial perplexity of being in the world. The human experience of reality is inextricably linked with how the body perceives space and, conversely, with how it perceives itself in space. This chapter will explore this double dimension. In particular, I will focus on the loss of agency that the postmodern experience of space brings to the individual, the bewilderment of not being there.

The short film *Marisa* (2009), by Spanish director Nacho Vigalondo, provides a clear example from where to begin the study of the transgressions of body and space. The film starts with the story of a woman, Marisa, whose mood oscillates according to her location. While initially this might seem unremarkable, her disorder gets more complicated when, as the narrator tells us, after a while her entire persona becomes susceptible to changes of position in space; depending on where she is located, she becomes different Marisas ("her changes of personality related to her position in space, with a sensitivity of less than a square meter", narrator in *Marisa*).[1] Here the narrator's struggle to find "his" Marisa starts: as he begins the search for her specific physical position in space. After a while, he discovers these specific coordinates. It is when Marisa is at the playground that she is the person whom the narrator had met, 'his' Marisa. Position, for Marisa, encompasses physical as well as existential emplacement. 'To be out of place' is interpreted literally in this short film as being someone else. The situation becomes more complicated still: Marisa ends up changing identity even when she is still in the same spot. When this occurs, the narrator realises that to find Marisa he would have to identify not only the right place but also the right time.

Another example of transgression of body and space is *Skhizein* (2008), a short film by Jérémy Clapin, often interpreted as a parable of schizophrenia. Henry, the protagonist and narrator, tells of how a meteorite has impacted his life: he is now exactly ninety-one centimetres from himself (see Figure 2.1). The opening sequence shows Henry's conversation with a psychologist. Henry tells him his story with the following words:

> I haven't always been here. Before, I was normal. Before it happened, I would have been there, on the couch, not over here, in mid-air, 91 cm from the couch, precisely 91 cm from where I should be.
>
> (*Skhizein* 2008)

A second meteorite displaces him further; where the first one had provoked a slippage sideways, this second one provokes a slippage of seventy-five centimetres downwards. As a result, Henry has to learn to live literally displaced from all the objects and people that surround him (see Figure 2.2). This dislocation triggers an existential crisis; he is "beside himself" ("*à côté de la plaque*"), a pun that indicates this displacement is not only physical but also mental. The entire short film revolves around the fusion between physical displacement (which is the fantastic motif) and shifts in personality, identity and in how one perceives others and is perceived by others (see Figures 2.3 and 2.4).

Figure 2.1 Henry's Displacement from Himself (© Dark Prince).

Figure 2.2 Learning the New Distances (© Dark Prince).

Figure 2.3 Henry's Dislocation (© Dark Prince).

Figure 2.4 At the Mont-Saint-Michel, Trying to Attract a Meteorite and
   Reverse the Slippage (© Dark Prince).

The space/body/subject triad has proved to be central in the schemes of the
real as interpreted under the lens of Phenomenology and Existentialism
such as is seen in Maurice Merleau-Ponty's philosophy on spatiality of
human existence and in Martin Heidegger's existential approach to space,
particularly reflected in his piece "Building, Dwelling, Thinking" (1951).

In *Phenomenology of Perception* (1945), Merleau-Ponty extensively elaborates on the perception of reality through the corporeal. He
develops a phenomenological insight into reality, understood as an experience mediated through our senses. In the experience of reality, physical
space is an experience both perceived and constructed by the individual's
corporeal awareness. At the heart of this experience, he argues, is the
body. The human body is a starting point that anchors all spatial relationships and experiences of distance, direction and location: "When I
say that an object is *on* a table, I always mentally put myself either in the
table or in the object, and I apply to them a category which theoretically
fits the relationship of my body to external objects" (1962:101, emphasis
in the original).

That the spatial environment is produced by the subject and the subject is
produced by space is the core idea of Merleau-Ponty's work, captured by for-
mulations such as "the body is our anchorage in a world" (1962:144), "the
body is our general medium for having a world" (1962:169) and "I regard

my body, which is my point of view upon the world, as one of the objects of that world" (70), all of these echoing the opening quote to this chapter.

Pursuing the same line of thought and drawing from the phenomeno-logical philosophy of Merleau-Ponty, architectural scholars and human geographers—among whom are Rasmussen (1959), Ching (1975), Tuan (1977), Pallasmaa (1996) and Saldarriaga Roa (2002)—have applied Merleau-Ponty's views on spatiality to built space:

> We believe that the most essential and memorable sense of three-dimensionality originates in the body experience and that this sense may constitute a basis for understanding spatial feeling in our experi-ence of buildings.
>
> (Moore and Yudell in Ching 1996:227)

> The world is reflected in the body, and the body is projected in the world. [...] Understanding architectural scale implies the unconscious measuring of the object or the building with one's body, and of pro-jecting one's body scheme into the space in question. We feel pleasure and protection when the body discovers its resonance in space.
>
> (Pallasmaa 2005:45–67)

These excerpts converge in one idea: architectural space is also experienced through the body. From a phenomenological angle, the body is the start-ing point of (spatial) experience. It serves as a referential axis in establish-ing spatial structures (vertical-horizontal, left-right, top-bottom), which are the positions of the body extrapolated onto the coordinates of space (see "The natural coordinate system", Bollnow 2011:44–54). When regarding material space as a sensorial experience, the codependence between body and space is asserted. As Finnish architectural scholar Juhani Pallasmaa expresses, "architecture strengthens the existential experience, one's sense of being in the world, and this is essentially a strengthened experience of self" (2001:41).

Implicit in this quote by Pallasmaa is an idea earlier developed by German philosopher Martin Heidegger. The existential awareness of 'being' (a 'subject') through this dialogue between body and space is the pivotal thought of his essay "Building, Dwelling, Thinking" (1951). As the title indi-cates, Heidegger elaborates on the existential relationship between being and dwelling, originating from the sensorial dimension of the built environ-ment. By 'dwelling', he means 'to inhabit the world'. But more importantly, the corporal experience of 'being in space' is equated with the act of being aware of the self. In other words, the subject perceives himself in relation to the space he occupies. The notion of 'being' for Heidegger associates insepa-rably this double existential and situational dimension, an opposition that, in contrast to other languages (e.g., the Spanish *ser* and *estar*), the English and German language merge into one single verb (to be; *sein*). Heidegger resolves this by adding a spatial deictic ('*da*', German for 'there'), resulting in his central term *Dasein*. The German philosopher thus stresses the inter-relation between ontology and position, between *being* and *being there*. To know that we exist is to know that we have a body that inhabits space and generates space—that we *take place*—a thought that coincides with Merleau-Ponty's view of corporeal perception as a way of stating 'I am in the world'.

What these phenomenological and existential views of spatiality recall is that the notion of physical reality (whether textual or actual) cannot be separated from that of emplacement or physical position. Just as there is no space without a body that experiences it, as Merleau-Ponty argues, there is also no body if there is no space for it to be in. From this, it can already be inferred that, in considering transgressions of space in fantastic narrative, the body/reality dyad will be crucial.

In the literary realm, in the volume *Raum und Bewegung in der Literatur* (Hallet; Neumann [eds.] 2009)—dealing, as the German title indicates, with space and movement in literature—the editors argue that the notion of spa-tiality (*Räumlichkeit*) is correlated with that of spatial experience (*Raumer-fahrung*): there is no space without movement, movement thus perceived as the dynamic act of a subject who observes space rather than necessarily as the physical displacement around (2009:20–21,66). Accordingly, space can-not be dissociated from the corporal experience of the one who perceives it. For this reason, the editors of the volume argue, the codependence of 'body' and 'narrative space' should be taken into account in any study on textual spatiality.

Remarkably, this basic premise is overlooked in the model of reality used by Todorov's well-known study on the Fantastic, originally published in 1970. Driven by the need to create a thematic study based on abstract cate-gories and not on lists of motifs, Todorov seeks reference in something more abstract: the scheme of human experience formulated by Witold Ostrowsky in "The Fantastic and the Realistic in Literature: Suggestions on How to Define and Analyse Fantastic Fiction". This schema comprises eight catego-ries, which I reproduce (in Todorov 1975:102):

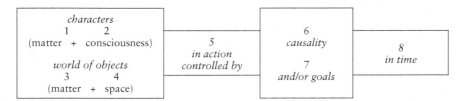

According to this schema, space is a category in which only objects are located, thus disregarding the physical emplacement of characters. But are characters not also in space? And could objects not also be characters of the story, as frequently happens in the Fantastic? This seems to indicate that

this scheme prioritises the temporal (the plot) over the spatial. While everything happens in time (category 8), the dimension of space is restricted to
an emplacement for objects (and thus, to being a neutral setting or physical
stage).

These significant omissions can be addressed by including space as a category in which *both* characters and objects *are*; since objects, especially in
narratives of the Fantastic, are frequently animated and thus endowed with
the potential agency of human characters. As a consequence, the potential
is opened up for a thematic field on the transgressions of physical bodies
(whether objects or characters) and/in space.

The transgressions of the body in space are of particular relevance in the
postmodern context and for the postmodern fantastic text. While phenomenological and existential analysis is rather a-temporal and remains on the
margins of sociocultural particularities, over the past few decades a large
number of critics have exposed how the relationship between the corporal
and the spatial becomes even more troubling in and by the Global era.[2] This
topic has been present to a significant degree in the postmodern discourse
of human geographers, who have sought to understand how the dialogue
between body and built space has failed, particularly in the late twentieth
century.

The fluctuating relationship between body and space is, according to
Fredric Jameson (1991), best seen in postmodern architecture. Taking the
architecture of the Westin Bonaventure Hotel in Los Angeles as the paradigm, Jameson draws a parallel between the building and a text (or texture)
whose meaning is to be completed by the movement of a body. He concludes
that the elusive and disorienting nature of this building repels the human
figure; it deconstructs hierarchies and the body cannot anchor itself in it.
There is no possible orientation nor apprehension of materiality, distance
and structure. This is paradigmatic of what Jameson denominates "postmodern hyperspace", a spatial experience that exceeds human perceptual
capability, a phenomenon of disengagement between the body and space
that profoundly affects the experience of the real. The postmodern production of space, as Jameson asserts, "has come to be felt as incompatible with
the representation of the body [...] The privileged space of the newer art is
radically antianthropomorphic" (1991:34), indicating an "alarming disjunction between the body and its built environment" (1991:44).

Anthony Vidler's view on the subject matter (1991) coincides with
Jameson's explanation of this phenomenon of corporeal fracture. Vidler's
thesis also establishes that Postmodernity (which he calls 'late modernity')
has given rise to a progressively disengaged relationship between space and
body. Going back to Vitruvius's references to the human finger, palm and
foot in architectural history, the view of built environment as a reflection of
the human body predominated for centuries. The dialogue between body
and built space finds its canonical example in *the Golden section*, that perfect proportion and scale where space and body feature in a harmonious

dialogue, which has fascinated artists and architects since Antiquity. By the nineteenth century, there was a progressive shift away from considering the body taken as the origin and essence of harmony. Increasingly, the modern— and even more so the postmodern—body no longer serves "to center, to fix, or to stabilise" (Vidler 1992:70).

This gives rise to a conception of material space as progressively detaching itself from the human figure. In the nineteenth century, architecture— influenced by the animistic ideals of Romanticism—begins to be conceived as an organism embodying states of the body and of the mind. During the later decades of the twentieth century, this process accelerates. The idea of space as no longer subject to the sovereignty of the human body is crystallised in Postmodernity. This period leads "inexorably to the final 'loss' of the body as an authoritative foundation for architecture" (1992:70). Ultimately, the 'bodily-analogy' is "abandoned with the collapse of the classical tradition and the birth of a technologically dependent architecture" (1992:69). The consequence leads to what Vidler calls the "architectural uncanny": the strange experience of built space perceived as animated, no longer reflecting proportions of the body, a detachment from the surrounding built environment. A decade after the publication of Vidler's text, the Dutch architect Rem Koolhas brought this idea of the architectural uncanny to the extreme in his article "Junkspace" (2002), where he argues that the loss of the 'bodily-analogy' in the late twentieth century is related to the growth of a dehumanised architecture, largely based on technologically dependent 'bubble buildings', such as the air-conditioned shopping centre.

Jameson, Vidler and Koolhas, among others, emphasise the loss of human dominance over the spatial environment, a phenomenon—as they argue— particularly prominent in Postmodernity. A central argument of these thinkers is that the fracture between body and spatial experience weakens the experience of 'being', also weakening the experience of factual reality. These aspects are of special interest in the exploration of the fantastic transgressions considered in this chapter.

2. CANNIBAL SPACES

In this section, physical space in the text is considered not as a simple inanimate entity, an innocent setting in which characters are present and where events unfold, but as quite the opposite: all the texts that follow have in common some type of space—a house or a room for instance—that is presented as an entity capable of devouring the human subject. This motif can recall for the reader the vampire or other fantastic blood-sucking creatures for whom the human body is a vital source. Finné, in referring to the American fantastic, notes that it is precisely when the figure of the ghost who haunts space disappears from fantastic literature that the motif of the predator-place appears (2006:11–44). This phenomenon is particularly identifiable in late-twentieth-century literature, which produced a myriad of novels and short stories featuring an evil, vampire, perverted, or sadistic house. "Le Jardin malade" ("The Sick Garden", 1941) by Michel de Ghelderode, Shirley Jackson's *The Haunting of Hill House* (1959), Richard Matheson's *Hell House* (1971), Anne River Siddons' *The House Next Door* (1978) and Stephen King's "1408" (2002) are classic texts of the Fantastic that present an evil and all-powerful space, capable of destroying whoever enters or finds himself in it.

A much more unusual and interesting text with this motif is "La casa" ("The House", 1975), by Peruvian writer José B. Adolph. Despite the fact that the author is acclaimed as one of the twentieth-century masters of the Peruvian Fantastic (Belaván 1977:160–171; Portals Zubiate 2009; "Tinta Expresa" 2010), Adolph's work has gone quite unnoticed in other countries, with only a few exceptions. Critical attention has focused on the elements of his oeuvre that fall into the conventions of the science fiction narrative (Lockhart [ed.] 2004:3–6). Nevertheless, some of Adolph's texts undoubtedly correspond to the definition of the Fantastic adopted in this book, with "La casa" one of the most famous of these.

"La casa" is a revolutionary text in the relationship between spatiality and the Fantastic that it presents. The text breaks with traditional patterns concerning the portrayal of the predator (as evil or menacing), the reasons for the human depredation of this predator (typically to keep itself alive or eternally young) and the subject's reaction to such an act (almost always fright or fear). Adolph's text offers, by means of a simple plot line, a clear example of the transgressive relationship between space and body. The story concerns a character referred to as A. who, immersed in his daily journey to work, finds himself inside a house he had never been to before. What seems to be an ordinary house quickly turns out to be a predator-place, a fact that A. realises when he experiences his body being slowly devoured by this house. Following the proposed methodological model in Chapter 1, I will take a closer look at this text through the four dimensions identified in that model—choice of setting, rhetorical construction, functions of space in the plot and examination of the spatial transgression in the context of the postmodern Fantastic.

Location: A Random House

In this short story, there are two central spatial frames: the exterior and interior of the house. It is in the latter that most of the action is concentrated. The function of the exterior frame is mainly to emphasise that the house is located in an ordinary neighbourhood. Right at the beginning, the reader is told that the character ends up in this house because he deviates from "the sweet monotony of the known path" (2009:585).[3] This phrase serves to segregate two domains: the known space, located in the exterior, and the exceptional, which will be found in this particular house, the characteristics of which are, at least at first glance, completely unremarkable.

In the first paragraph, the author brings forth the mundanity of the setting by describing the character's routine trajectory, which he follows every morning. He takes his everyday setting so much for granted that only "a true catastrophe" (2009:585) could make him aware of any modification in it.

The choice of a banal setting in the story establishes a contrast with the literary topoi of the haunted house and other classic horror-doomed spaces. Very little text is devoted to the description of the house itself, or to the specification of its geographical location. Aside from a few details that establish the house as one of many in a normal neighbourhood, there are no spatial referents; neither street nor city names are given to help us determine where the action takes place. There is initially nothing fearful or strange about this house. On the contrary, it is an unremarkable house containing typical domestic objects, all of which creates the impression of an ordinary inhabited building.

Another important spatial element is the threshold of the house. The function of this threshold differs from the importance often ascribed to thresholds in classic fantastic fiction (discussed in Chapter 1, section 3). There is a significant contrast with the Fantastic of Place, in which the physical boundary of the threshold differentiated both domains and acted as the frame or turning point in the plot when it was about to be crossed. In this case, the threshold is still a physical boundary segregating the natural from the supernatural domain; however, how and when it is crossed by the protagonist is as imperceptible as it is irrelevant. Instead, a strange 'logical' concatenation is implied: because the character is distracted, he ends up entering this supernatural domain of the house. There is neither anticipation nor description of him accessing the house. The exterior ("the sunshine" [585]) is abruptly replaced by the interior ("the pleasant darkness of a closed building" [585]) in the next scene.

Discourse: Fantastic Oxymorons

We know as little about the house as we know about the character. One of the few details provided about the protagonist is his name—solely the initial "A." (probably for "Adolph", paralleling Kafka's classic "K."). Therefore, most of the rhetorical devices are concerned not with *where* or *who* but rather with the interaction between the two—subject and space. What matters is *how* the devouring process takes place and how, then, this is perceived by the character.

The brutal and explicit devouring process contrasts with the submissive reaction of the character. The action starts with a force that strips A. naked, this section narrated in the passive form and thus omitting the agent responsible: "his cloths were being taken off" (586), "he was being dragged towards the living-room" (587) and "he was being attracted towards the second floor" (587). This does not cause alarm in A. but instead "indifference" (587) and a "sensual curiosity" (587), ending up in a "semierection" (587). This strange reaction turns to anguish when he realises it is the house that is causing his body to disappear, a fact that he quickly determines to be irreversible ("the impossibility of keeping totally isolated from the house and its intentions" [587]). However, at this point, our bewilderment as readers is but beginning.

From the moment A. decides he cannot fight the house (or so he thinks), he resolves to celebrate his physical dissolution with relief. A variety of references to the semantic field of comfort irrupt in the violent scene. That which is being told and how it is told seem disjointed, in what I will call 'Fantastic Oxymorons'. This is what forms the rhetoric of the Fantastic in this short story.

His head, about to be eaten up, lay "reclined in a *luxurious* manner on the fresh pillow" (588, emphasis added); "From now on he would be the tributary of the world, but vice versa. He would have liked to cross his hands around his neck; he did this gesture mentally" (588). The joy with which the character accepts his physical destruction gives the horrific scene a grotesque touch of humour, especially when the character starts considering the practical advantages of not having a body:

> A. sighed, comfortable, relieved. He started analysing, quickly, his possibilities in the world, his reinsertion, the easiest way to arrange his disability pension. [...] What did the loss of arms and legs mean? Did he ever really use them? And concerning his sexual organs, was man not essentially intelligence and soul? (588)

The contrast between the cannibalistic act and the happy, submissive, even eroticised reaction of the character is further accentuated in the final scenes. The house starts vibrating, "while it devoured the slim body of A., who closed his eyes, smiling ..." (588). The tale closes with the atomisation of his body into pieces that the house expels into the exterior, while the remains of his eyes "gave a delirious gaze at the impeccable and cozy ceiling" (588). The "delirious gaze" (588) and the two adjectives "impeccable" and "cozy" once more reinforce the idea of an individual who welcomes the physical dissolution of his body, absorbed by this house.

Another disjunction is centered on the tempo. The abrupt and rapid disappearance of the character's body parts is juxtaposed with the calm ambiance and tempo of the devouring, as seen in these excerpts:

> It was as if a solicit butler urged him, with quiet paternalism, to take off his jacket. (586)

> The bed started to vibrate, making him sleepy, while it devoured with infinite patience [...]. (588)

Equally disconcerting is the character's submissive and positive attitude to this act. This is highlighted by the lack of discourse on evil or horror surrounding both the house itself and the actual event. This fact could also be regarded as oxymoronic: very frequently the motif of the 'doomed' space appears hand-in-hand with that of the 'evil' space. In this way, the supernatural features of a space are explained in connection with its desire to harm (physically or psychologically) its inhabitant, thus the plot is centred on how to escape from this diabolic space. Among the various examples mentioned in the introduction to this section (*The Haunting of Hill House*, 1959; Matheson's *Hell House*, 1971; King's "1408", 2002), the best example is Anne R. Siddons' house (*The House Next Door*, 1978). Amidst the quiet and perfect American suburban life, this house is capable of corrupting those who enter it, by pushing them to commit adultery for example. The house/neighbourhood relation is based on the categories of evil/good; therefore, the entire story deals with how to avoid the perverse influence of this building. In "La casa", in contrast, the devouring is not presented as evil, as might be expected, but instead as surprisingly pleasant; the anthropophagous act is portrayed with absolute lack of moral judgment.

Story: Banalisation of the Fantastic

When it comes to assessing the role that space performs in the story, "La casa" is a good example of a fantastic text that prioritises neither place nor character but emphasises instead a 'spatial event': the anthropophagous act by the house. This action is presented as banal: the figure of the predator is an ordinary place; the finality of the action, random and the character ends up submissively accepting this supernatural destruction with joy.

These three elements point to the tradition of the Fantastic inaugurated by Kafka's *Metamorphosis*, in which the physical transmutation is accepted by the character with abnegated passivity. In Adolph's short story, the reason or motivation for the house's devouring of the body of the protagonist is not even alluded to and—very much in tune with Kafka—the source of anguish is precisely the randomness of the act. The influence of the Czech author is also explicitly stated in the epigraph preceding the story.

The exact idea or topic drawn from Kafka's work is not specified. Perhaps the figure of prison space, in whose complex structure and mechanisms the subject is entrapped (cf. *The Castle* or *The Trial*)? Maybe the theme of random physical mutation or effacement, central in *Metamorphosis*, "A Hunger Artist" and "In the Penal Colony"? An entry in Kafka's diary (1913) was found to feature a scene that coincides with the central idea of Adolph's short story. In it, Kafka blends the motif of a threatening space with that of corporeal devouring, in an image that bears strong parallels with the anthropophagous space of "La casa" (cf. Osborne's analysis of "The Hunger Artist", 1967):

> To be pulled in through the ground-floor window of a house by a rope tied around one's neck and to be yanked up, bloody and ragged, through all the ceiling, furniture, walls and attics, without consideration, as if by a person who is paying no attention, until the empty noose, dropping the last fragments of me when it breaks through the roof tiles, is seen on the roof.
>
> (Kafka 1965:291)

This anguished Kafkian dream illustrates the horror of being exposed to a random power beyond human control, without the possibility of resistance or escape. The cause of the mutilation in Kafka's paragraph is almost banal: simply "a house" (1965:291), with no further spatial markers.

Similarly, in Adolph's story, the function of space is displaced from the 'where' in which it happens to the 'what' that is causing it, from setting to agent. This corporeal transformation, or destruction, in "La casa" reveals an existential dimension of the supernatural. Adolph's treatment of this event is remarkably different to Kafka's. The character's reaction is the key in "La casa": he not only accepts his dehumanisation with passivity (as Gregor Samsa does), but he goes so far as to celebrate it with joy.

The Body-Less Subject

The reader's reaction is expected to be quite different where the subject accepts his new state in a calm manner. The oxymoronic construction of the scene and the randomness of it are what render the transgression particularly abrupt, surprising and unpredictable for the reader. Quite apart from the lack of finality, there is no transition scene marking when and how the character has entered the house. Nor is there any indication as to why those particular space and time coordinates caused events to unfold as they do. As mentioned, this is a significant innovation on the traditional motif of the all-powerful, doomed or evil space, in which finality and causality are explicit.

Even more shocking for the reader is the character's joyful apprehension of his own brutal destruction. A., after a brief moment of panic, resigns himself to his new condition and trades his physical position in the world in exchange for a better plane of existence. Strangely, A. is certain that losing his body does not equate with death. In a moment of epiphany, he realises that by being body-less he will occupy a 'better' position (if not physical, existential) in the world.

Kafka's "involuntary complicity", as Adolph writes in the epigraph, is indeed strongly present in "La casa", both in the theme itself as well as in the story's random and illogical elements. By emphasising the natural acceptance of the supernatural event by the character (for example in *Meta-morphosis*) while this supernatural event would still be presented as prob-lematic within the textual world—and so conceived as 'fantastic' (and not as 'marvellous') by the reader—Kafka's use of the fantastic element marked a turning point in the Fantastic.[4]

However, Samsa's supernatural metamorphosis globally expresses an existential anguish over exclusion. This seems to be overcome in Adolph's text by A.'s acceptance of the new supernatural condition of being body-less. In so doing, Adolph's text displays a typically postmodern feature: it is both a continuity (the supernatural is accepted with abnegation) as well as a rupture (while it is accepted, it is not threatening and even celebrated) with the tradition of the Fantastic.

In "La casa", this new state of being incorporeal is presented not as a potential sign of exclusion but rather as one of inclusion. A. shows a distinct lack of fear of being rejected by society; instead, he quickly starts thinking of possibilities of "re-adaptation" (588) and of the advantages of his new plane of existence. What is suggested in the text is that by accepting this irremedi-able and illogical situation, the subject can find his position in the physi-cal world. Physical devouring is no threat because the body is presented as unnecessary. What is truly Fantastic is that the idea of not occupying a physical position is still accepted as an ontological possibility: a not-being-in-space, to invert Heidegger's concept.

What is more, this experience is ecstatic, as is very clearly shown at the end of the story. In the process of his body being torn apart, A. embraces with joy his imminent body-less condition ("maybe it will be more comfort-able to live away from the fruitless tensions and threats of the world: with-out moving, without acting, without enjoying and without suffering" [588]), and in the last paragraph he exclaims: "life is beautiful" (588).

3. MAGNET-SPACES

The character of "La casa" welcomes the disintegration of his body with joy and as a relief because for him being body-less does not imply not being in space. The texts of this following section, however, consider characters that are completely deprived of their own agency; they cease to be *subjects* to become *subjected* to the space they live in. As a consequence, the fantastic transgression of space goes beyond the point to a more profound examina-tion of the notion of personal space.

The bond between a character and a place is one of the key themes in, for example, "The Fall of the House of Usher" (1839), where the family line is embedded in the house, so much so that the end of the family line is manifested in the crumbling of the house. The transgression of Poe's text is related to a common conception in Romanticism of nature as organism, where space is a metonymic or metaphoric expression of the character. The unity between nature and human beings is literal in this short story, where environment and character are one single, united and codependent entity.

The sample texts selected for this section also play on this correlation, but, in contrast to the Romantic ideal, subject and space are not in harmonic equity in them. The impossible element is centred on the domination of space over the individual, to the point where physically leaving the space becomes impossible, resulting in an irrational and unavoidable attachment to the place in question.

An earlier allusion to this type of transgression is found in the novel *The Haunting of Hill House* (Shirley Jackson 1959). However, the attractive force of space, although suggested, is here explained as one of the various evil characteristics of this Gothic mansion: "The house was vile. She shivered and thought, the words coming freely into her mind, Hill House is vile, it is diseased; get away from here at once" (1999:33).

The story tells of an old and remote house with a history of deaths and other strange occurrences. A group of four people resolve to spend some time in it to discover more about its hauntings. Among them is Eleanor, the most fragile of the group and catalyser of the supernatural. The attractive force of the house manifests when she drives towards it. Despite warning voices, she cannot help but enter the house. Also, despite her colleagues' advice to leave the house for her own mental health, she is determined to stay and ends up developing a strange bond with it, a bond that will crystallise in the macabre ending of the tale: immediately after leaving the premises, Eleanor crashes into a tree and dies.

As the story develops, the authority of the building over its inhabitants becomes clearer. The house seems to have its own specific norms that have to be obeyed and respected. "'The linen,' Mrs. Dudley said, 'belongs in the linen drawers in the dining room. The silver belongs in the silver chest. The glasses belong on the shelves'" (1999:101). The repetition of "belong" shows that the house is portrayed as a space with elements that appertain to it, with their specific emplacement and function, as if they were the organs of a body whose distribution must not be altered if they are to function properly. With this system of rules, the mansion is presented as a closed-off system. The house is a world apart, with its own rules. Even the characters refer to the house as a desert island ("'We are on a desert island,' said Luke. 'I can't picture any world but Hill House,' Eleanor said" [151]).

Whoever inhabits this house becomes an integral part of it. Whoever is in it is stripped of his/her independence to act and think. This idea is transmitted through the image of an all-powerful space that is not willing to let any of its inhabitants go: "The house. It watches every movement you make" (85), "The gates are locked. Hill House has a reputation for insistent hospitality; it seemingly dislikes letting its guests get away" (67). This is most clearly seen in the last scene, as Eleanor dies the instant she is exposed to the exterior. Outside of the house-organism, its parts cannot survive: "I *won't* go, she thought, and laughed out aloud to herself; Hill House is not as easy as *they* are; just by telling me to go away they can't make me leave, not if Hill House means me to stay" (245).

Shirley Jackson's novel is an early example of space as a transgressive element in fictional reality. Hill House goes beyond the traditional role of space as an inanimate physical container and becomes a subject with a specific agency: namely, the capability of mesmerising the character and exercising an unavoidable power of attraction. Despite this, the treatment of this fantastic space—especially in the choice of setting and plot structure—cannot be said to be hugely innovative. Jackson's text stays very much within the conventions of the Gothic haunted house frame. This is seen, for example, in the geographical isolation, intricate labyrinthine structure of the building, the uncanny aura surrounding it and the motif of "the purposeful exploration of the haunted house to determine its true nature and restore it to its original condition" (Aguirre 1990:93). All this leads to the conclusion that although Hill House is presented as an impossible element in the novel, it is its role as generator of the gloomy atmosphere that is to the fore. There is very little development on the way in which this building alters the physical laws of space.

A more innovative use of the motif of the magnet-space is found in two short stories selected as models for this section. The first text is "El museo" ("The Museum", 1982) by José María Merino. The second one is "Habitante" ("Inhabitant", 2008) by Patricia Esteban Erlés. The Fantastic is one of the favourite narrative forms of Merino, the author having employed it consistently throughout his creative production as seen in volumes like *Cuentos del reino secreto* (1982)—from which "El museo" is taken—*El viajero perdido* (1990), *Días imaginarios* (2002) or *Cuentos de los días raros* (2007). His contribution to the postmodern Fantastic has also attracted substantial critical attention (Andres-Suárez 1997; Alonso 2000; Roas in Andres-Suárez and Casas [eds.] 2005).

The second author, Patricia Esteban Erlés, is a young yet already established voice of the contemporary fantastic short story. In her stories, the Fantastic recurs but with a distinct innovative approach to traditional themes, as the analysis here will demonstrate.[5]

These two short stories are clear examples of the figure of the magnet-space and offer a distinctive treatment of the fantastic element that is closer to José B. Adolph's presentation of the devouring-place in "La casa" than to the classic space of Shirley Jackson's Hill House.

Location: Strangely, At Home

José María Merino's "El museo" tells of a young anthropologist who visits his uncle in a small village in Spain. This uncle had set out to create a museum composed of all sorts of everyday objects of his house. During the visit, the uncle offers to bequeath the collection to his nephew. Accepting this offer, however, requires a permanent stay at this museum-house. For the nephew—who is the narrator—this idea of being confined to an isolated country-house is ridiculous, going against his desire to travel the world. And yet he ends up accepting the offer, although initially only for a short while. From then on, and for more than forty years, leaving the museum becomes impossible. During all that time, despite the narrator's plans of going somewhere, an irrational force keeps him tied to the space.

The museum-house is, then, the main setting of this story and is located in the Valley of Omaña, a rural area of the Spanish Province of León. The volume of collected works from which the story is taken devotes a great deal of attention to spatial descriptions, using real referential spaces to strengthen the effect of a realistic environment. However, it is important to note that Omaña, for example, is less relevant as topos than as realistic space. The fact that the author has chosen a specific real place in which to set his stories is not so much to testify to the magical potential or to refer to the superstitions of this location, as some critics have claimed (Candau 1992:43). Instead, this referential setting is employed to strengthen the effect of realism in contrast to the fantastic effect. As Roas emphasises, it "would work equally well (talking exclusively about the fantastic dimension) if his stories were set in Madrid, Barcelona or Cádiz" (Roas 2005:162).

Equally mundane is the setting of "Habitante". In the compilation from which this story is taken (*Manderley en venta*), spaces are again important; more specifically interior space functions as leitmotif. As stated in the back cover description: "*Manderley en venta* is a book of interiors [...]. In almost all of them, the house, life indoors, has a prominent role in the narration; it is one of the characters, silent but constant".

"Habitante" is the only short story of the volume where a place not only hosts the Fantastic but is also an active agent of the transgression. In the space of five pages, the author manages to create a disturbing scenario that culminates in a surprising ending. A young woman finds precisely the exact apartment she had been looking for, an idea that is recurrently emphasised. In this apartment, there are still some remaining traces of the last owner Virginia (her name on the metal plate, her black swimsuit, her marks left on the chopping board), who drowned in the swimming pool. For most of the story, the narrative could represent anyone's experience of moving into a new place in the awareness that it previously belonged to someone else. However, the last lines of the story turn this seeming normality upside down: when someone rings the doorbell one evening asking for Virginia, the protagonist unexpectedly answers that she will be down in a second, puts on the black swimming suit and leaves the apartment.

The story thus presents many open questions and a variety of readings: did the protagonist assume Virginia's identity? Was she somehow driven to the house to replace Virginia? Will she undergo the same fate as the previous inhabitant? The author could be playing with the classic motif of the exchange of identities, as typically reflected in Julio Cortázar's short story

"Lejana" (1951). However, the characters of both Virginia and the narrator are very scantly developed. The same applies to the locus of the action. In contrast to the specific setting of "El museo", here very little is mentioned about the location of the apartment. The reader knows only that it is number 27 on Hobson Street, located in a compound with a swimming pool. These few details are in contrast to the extended account of the relation between the house and the narrator.

What is remarkable about the settings of both stories is precisely how unremarkable they are: a countryside house and a modern urban apartment. Similar to "La casa", and in contrast to Jackson's intricate Gothic Hill House, there is nothing extraordinary about the buildings themselves, other than the random attraction they seem to provoke in the two protagonists.

It is not the setting, therefore, but rather another aspect that is striking, an aspect related to the concept of home. In "El museo", 'home' is a museum of "undecipherable domesticity" (1982:150), whose "appearance of being lived" (1982:150) strikes the character from the start. Also peculiar is the title of "Habitante". Even though the apartment is the heart of the action, "inhabitant" inherently alludes to how a particular place is *lived*. Inhabiting means the appropriation of space as habitat, this being reflected in the fact that the apartment from the start is perceived, strangely, as home. Therefore, the fantastic element in these short stories is not just a place with supernatural qualities as in "La casa"; what is at stake here is a question of relation between 'home' and 'inhabitant'.

Discourse: The Physical Bond

In "El museo" and "Habitante" any physical body is conceived as an integral part of it, in a manner that preserves this "strange harmony" (1982:150) among the elements that belong to this space. The fantastic relation between body and space is based on a specific understanding of the word 'belonging'. The Oxford English Dictionary differentiates between three contexts in which the verb 'to belong' appears:

1 "to be the property of" or "to be dominated by";
2 "to be a member of", and [*usually with adverbial of place*, emphasis in the original] also to "have an affinity for a specified place or situation";
3 referring to emplacement, once more with an adverb of place, "to be rightly placed in a specified position".

In these two short stories, the three definitions merge: position in space is equated with being part of space, being dominated by and being a property of it.

The fantastic relationship between subject and space is constructed around three elements. There is the image of a strange attraction between character/ house, best observed in "El museo". The second strategy refers to a strange familiarity between the two, an idea more developed in "Habitante". In the third, this space is portrayed as an organism with its own rules, an aspect strongly present in both stories.

In "El museo", the power of attraction of space upon the body is explicitly described as the character plans to leave for the first time on a trip but, as he says, "all efforts to get away from the house and the valley were pointless" (1982:156):

> I perceived then an unexpected irritation in me. Looking at the path that wound down the valley, I sensed my look and my presence being reclaimed by the museum as a fervent wish not willing to let me leave. I realised that I could not go, and told the valet to unload the luggage.
>
> That was the first time that I felt mysteriously tied to the museum, [...] to be entrapped in the domain of an arcane power that did not allow me to move away [...]. (156)

As these passages show, the house is portrayed as exercising a strong magnet effect over the human body from the very moment the narrator resolves to live in it, this done using expressions from a domain which the reader does not usually associate with the semantic field of inhabiting a space (cf. "semantic impertinence", Casas 2010:11) as, for example: "mysteriously tied to the museum" or "the domain of arcane power" (1982:156).

While the plot of "El museo" is built around this attractive force, what is striking in "Habitante" is that the character and the building are in a relationship of 'excessive familiarity' from the start. The short story begins *in medias res*—"It cannot be possible" (2008:53), an expression that plays upon a double reading between astonishment vis-à-vis a coincidence and the reaction when faced with something impossible. This sentence is uttered at the start by the protagonist, who finds out that the building that had captured her attention a while ago is now for sale. The ambiguity of this first sentence is extended to other expressions such as "it is precisely what I was looking for" (2008:53), "unmistakable, it cannot be another one" (2008:53). She then circles the newspaper ad, an action equated with an establishing of the confines of this space that, she is certain from the start, belongs to her ("to delimit my territory" [54]). The idea of premature possession, before she has even moved in, is best expressed in the sentence: "This apartment is morally already mine" (in the Spanish original, literally "ya es moralmente mío" [55]). As if the house represented her system of values, or even as if the house represented her, the adverb 'morally' stands out in this sentence. Another element that stands out is the temporal ambiguity between "is" and "already". Once again, this ambiguity might not be random; the expression can be taken literally as being in the present tense, indicating that she belongs there even before having physically been in it. This would explain her anxiety over someone else taking the apartment *from her* and not just before her.

This 'excessive familiarity' is reinforced with the use of the grammatical articles. From the beginning, without introduction, it is directly referred to as 'the' house, a definite article that makes it exclusive and univocal ("The house is unmistakable" [53]). This determinant seems to presuppose that the encounter of house and protagonist recounted in the story is not the initial encounter with this building, even when in reality it is.

As the story evolves, this idea of the house belonging to the narrator is inverted to her belonging to the house, an aspect present in "El museo" from the start. The house even has its personal system of norms. There are various details indicating that the interior of the building has to be preserved as it is; it does not tolerate any modifications by the narrator. For example, the house of "Habitante" reclaims its original wall colour: after the protagonist starts painting one in blue, she feels a strong urge to change it back to its original white colour. Only then is she at peace ("I sigh with relief when I finally get to leave it as it was before" [56]). In "El museo", the elements that belong to the museum relate to each other in "a strange harmony" (1982:150), as if those objects that otherwise would never be related formed a coherence. Also, the presentation of space as organism is reinforced by its sharp segregation from the outside: "The world is still out there, waiting for me. A world different to the museum. After forty years, six months and seventeen days" (1982:158).

Story: Stratigraphic Space

One of the central functions of the museum and the house in the short stories is to convey the idea of cyclical plot. In this sense, time also plays a role in the Fantastic. The house and the museum are generators of a temporal transgression, this being the strange repetition of events that Freud identified as a source of the uncanny ("persistent recurrence", Freud 1993:145). In both cases, the imprint of the past is fundamental. In geocritical terms, the "stratigraphic" property of space (Westphal 2011a:137–143)—the history embedded in the house and the museum—is a responsibility that weighs on the characters. Only by appointing the next successor can the protagonist of "El museo" leave this space for good, as happens in the end. The protagonist of "Habitante" also ends up repeating the steps of her predecessor.

The temporal imprint on space is immediately brought to the foreground by the title itself, "El museo". The original owner decided to make a museum of his own life, represented in a vast catalogue of objects in what is otherwise an ordinary house. Just as the notion of museum responds to the desire to preserve identity over the passing of time, so too does it involve the physical representation of memories so that they can be exhibited to the exterior. The Bachelardian view of home as the site of intimacy and self-development (1958) is turned upside-down; domestic space is converted into a display window for voyeurs. The character abandons his dreams and personal needs in order to dedicate himself entirely to the preservation of the museum; the subject becomes an object within the museum.

The protagonist of "Habitante" also succumbs to the past that is embedded in the house. She answers the call for Virginia, puts on the swimming suit and goes down, maybe following the same fate as the previous inhabitant, who herself might also have followed a predecessor's steps. As in Adolph's "La casa" and Merino's "El museo", there is no intention of rationalising the situation or of resisting it. The building exercises its power of attraction, persuasion and, at least in "Habitante", possibly lethal agency over the subject. Furthermore, this space has its own rules by which the human must abide. And, finally, it not only contains a story from the past but also generates the repetition of this story: the character is trapped not only in the confines of the place but also in the confines of its history.

Although both houses are presented as physically unremarkable, they exert a mesmerising, overpowering force upon the human characters, to the point where these spaces bend the individual's will power. Once more, what matters is not the specific place but the influence it exerts and how it distorts the laws of reason; the fantastic element is found in the magnetic force of a space presenting an illogical, irresistible attraction. The subject, on the other hand, is presented as an entity whose willpower and independence to act freely are annihilated. The temporal charge of space accentuates the image of, literally, a burdening chain preventing free movement. The subjects are conditioned by the past, embedded within the four walls of the different spaces they inhabit. This could be read as a hyperbole for isolation and as a dependence on one's own comfort zone, which results in a type of paralysis when attempting to leave, just as occurred to the character of "Eveline" in James Joyce's *Dubliners* (1914).

To return to the Heideggarian correlation between 'living' and 'being': in "El museo" and "Habitant" 'living' is equated with a loss of individuality—'physical position' inside these buildings means 'being possessed by these buildings'. Thus, fantastic transgression could be regarded as a literalisation of the Heideggerian 'being', merging the existential emplacement with the physical. Being (*located*) inside literally means being (*part of*) the inside. The characters are then urged to accept the implications of being the 'inhabitant' of this space, "with all the horror it hosts", as the epigraph of "Habitante" anticipated.

The Captured Body

Notwithstanding plot differences and divergent locations and endings, common to both short stories is that the protagonists abandon who they are in order to replace the previous inhabitants; what is more, by the end of "El museo" the character has found someone to take his place. Not only do the characters surrender from the start to the power of attraction exercised by the house, but they also hand themselves over to its will and become

part of its story. This is significantly different from the Romantic conception of space, where space is conceived of as an organism at one with the
subject in a mutually influencing relationship. In these stories, by contrast,
space inhibits and overcomes the subject. This is expressed in the motif of
being attached to a particular place, of not having any free will in that place
and, literally, of losing the capability of physical movement when away
from it. The subject's loss of agency is absolute.

Just as the vampire may need human victims to survive, this doomed
space always requires a human captive. A further example in which the
same motif is present is "La habitación maldita" ("The Doomed Room",
2004) by Fernando Iwasaki. In this micro short story, the protagonist spends
the night in a hotel room. During the night, something awakens him whis-
pering that, this time, he will be the one staying. Only by finding a successor,
another guest who will spend the night there and take up his position, will
he be liberated from the room.

In the final text of this chapter, the dissolution of the body (as in
"La casa"), and physical and mental surrender (as in "El museo" and
"Habitante"), merge into one last figure—the most radical of all transgres-
sions of emplacement.

4. PRIVATOPIAS AND THE PSYCHASTHENIC EXPERIENCE

Of all the fantastic transgressions of body in/and space dealt with in this
chapter, this last is perhaps the most complex. This transgression can be
labelled as 'psychasthenia', a term used here to refer to a subject incapable
of demarcating himself/herself from the physical environment. The Fantastic arises when, by mimicking space, the human body becomes the space it
occupies and, as a result, the notion of position or physical emplacement
ceases to exist.

From the Greek *psykhe* (soul, mind) and *asthenia* (weakness), psychasthenia was a term that referred to a mental pathology of the mind related
to anxiety and obsessive-compulsive syndrome (Jakes 1996:63–75). Most
relevant here, however, is how this term was employed by the sociologist
and scholar of the Fantastic Roger Caillois in an article entitled "Mimicry
and Legendary Psychasthenia" (1935). Although in his article Caillois does
not refer to the Fantastic specifically, his idea of psychasthenic experience
bears strong parallels with the topic developed in this section. Caillois
starts by asserting the importance of distinction in any form of knowledge:

> Among distinctions, there is assuredly none more clear-cut than that
> between the organism and its surroundings; at least there is none
> in which the tangible experience of separation is more immediate.
> (1938:86)

He then proceeds to wonder what causes the phenomenon of mimicry in the natural world, since there is evidence that physical fusion cannot simply be attributed to a desire for self-preservation from predators. His hypothesis is quite daring: this behaviour of certain species, which includes mechanisms such as chromatic mimicry (colour copy) and homomorphy (adaptation from form to form), is not simply a strategy for survival. It is pathological. This pathology is what he terms as "legendary psychasthenia" (1938:111), essentially "a disturbance in the perception of space" (1938:111).

Psychasthenia is a mechanism that juxtaposes the perceived with the represented experience of space, the mental with the physical. Simply put, *the entity thinks it is the space it occupies*. While Caillois is referring to a pathology in certain types of animals, psychasthenia is a notion that can be extrapolated productively to the fantastic text. It designates a distortion that takes place when the subject begins to regard himself not as self but as a particular place. And so the notion of emplacement—of body in space—vanishes:

> It is with represented space that the drama becomes specific, since the living creature, the organism, is no longer the origin of the coordinates, but one point among others; it is dispossessed of its privilege and literally no longer knows where to place itself.
>
> (Caillois 1938:110)

Of particular interest is Caillois' description of how this mechanism affects the notion of individuality, or of 'being'. As mentioned in the introduction, it is a basic phenomenological and existential premise that the human being distinguishes herself/himself from the surroundings by being aware of the position the body occupies. Caillois mentions that psychasthenia is not a mere technique of camouflage; it is also a mental transformation that necessarily implies some self-renunciation for assimilation into the environment to occur:

> Then the body separates itself from thought, the individual breaks the boundary of his skin and occupies the other side of his senses. He tries to look at himself from any point whatever in space. (1938:111)

The concept of psychasthenia has been recently readapted in the field of urban sociology to refer to the dissolution of the subject in vast extensions of space. As exemplified by the following paragraph, in her book *Megalopolis* (1992), Celeste Olalquiaga uses the term "psychasthenia" to refer to a form of urban malaise in the experience of the contemporary urban environment:

> [...] a state in which the space defined by the coordinates of the organism's own body is confused with represented space. Incapable of demarcating the limits of its own body, lost in the immense sea that circumscribes it, the psychasthenic organism proceeds to abandon its own identity to embrace the space beyond.
>
> (Olalquiaga, in Soja 2000:151)

In the realm of the Fantastic, one author has extensively explored this theme: British writer J. G. Ballard. In an essay entitled "Which Way to Inner Space?" (1962), Ballard revealed his interest in physical and psychological interiors to be a source of creativity in his work: "the biggest developments of the immediate future will take place, not on the Moon or Mars, but on Earth, and it is inner space, not outer, that needs to be explored" (1962:117). In this essay, the author was specifically referring to science fiction, manifesting his desire to distance himself from these traditional forms so that he could exploit in his writing the potential of the genre as a means for self-exploration. This idea gave birth to one of his distinctive features—Ballard's "psychogeographies"; the fusion of mind and built environment populate his novels and short stories, as well as his fictionalised autobiographies. Examples of "psychogeographies" are illustrated in the following excerpts from two of his most famous short stories:

> It was almost as if the barriers between the deepest levels of the nervous system and the external world had been removed, those muffling layers of blood and bone, reflex and convention.
> ("The Giocconda of the Twilight Moon", 2006:114)

> [...] this island is a state of mind.
> ("The Terminal Beach", 2006:30)

As these quotes show, when the boundary between the external world and the internal perception of the character is diffused, there is no sense of objective tangible reality, only "a state of mind" (2006:30). This feature of Ballard's writing has prompted a great deal of scholarship focusing on the influence of Surrealism upon his construction of territory (Delville 1998; Baxter 2009).

Space occupies a primordial position in Ballard's texts, insofar as it transcends its ordinary function as a "place of action" to become an "acting place" (Bal 1997:136). In most of his fiction, space influences story and story becomes subordinate to the presentation of space. Closed spaces particularly illustrate the conflictive relationship between the modern subject and his environment. Ballard's own biography, marked by a disaffiliation with the different places in which he lived, has been considered as being a source of inspiration to his writing (Luckhurst 1997; Gasiorek 2005). Ballard himself states this in his most autobiographical works, *Empire of the Sun* (1984), *The Kindness of Women* (1991) and *Miracles of Life* (2008). He was born in the Shanghai International Settlement, where the lives of expatriates were lived in a bubble that reproduced the patterns of the British lifestyle. After the outbreak of the Sino-Japanese War, Ballard was lodged in the Lunghua Internment Camp, another insular space that was to become central to his work *Empire of the Sun* (1984). After the war, he moved to England, a country that was always to remain alien to him and from which he always kept a critical distance.

The critical overtones of Ballard's constructions have enabled him to transcend the literary sphere; he has become an important "fictional architect" of the modern world. Baudrillard, for instance, refers in his influential *Simulacra and Simulation* (1994:111–123) to Ballard's *Crash* (1973) as a basis for explaining his theory of simulacrum. Jameson praises Ballard's alienating constructions as providing warning lessons on the risk of being absorbed into the high-tech impersonal space around us (2007:369). Similarly, in literary criticism, many scholars have identified Ballard's work as constituting a "forum for contemporary debates" (Delville 1998:6), addressing how the subject's disengagement from others and from himself is related to the architecture surrounding him. His fiction has been said to be technically and generically "homeless" (Luckhurst 1997) and his characters to form part of a post-emotional society (Delville 1998:8). It is indisputable that this depiction of the "spaceless-ness" of the contemporary being in a postmodern society is fundamental in Ballard's spatial universe.

Ballard exploits the fictional built environment as a mirror of the psychological alienation of the character and clearly states in his fiction that physical space affects the perception of the self. In this sense, a leitmotif of his fiction is the exploration of how a particular physical structure influences those inhabiting it, dictating social patterns of (uncivilised) behaviour and annihilating the experience of individuality. Ballard's use of narrative space is one of the greatest exponents of the postmodern non-place (e.g., Augé 1995), with a constant emphasis on how impersonal, mass-produced spaces modify the human's psychological stability. Motorways (*Crash*, 1973 and *Concrete Island*, 1974), vast shopping malls (*Kingdom Come*, 2006), empty parking lots and swimming pools (*Cocaine Nights*, 1996) "displace and evacuate the accretions of 'anthropological place'", as Luckhurst states (1997:131). Always very critical of the contemporary built environment, if there is one central aspect in the literary universe of J. G. Ballard, it is that narrative space is never innocent.

"The Enormous Space" is a representative short story of the phenomenon of the dissolution of subject in space. The main character of this text perceives himself, not devoured and not dominated by space as in the previous sections, but as being *incorporated* into the physical space surrounding him: as becoming the house, in a form of extreme identification with space. The fantastic event affecting the character of the model story could be interpreted as simply a mental delusion, but, in any case, this event has a physical impact on the body of the character (hence the fantastic component).

The story is told by a narrator who, by shutting the door of his house and not leaving it again, cuts off all contact from the outside world after divorcing his wife. Determined to live on the means this space provides (food remains, animals, humans), he soon realises that the physical boundaries of the house are increasingly expanding. This expansion is viewed by him as a sort of epiphany that enables him to access a 'truer' reality embedded in the space of the house; finally, by locking himself into the freezer, he waits for his final integration into this 'truer' reality.

Although it is suggested that all the events might be no more than hallucinations of a man in a state of physical and mental deprivation, this is never specifically clarified. For this reason, this text can be considered a borderline case of the Fantastic, since the supposedly impossible event (the physical disappearance in space) can be read as merely the perception of a character in a state of mental dysfunction. If we accept this rational explanation of the Fantastic element, this short story would be labelled as "pseudo-fantastic" (Roas 2011:62–67). Roas creates this category to refer to narratives that employ the structures, motifs and devices of the Fantastic but where the impossible event is rationally explained in the end (e.g., resulting from a dream or madness). In this case, the idea of madness is a strong candidate in the potential explanation of the supernatural phenomenon. For instance, at the end of the story, the character goes as far as to lock himself into the freezer, waiting for the final physical dissolution and transcendence. However, no further details are given after this scene; for example, it is not clarified whether he is found dead after, a fact that would demonstrate his psychological disturbance, or whether he really is incorporated into his house, a fact that would demonstrate the impossible event. There is, therefore, no explicit rationalisation of the fantastic phenomenon, and so the ambiguity as to how the events of the story are to be read is retained. This situates this narrative as belonging alongside "Le Horla" (Maupassant 1887) and *The Turn of the Screw* (Henry James 1898), in which the reader oscillates between interpreting the supernatural as a phenomenon of the mind—and thus "pseudo-fantastic" (cf. Roas 2011:62–67)—or as a fact taking place in the story—and thus as a fantastic element.

Location: the Privatopia

"The Enormous Space" (1989) is set in one of the most recurrent tropes in the fiction of J. G. Ballard: the gated community. The entire action takes place in a suburban house, where the protagonist is entrenched. This residential area reproduces the pattern of many other novels and short stories: it is turned into a sort of cocoon disengaged from the norms and codes ruling the exterior. The subject, once in the confines of a closed-off system, immediately becomes part of the social structure dictated by this system. Another clear example is the 40-storey apartment block in London from Ballard's claustrophobic novella *High-Rise* (1975). In this apartment block, there are schools, shopping centres, banks and swimming pools, so that the building's interior caters to every need and provides every comfort for its inhabitants, who rarely leave it. The harmonious analogy between building and inhabitant does not last for long. When lifts, stairs and other 'organs' of this building collapse, the entire community housed within breaks down into outbursts of violence and anarchy, which corrupt this "vertical city" (*High-Rise*, 2006:9). The built structure, the physical characteristics of which mirror the action that follows, encapsulates the idea that monstrous constructions create monstrous beings. Ballard's architectures are experiments to test the psychological cohesion of the communities that they enclose, and frequently prove to be failed contingent structures. This pattern is repeated in many other of his works, such as in the suburban colony of *Concrete Island* (1974), the ex-patriate holidays complex of Estrella de Mar in *Cocaine Nights* (1996), as well as that in Las Palmas in "Having a Wonderful Time" (1978) and in the business-park of Eden Olympia in *Super-Cannes* (2000).

In "The Enormous Space", the setting also follows this pattern. The action is set in a suburban colony, populated with identical houses (and individuals). Urban sociologist Edward W. Soja refers to this phenomenon as "privatopias"; areas protected by physical, restrictive and exclusive boundaries, for example, by means of restrictions on access through verification by cameras or identity badges, the paradigmatic example being Silicon Valley (California, USA). From a socio-urban perspective, the privatopia is less of a *place* than a spatial *phenomenon*; it is a reactionary symptom against the dissolution of boundaries in an increasingly globalised urban space. This provokes a proliferation of niched or fortressed cityscapes, which in turn produce fortressed individuals, a key theme of Ballard's short story: "Centrifugally spinning ever outward from the Forbidden Downtown is a growing constellation of luxury island sanctuaries, residential areas with 'clout' enough to partition themselves off fearfully from the real and imagined spaces of the criminalized poor" (Soja 2000:313). Soja's theorisation of the privatopia is largely based on Davis' *City of Quartz* (1990), in which this phenomenon is discussed within the frame of Los Angeles: "[N]ew luxury developments outside the city limits have often become fortress cities, complete with encompassing walls, restricted entry points with guard posts, [...]" (1990:244–246).

"The Enormous Space" is one of the few Ballardian texts (along with "Motel Architecture", 1978) in which the Fantastic intervenes to explore the relation between gated community and individual, a theme that will reappear in Chapter 5 of this book with the text "Une dure journée" ("A Hard Day" by Jean-Paul Beaumier 1988) (although there as part of a different spatial transgression).

The socio-urban privatopia is strongly anchored in the utopian enclave, a topos that is both differentiated from the exterior as well as protected from it. While both utopias and privatopias allude to the same principle of separating the dystopian by establishing clearly defined borders away from it, there are, however, significant differences between both concepts. Literary utopias are very often places with no extratextual spatial referents and are often outside the scope of time (eternal or atemporal). Privatopias, on the contrary, are anchored in specific temporal and spatial coordinates; frequently, they manifest as suburban housing estates, increasingly so during the second half of the twentieth century. The utopian enclave is very much related to the literary tradition of exotic exploration and travel narratives, one of the best examples being *Gulliver's Travels* (1735). Utopias are generally founded on the premise of displacement into a geographically isolated area, often unreachable by land (e.g., Thomas More's island, 1516), if on this earth at all (e.g., St. Augustine's *City of God*, 412–426 A.D.). But while the utopian impulse crosses boundaries and moves toward the exterior (the need to explore), the privatopia imposes boundaries with walls, barriers, cameras and other closures to build a retreat from the exterior.

Ballard's suburban house of "The Enormous Space" is part of the urban landscape, but its integral and autonomous status is achieved through the mechanisms of definition that are described in the next section.

As with the motif of the magnet-space, a parallel with the Romantic tradition of man/environment projection can be seen, as well as a retreat for personal exploration. Yet in this case, it is not a natural environment that constitutes the cosmic experience but rather a simple suburban house—one of the many near-identical buildings in a housing estate on the outskirts of London.

Discourse: Construction of the Microcosm

In this short story, one of the most interesting elements is that the Fantastic is not given as an external fact that suddenly appears, as is the case in most fiction of this narrative form. In contrast, the Fantastic properties of this house are progressively 'built' by the protagonist, in a process embracing three stages: delimitation of the fantastic territory, purification from the exterior and achievement of autonomy.

First, the retreat from the outside is conveyed through expressions such as "closing the door" (2006:698), "to secede from" (698), "to break off" (698) and "to shut out the world" (698). This last example is of particular relevance since it denotes that the separation from the exterior is not only physical. It also implies a more profound existential differentiation from the rest: "by closing the front door I intended to secede not only from the society around me [...] I was breaking off all practical connections with the outside world" (698). In this process, the threshold of the door is very important; the character defines his house as his personal world. He thus conceives the threshold as a physical and ontological boundary that will define the house in opposition to the exterior and will turn it into a space with its own system of values:

> [...] I could change the course of my life by a single action. To shut out the world, and solve all my difficulties at a stroke, I had the simplest of weapons—my own front door. I needed only to close it, and decide never to leave my house again. (698)

Much like a ritual of territorial possession, space is delimited, the "declaration of independence" typed (698), his regime "stabilised" (700), and so his microcosm is founded.

Once this is achieved, the character exposes this newly founded space to a process of depuration, conveyed in the text through images of erasure, incineration and elimination ("I have pulled down the heavy curtains" [701]). His previous life is literally burned, including passport, birth and degree certificates among other "[d]ocuments of a dead past" (700–701). After this process of cleansing, for the first time, the motif of the light as a liberating agent, as that which provides security and stability, appears. The house attains a state of purity when he removes the curtains and other accessories: "Light has flooded into the rooms, turning every wall and ceiling into a vivid tabula rasa" (701). The image of the *tabula rasa* transmits this desire to abolish who he was before facilitating a fresh start in a new world. It is as if the building was physically liberated from the outside, it "can breathe" (701) ("The rooms seem larger and less confined, as if they too have found freedom" [701]).[6] This space is perceived by him as a state of purity, consisting simply of the "essential elements of existence" (701), these being light, time and space. To emphasise this process of purification, he even contrasts his situation with that of Crusoe:

> In every way I am marooned, but a reductive Crusoe paring away exactly those elements of bourgeois life which the original Robinson so dutifully reconstituted. Crusoe wished to bring the Croydons of his own day to life again on his island. I want to expel them and find in their place a far richer realm formed from the elements of light, time and space. (700)

In his study on utopian literature, Jameson writes that a perfect world only acquires definition against the horrendous world it excludes. The utopian enclave arises as a demarcation of a smaller ground when society outside is presented "as a bewildering chaos, whose forces are indiscernible" (2007:14). Similarly, in Ballard's text, there is a prominent demonisation of the exterior. In the story, the lethargic exterior world is in sharp contrast to the character's interior life: "the lack of any response reflects the tranquil air of this London suburb" (697), "a more limited world, [...] that everlasting provincial melodrama called ordinary life" (704), the outside world that threatens to intrude his sanctuary with junk-mail and free newspapers among other "irrelevant messages" (703).

The house goes from being an ordinary suburban construction to being founded as a microcosm segregated from the exterior, to finally becoming a self-sufficient system, independent from the external world with its own sources of food and maintenance. To achieve this, the character is determined to survive on the resources that the house provides. When he has exhausted the food, he feeds on the intruders that fall into his traps, such as neighbouring pets and visiting human beings: "I would depend on the outside world for nothing. I would eat only whatever food I could find within the house. After that I would rely on time and space to sustain me" (698). This is what for him is conceived as freedom, from the exterior and, most importantly, from himself: "Above all, I am no longer dependent on myself. I feel no obligation to that person who fed and groomed me, [...]" (701).

In contrast to the Romantic ideal of self-exploration in a state of isolation, the psychasthenic experience starts with this self-renunciation. The house begins to integrate the character into itself. In this final stage, the house, now internally cohesive and an externally independent organism (at least from the character's perspective), is definitively established as an active character within the plot.

Story: One-Person World

As in Adolph's "La casa", in this short story, the entire action is concentrated on the relationship between one single character and one single space. This type of textual dynamics can be best understood with the concept of One-Person World (Doležel 1998:37–73). This storyworld typology applies to, for example, *Robinson Crusoe* (1719)—as mentioned, also quoted in Ballard's text. The One-Person World macrostructure is organised around the principle of a single space for one individual or, employing Doležel's terminology, a one story-world with one single character. The totality of the action is transmitted from the point of view of this character, with no contrasting external perspectives.

Doležel mentions that, although theoretically stimulating, One-Person Worlds are quite limited in their narrative potential and can be rather tedious due to the absence of interpersonal conflict to generate plot turns (1998:74). In "The Enormous Space", however, several textual mechanisms compensate for this. The integrity and singularity of the house are challenged several times through various attempts at human interaction (by his ex-wife, the policeman and his secretary). These occur in liminal spaces: thresholds, windows and doors that frame and protect the founded microcosm. The presence of these 'viruses' disrupts the stability reigning over the character's sanctuary, and this unexpected confrontation with the external world provokes a subsequent crisis.

The realisation of the Fantastic first takes place when he discovers that the house is literally growing ("the rooms *are* larger" [704]). This impossible displacement affects the idea of body as referential point; the house "pull[s] back" (705), "sheers away from [him]" (705), "pushed back" (705), "the house enlarges itself around [him]" (707). He becomes increasingly incapable of keeping a grasp on this space, as condensed in the fantastic motif of the ever-expanding house: "Already I can feel the walls of the kitchen distancing themselves from me" (708), "already the walls of this once tiny room constitute a universe of their own" (708), "the almost planetary vastness of this house" (708).

The expanding microcosm-house strongly evokes an urge to be protected from the exterior: "This conventional suburban villa is in fact the junction between our small illusory world and another larger and more real one" (706). The character is eager to transcend into what he considers a higher reality by physically merging into this space he has created.

The Cocoon-Subject

Ballard's character is neither capable of nor interested in mapping his position in external physical space; this leads to what Caillois calls "psychasthenia": a "depersonalisation by assimilation to space" (1938:112). It is this loss of position in space equated with the loss of individuality that destabilises the character's experience of reality.

There is no lack of examples in fantastic narratives featuring the literal incorporation of the subject in space. For example, a similar transgression takes place in "Valle del silencio" ("Valley of Silence", José María Merino 1982), although the existential dimension is less developed in that case. The disappearance of Marcellus is later 'resolved' when his friend realises he had fused into the rock of a cave:

> [...] under the humid moss that Lucius Pompeius' fingers separated, an eyelid appeared and an eye opened after that amazement of absolute self-absorption. [...] Marcellus' body had incorporated in the very substance of the valley. (1982:84)

Another character who undergoes a similar fate is the narrator of "Le Corps éparpillé" ("The Scattered Body", Michel Dufour 1991), who wakes up one morning feeling his body not only dispersed all over the room but also *being* each object in the room: "Besides, in my position, I cannot go too far. As an object that one ends up forgetting by force of habit, I am from now on part of the setting" (1991:100).

As mentioned in the beginning of the analysis, some motifs of Ballard's text strongly echo those of the Romantic tradition, where the individual seeks an isolated retreat in nature to explore his sense of individuality. However, Ballard exploits this in a distinctively postmodern fashion: the sublime experience takes place in an ordinary suburban house. What is of relevance is the way in which the subject appropriates this otherwise undifferentiated space and 'constructs' it as a personal, unique and literally exceptional enclave. This is also an unusual presentation of the Fantastic within the history of this narrative form; instead of the Fantastic occurring as an external factor, it is the subject who provokes it (whether in his mind or taking place in physical reality). The story develops from the initial animation of space (the house realised as an organism), to the actual spatialisation of the individual. And so, unlike the Romantic ideal of synthesis between individual and space, isolation does not strengthen the experience of individuality. Instead, it leads to a (happy) dissolution of the self.

The character shifts from a need to be in a personal space toward an urge to become that space. The end of this short story, where he decides to lock himself in the compartment of the freezer in order to finally dissolve into the space he has created, resembles very much the end of another short story by Ballard: "Motel Architecture" (1978). Here, the character, who lives secluded within a solarium, kills himself, "eager to merge with the white sky of the screen in which he would be rid forever of himself, of his intruding mind and body" ("Motel Architecture", 2006:516). This subject seeks the ultimate physical dissolution into space precisely because it will entail a transcendental experience. But a transcendence to what? The experience of disappearing in space is taken by him as the announcement of an imminent cosmic revelation: the 'true' dimensions of the world it encircles. This dualistic conception of an external weaker 'real' and an ideal 'real' strongly recalls the Platonic view of the physical world as ontologically inferior to the world of ideas. The gradual disassociation from the world that the house excludes enables the protagonists to access a 'reality', "which the visual centres of our timid brains have concealed from [him]" ("The Enormous Space", 707). It also recalls the Platonic process of *anamnesis*; what the characters assumed as their perfect world shatters, leading to the remembrance of a metaphysical more 'truer' realm beyond the empirical physical world.

The question is *what* or *where* is this 'truer' reality? This 'more realistic real', the character asserts, is to be found when he dissolves into his house, into the reality he has fabricated. The protagonist's body is obsolete; it ceases to be regarded as a necessary anchor to external reality. He is happily entrapped in this cocoon. He becomes his one and only reality, "uncluttered by the paraphernalia of conventional life" (705). Therefore, by giving up his human 'position' in the world the subject is upgraded beyond that polluted, unreliable and "over-worked hologram called reality" (702), revealing a typically Ballardian dismissal of the accepted (and constructed) idea of external reality.

The physical space of the house acts as a metaphor for his personal enclosure, with no interaction with the exterior reality. He refers to this in the last paragraphs: "By shutting out the world my mind may have drifted into a realm without yardsticks or sense of scale" (709). The segregation from the physical exterior is equated with the loss of his grasp of ordinary, consensus reality. With external reality despised and distrusted, the only 'true' reality for the character is interior. There is no exterior, objective reality but instead only a subject who creates his own perception of it, an idea which will reappear in the next chapter of this book.

***

The three transgressions presented in this chapter deal with the transgression of the principle of 'body in space', according to which individuals perceive themselves through and in space. All the analysed texts demonstrate distinct postmodern features in the manner in which they approach this theme. Cannibal spaces devour the body of the protagonist, but, in a deviation from the classical motif of the evil space, the act seems completely random, performed by an ordinary house and welcomed with pleasure by the narrator. This narrator becomes a body-less entity which—or *who?*—still conceives himself as subject in space. Magnet-spaces attack the freedom of movement of the body in space. This is presented by a subject who cannot release himself from the physical and mental influence of a particular place. Finally, the psychasthenic experience describes the incorporation and dissolution of the subject into space; a literal inscription of body in space. This is the most radical transgression of the principle of 'body in space'; the fantastic transgression of psychasthenia presents a subject who ceases to *be* in space (physically, existentially and ontologically) to *become* space.

If the body is a central referential axis by which human beings apprehend the physical space around us, this apprehension occurs through a demarcation of ourselves from the external world (hence the double physical-experiential dimension). The process of demarcation inherently refers to the notion of 'boundary', which is the spatial protagonist of the next chapter.

NOTES

1. The dialogue translations of *Marisa* and *Skhizein* are mine.
2. See in this respect Robert Tally's section "Anxiety and a Sense of Place" and "An Aesthetic of Cognitive Mapping" (2013:64–74), where he connects Lukács' "transcendental homelessness" to existential *angst* in order to explore the importance of Jameson's concept of "cognitive mapping" in postmodern human spatiality.
3. Since there is no official English translation of the short stories in Spanish analysed in this chapter, all translations are mine.
4. Todorov's study ends with the polemic statement that the Fantastic in literature of the late twentieth century is forcefully dead. His main argument is that the category of 'real' (and thus textual realism) disappears in a context where "we can no longer believe in an immutable, external reality, nor in a literature which is merely the transcription of such reality" (1975:168). Taking Kafka's *Metamorphosis* as the turning point of this paradigm shift, he argues that the Fantastic no longer exists since fiction has already become reality. In this light, all (postmodern) literature would be considered 'Fantastic'.
5. This has qualified her to be included within the most influential new voices of the Fantastic in the recently published anthology *Perturbaciones. Antología del relato fantástico español actual* (2009).
6. The motif of the blinding light is often an element of epiphany in the poetics of Ballard, possibly deriving from his own personal experience. As he expresses in *Empire of the Sun* (1984), for Ballard the explosion of the atomic bomb was followed by liberation from the camp. Jordi Costa notes that, in the film adaptation of this book, Spielberg devoted special attention to this element when shooting the transformation of the character from child into adult (2008:22).

3 Boundary
Liquid Constructions

"Men manage reality by their constructions"

(Ihab Habib Hassan)

1. CIRCUMSCRIPTION, STRUCTURE, REALITY

In order to apprehend what surrounds us—what we call 'reality'—we strive to articulate it as a more or less coherent system. In this process, a central spatial ally is the notion of boundary. An illustrative example of this phenomenon goes back to the historical evolution of the concept of space from the Middle Ages to the Renaissance. It was in this latter period that the rise of geographical knowledge was largely made possible through new techniques of measurement of physical space (and time): the compass, the telescope, the rediscovery of the Ptolemaic map and Martin Behaim's terrestrial world ("*Erdapfel*") set boundaries to the unknown and engendered drastic changes that reconfigured the worldview. A new mapping tradition distanced itself greatly from theological fantasies in search of the means of representing reality 'as it really was'.

As Harvey reminds us, the Ptolemaic map played a central role in the Renaissance, since it located all the countries of the world in a single spatial frame and in so doing presented "the globe as knowable totality" (2008:246). By imagining how the globe would appear if looked at by a human eye, Ptolemy was also implicitly reasserting the 'objectivity' of optics and the capability of the individual to represent truthfully the seen. New mapping systems legitimised knowledge and power through a (supposedly) objective representation of space as something conquerable and containable.

This self-proclaimed domination of space, time and nature was a necessary condition for human development. It favoured the emergence of some of the most influential theories on spatiality such as those of Copernicus, Galilei or Descartes, culminating in the Newtonian revolution of the seventeenth century. This need for delimitation as a synonym for knowledge and control over reality was captured in one of the most famous quotes by Galileo Galilei: "Measure what can be measured, and make measurable what cannot be measured" (in Gaarder 1994:157).

It is through the notion of a referential boundary that spatial oppositions like 'up/down' and 'in/out' are conceived. Without such a boundary, space becomes an incomprehensible and unattainable 'something': there would be no volumes against which bodies could be measured and compared. Equally, the notion of distance and location would have no meaning in the absence of any referential system of coordinates. As Roas reminds us, we humans need to "enclose [*acotar* in the Spanish original] our world in order to function in it" (2011:35). In consequence, the human perception of reality needs a stable and referential boundary through which orientation, measurement and articulation are possible.

The field of anthropology of space offers plenty of examples of how, in the history of humanity, the experience of the real has been equated with that of bounded space. Anthropologist and philosopher of space O. F. Bollnow shows how the horizon—a fusion between the body and the boundary as axis of the spatial experience—was a physical as well as an ontological limit for many ancient civilisations ("[...] beyond the borders of the known inhabited realm, the world simply stops", Bollnow 2011:60). Drawing on Heinrich Brunner's study on the concept of space in ancient Egypt, Bollnow emphasises that only the space delimited by the human eye was conceived as a possibility; as their 'reality'. Beyond that founded terrain was the surrounding chaos, conceived of as an unknown domain that did not belong to the real. Rather than being a 'space', this chaos was "spaceless" (2011:61).

Another example of the same phenomenon is found in ancient Greece. The *chorismos* (or separation, boundary) was a way of articulating what would otherwise be a boundless and chaotic something. *Chorismos* was the limit of physical space that the eye could meet (the *Kosmos*), and beyond this boundary laid the inapprehensible; the infinite (the *Kaos*).[1]

Westphal also emphasises the literal association between the horizon and the physical border—or limit(ation)—within the medieval concept of space (2011b:68–93). Man was not allowed (nor was he capable) to transgress that boundary. The act of doing so was considered a heresy, a mindset that was to be completely modified during the voyages of discovery in the Renaissance.

Embedded in this spatial idea of the construction of a reality is once more the etymological root of the term 'architect' as described in the Introduction to this book; the one who transforms the formless origin into a structure on which the human being can rely. The divine figure of the architect articulated and organised our reality by confining space "so we can dwell in it, [creating] the framework around our lives" (Rasmussen 1995:10). Building space was, therefore, originally conceived as a god-like activity that provided mankind with the impression of being in a structured, solid reality. This coincides with the existential dimension of space highlighted in Chapter 2: architecture, in its etymological sense, provided the existential awareness of 'being in time'. As the anthropologist Marc Augé, among others, has argued, a central function of built space is, or at least traditionally was, to organise society's concepts of time and space:

> Without the monumental illusion before the eyes of the living, history would be a mere abstraction. The social space bristles with monuments—imposing stone buildings, discreet mud shrines—which may not be directly functional but give every individual the justified feeling that, for the most part, they pre-existed him and will survive him. (2008:49)

To return to the literary realm: in the textual world, as Ryan (2012) has emphasised, physical boundaries are among the most fundamental elements of narrative space in creating and defining "the physically existing environment in which characters live and move" (Ryan 2012:8). In the absence of consensual terminology, I borrow from Ryan's definition of "spatial frames" as "the immediate surroundings of actual events, the various locations shown by the narrative discourse or by the image (Ronen's 'settings' [1986]; Zoran's 'fields of vision' [1984])", delimited by two elements: spatial boundaries (clear-cut or fuzzy) and hierarchical relations (being within a space) (Ryan 2012:9). Despite their terminological differences, the approaches of Ronen, Zoran, Bal and Ryan to narrative space converge in one aspect, namely that they analyse how physical space *constructs* the storyworld. All refer to the stabilising function of spatial frames in the articulation and reinforcement of the "reality effect" (Barthes 1968).[2]

Indeed, these spatial frames are a crucial realistic device in the building of a fictional world. The notion of boundary in a realistic text is perhaps so intuitive and is taken for granted to such a degree by both author and reader that it is not until these boundaries are destabilised (for instance, through the Fantastic), that the reader is aware of how important their architectural function is.

Mieke Bal, for instance, establishes that there are only two possible relationships between characters and space in terms of location: a character is situated in a frame or outside a frame (Bal 2009:134). Through this frame, the dichotomies of being 'inside/outside' are established. She illustrates this with the following example:

> For hours, he wandered through the dark forest. All of a sudden, he saw a light. He hurried towards the house and knocked on the door. With a sigh of relief, he shut the door behind him a moment later.
> (Bal 2009:134)

In this quote, boundaries enhance the textual realism because they help the reader (re)construct a visual image of the narrative space described. Present in all realistic texts, this creation of boundaries is performed intuitively. The frame of a door separates the inside (house) from the outside (the forest). Thanks to this, both inner and outer spaces are meaningful categories. Their opposition confers both spaces with a wider symbolism—in this case, inside is the domain of safety, contrasting with the threatening exterior. Another example of a stable boundary is the motif of the threshold referred to in Chapter 1. In the texts mentioned as providing examples of a threshold, the function of this form of boundary is precisely to provide a stable spatial frame to separate the two domains. At times, the threshold separates and joins the natural from and to the supernatural domain; at other times, it might be the limit against which the transgression operates, as in the case of a ghost that crosses the physical frontier of a door or wall.

In contrast, some narratives call into question the function of the boundary as constructing relations of distance, reference and location. Quim Monzó's "La força centrípeda" ("Centripetal Force", 1996) and David Roas' "Excepciones" ("Exceptions", 2010) are clear—and complementary—examples. The first story describes a man who, every time he tries to cross the door of his house, finds himself back in the room he had just left. Roas' story provides the reverse of this: despite his continuous efforts to cross the threshold through the door, the protagonist cannot gain entry into the interior of his house. The spatial dichotomy of in/out is thus invalidated. Similarly, Jacques Sternberg's "L'Étage" ("The Floor", 1974) represents the invalidation of the dichotomy of up/down. Every time the character goes up the peculiar stairs of the story, he finds himself immediately back on the ground floor. This can also be read as a form of transgression of the principle of hierarchy (being inside of), an idea that will be further elaborated in Chapter 4 under the label of 'The Möbius Effect'.

The same principles are used in the impossible buildings represented in Giovanni Battista Piranesi's *Prisons* (1750), by M. C. Escher (e.g., *Belvedere Litograph*, 1958), or in Sandro Del Prete's *Inverted Chessboard* (1975). In all these constructions, the very notion of a boundary of 'inside/outside', 'here/there' and 'above/under' is annulled. This gives rise to a series of visual topological paradoxes.

Another example of a playing with the visual confines of structures, though in this case in the literary text, is Shirley Jackson's *The Haunting of Hill House* (1959), a story also considered in the previous chapter. On various occasions and in order to describe the unnatural aura of the mansion, Jackson employs the technique of anamorphosis, the distortion of the spatial form. And yet this does not necessarily imply a fantastic transgression. In the case of Hill House, Jackson creates the impression of an asymmetrical shape, with the impression received depending on the angle from which the mansion is viewed:

> No human eye can isolate the unhappy coincidence of line and place which suggests evil in the face of a house, and yet somehow a maniac juxtaposition, a badly turned angle, some chance meeting of roof and sky, turned Hill House into a place of despair, [...]. (1999:34)

However, while this technique plays upon the aesthetic dimension of the building to enhance the uncanny atmosphere, it is not fantastic in itself. The impossible nature of Hill House is not attached to the physical construction and shifting structure but rather to the psychological effects that this construction has upon its inhabitants.

The Postmodern Abolition of Permanence

Within the postmodern context, the notion of referential boundary has been contested in multiple ways. For example, Ihab Habib Hassan's quote opening this chapter expresses the need for a new construction of literary history since the traditional methods of literature have proven inadequate to the task of representing the actual context (see *The Dismemberment of Orpheus*, 1971). The idea of 'construction' was later to become central in theorisations of the postmodern, which viewed any construction as a subjective exercise of interrelating separate elements. The act of articulating produces a coherent discourse (an embraceable structure in terms of space) but also a constructed discourse that is thus always vulnerable to be conceived from a particular angle and point of view.

In the discourse of postmodern human geographers, represented by Marc Augé, Paul Virilio, Bernard Tschumi and Edward W. Soja, among others, it has been stressed that this organic function of architecture—the reassertion of an ordered and structured experience of space—has undergone a drastic change in the late twentieth century. The notion of architecture as construction is challenged. Urban sociologist Paul Virilio in particular has extensively elaborated on the 'liquefaction' of physical space through the rise of digitalisation, vehicular technologies (the conquest of space by transport systems) and transmission technologies (the conquest of time by electromagnetic means of communication). According to Virilio, this phenomenon necessarily leads to a new conception of dimensionality, in that boundaries cease to be stable and permanent, and in so doing heralds "the end of the vertical as an axis of elevation, the end of the horizontal as permanent plane" (Virilio and parent 2000:v). A practical application of this theory is found in Virilio's essay "The Overexposed City" (1997), where he elaborates on the transformation of the late twentieth city from bounded, defined space toward a limitless, formless entity.

Virilio recalls how previous methods of physical enclosure, such as gates and walls, have been overtaken by electronic systems of surveillance. These electronic systems constitute, in his view, the new (intangible, liquid) boundaries of the late twentieth century. The idea of physical consistency previously attributed to these delimitation systems is now, as he outlines, constantly challenged by immaterial devices.

Most interesting is the outcome of this transformation. According to Virilio, this lack of physical boundaries leads to the loss of traditional stability of spatial categories such as 'inside/outside' and 'near/far', which leads to a weakening impression of material reality: "a world devoid of spatial dimensions, but inscribed in the singular temporality of an instantaneous diffusion" (Virilio 1991:13).

Along the same line of thought, Bernard Tschumi, a scholar in architecture and sociology who is strongly influenced by Virilio, elaborates on this correlation between the lack of physical boundaries and a disjointed experience of the real in his volume *Architecture and Disjunction* (1996). Tschumi's thesis coincides with Virilio's in its contention that the acceleration of digital technology challenges what he calls "the appearance of permanence" previously provided by built space (Tschumi 1996:216):

> [...] architecture was first the art of measure, of proportions. It once allowed whole civilisations to measure time and space. But speed and the telecommunications of images have altered that old role of architecture. Speed expands time by contracting space; it negates the notion of physical dimension.
>
> (Tschumi 1996:216)

In an era where the foundations of "solidity, firmness and structure, and hierarchy" are not to be taken for granted (Tschumi 1996:218), architecture has, in the view of Virilio and Tschumi, lost its function of enabling us to structure our surroundings. This leads Tschumi to ask: "How then can architecture maintain some solidity, some degree of certainty? [...] No more certainties, no more continuities" (1996:219).

In Tschumi's view, urban life is no longer regulated by physical boundaries "delineating a coherent and homogeneous whole" (1996:217). Instead, TV, electronic surveillance and computer-generated images 'dis-articulate' and, in so doing, 'de-realise' our apprehension of physical space. Echoing Virilio's words, Tschumi states that "[t]he abolition of permanence confuses reality" (1996:218).

Very similar is Soja's theorisation of the "Postmetropolis", a form of postmodern urban development where "[t]he boundaries of the city are becoming more porous, confusing our ability to draw neat lines separating what is inside as opposed to outside the city; between the city and the countryside, suburbia, the non-city" (2000:150).

All these perspectives point to a distortion, or confusion, of the experience of reality caused by disarticulation of physical space, but not to a proper transgression of this reality in the sense in which 'transgression' is understood in this book (as a destabilisation of the real by the supernatural). Only in the fantastic text in the realm of fiction can this *distortion* of the real be represented as an ontological *transgression*. The aim of this chapter is, therefore, to show how this "abolition of permanence", a central preoccupation of postmodern discourse in the fields of urban sociology and architecture, is translated into the literary realm.

All the texts examined in this chapter destabilise the assumption of realistic physical boundaries established in the textual world. The common thread linking them is that the notion of stable boundary is transgressed with various techniques and plot devices and, as a result, the representation of reality as a graspable, reliable, orientating and consistent structure is similarly transgressed.

The fantastic transgression of "Rien n'a de sens sinon intérieur" ("Only Inner Sense Makes Sense", Claude-Emmanuelle Yance 1987) questions the very possibility of generating objective referential systems. The absence of a stable referent is as disorienting as the multiplication of boundaries that interconnect places. "Trastornos de carácter" ("Personality Disorders", Juan José Millás 1989) captures this. Finally, the motif of the absent boundary in space generates a vertiginous image of reality as boundless structure, as illustrated by the text "Tandis que roule le train" ("As the Train Goes", Éric Faye 1997).[3]

2. ELASTIC BOUNDARIES

"Rien n'a de sens sinon intérieur" is a work by Quebec author Claude-Emmanuelle Yance and was first published in *Mourir comme un chat* (1987). It was then included in the compilation *Le Fantastique même: une anthologie québécoise* (1997), a collection that testifies to the current vibrant state of the fantastic tradition in Quebec.[4]

The story tells of the following fantastic event: the narrator, a figure who remains anonymous throughout the whole story, has found the diary of the protagonist, Jean-Denis Vijean. In it, the latter has written with precision of the strange spatial experience that ended his life. Starting with a loss of balance sensed when looking through the window, he records how he sees the landscape progressively shrinking. The two buildings on both sides have been slowly approaching each other to form an elliptical shape. Aware of the risk of this being just an impression of his subjective perspective, he sets out to rigorously measure each displacement. The marks on the window leave no doubt that it is indeed happening. Later, he realises that the phenomenon is not taking place only outside his window, but it has also affected the interior of his room. The furniture on both sides is being displaced toward the chair where he sits, at the centre of the room. Finally, the ellipse reaches his body, as stated in his last record. He is found next to his diary, dead and huddled up on his chair.

Location: Exterior, Interior and Body

One of the first elements to be noted regarding the location of the story is that it could be set in any city, on any street and in any apartment building. Specific cultural and geographical references to Quebec are avoided, apart from the detail of the heavy falling snow. Other than that, there is a clear lack of explicit spatial referents. The locations of the text are constructed mainly by generic nouns ("the room", "the landscape", "his chair"). The attention of the reader is directed not to the emplacement of the action but to space and the role it performs in the events to come.

Therefore, instead of 'places' it is rather more useful to think about 'domains' of action. Exterior, interior and the body of the protagonist are the three spatial domains central to the action. As Vijean writes, the problem is "between his landscape, his window and himself" (1987:21), and how they relate to each other is significant to the generation of the fantastic transgression. These three areas are separated by physical frames: the exterior and interior by the window, while inside the chair serves as Vijean's reference in the later shrinking of the room. Window and chair are the frames against which the progressive ellipse of the buildings and furniture is measured. Moreover, these frames fail as contingent physical boundaries; the various buildings outside merge toward the window, the phenomenon trespasses from the physical exterior into the physical interior and finally the room shrinks around Vijean.

To aid the reader's understanding of where and how the fantastic phenomenon has arisen, maps are drawn and described on several occasions by Vijean in his diary. These provide evidence of the impossible event taking place, validating it as "almost as certain as a photography" (20). This view has different planes: a factory at the front, house and garage in the centre, and then the background. As the narrative advances, depth and width begin to contract toward an ellipse. In the second stage, when this shrinking enters the interior of the room, Vijean himself draws the layout of the room in his diary so that his testimony can be better understood and contrasted. The room, although rectangular, seems elliptical because of the pieces of furniture in each of its corners. From the centre, Vijean observes and records, with black marks on the floor, how the distance between the furniture is being reduced.

All these realist spatial techniques indicate, first, that we are located in an ordinary environment; second, that the person witnessing the event has carried out rigorous research and tracking of it in his diary; and, third, that the impossible movement of buildings did indeed take place according to the maps and measurements drawn.

Discourse: The Diary

A crucial space in the story is that of the diary. Vijean's adventure is recorded in this discursive space, which gives his account of the story and triggers the comments of the narrator upon his reading it. The narrator insists that what he reads is only 'one' perspective: "Certainly, it is important to remember that we do not dispose of other witnesses, the only version of the facts that we could evoke is that of Vijean" (25).

It is through this diary that the rhetorical construction of the Fantastic can be explored. Through this object we learn how the character himself strives to articulate the progressive loss of the referential boundaries of the physical space around him. As is frequently the case in fantastic narrative, the discourse of the 'unspeakable' is employed. The first entry in Vijean's diary clearly shows this:

> Indefinable sensation, painful, this morning, at my window. How could I say? I try to find the words which [...] Not an absence but [...] Something that worries my eyes. (19)

Another strategy Vijean employs to express that which has no referent in human vocabulary is the approximate comparison, a technique that was also used to designate the fantastic holes of "Mi hermana Elba" (*catachresis*, Chapter 1, section 4): "some sort of loss of balance" (19), "like in a vertiginous fall" (20), "like the form of an eye" (22). However, the indetermination prevailing in the discourse of the focalisor (Vijean) contrasts with rational and scientific discourse:

> Vijean has decided to study the subject in a methodical manner. (19)
> He will take great care in noting all his observations, [...]. (20)
> [...] he is seized by the evidence of the facts. (23)
> [...] observation ground, point of view, elements of the cause, interest of the observer, all are renewed. (25)
> [...] his intelligence relating to the phenomenon is extremely precise even if he does not know the cause. (27)

This oscillation between the unspeakable and the identifiable, the subjective and the objective, will be a key aspect in comprehending the wider meaning of the fantastic transgression.

Vijean's experience as tracked in the diary accelerates from a feeling of dizziness and instability to a vertiginous fall when he realises that the distance between the buildings is fluctuating. This is captured by a series of verbs and nouns that indicate movement and a change of states, like "a continuous displacement", "to swerve", "becoming" and especially the recurrence of the adverb "toward" ("*vers*" in the original text).

Apart from movement, "*vers*" in French language is also a vector; it captures the idea of relation, it indicates movement of two distinct bodies toward each other. At first, the buildings outside approach each other until their distance and distinction is cancelled. Vijean is then irremediably incorporated into the phenomenon, a fact also portrayed through relational expressions: "the connection ("*le rapport*") established between the shape of the landscape and that of his eye", "the concordance between word and reality" (21–22), and notably with the repetition of "*le rapprochement*", indicating both physical movement toward each other and an ontological connection of two things becoming similar to each other.

Imitating the structure of a vortex, the final movement between bodies is that of contraction. This progressive annihilation of distances is described by Vijean as the environment strangling him, where the chair ("a sort of little island for the shipwreck" [26]) is the only object left until the ellipse starts affecting his body.

The diary is not immune to this vortex. The space of the page mirrors the transformations taking place in physical space. This is when the concept of textual space is of great significance. The alignment of the signifiers, qualified by the narrator as "oppressive", also reflects the fantastic event: his writing projects this anguish through a frenetic and disjointed calligraphy.

Story: Relative Frames

In terms of the functions performed by narrative spaces in the plot, the first of these is to help define the character of Vijean. As discussed in the previous section, the discourse on subjectivity is juxtaposed with that of an obsessive search for objective validation. Vijean has tracked his experience using a scientific method of rigorous measurement and has taken precautions for occasions when the conditions are not favourable (in snow, for example). His attitude toward the event portrays him as a rational, ordered and meticulous being, remaining sceptical of the event until he has gathered enough evidence:

> He has the habit of sharp demonstrations, rigorous argumentation. And, in a certain way, he distrusts everything that touches upon impression, everything that relates to feelings [...]. (23)

The disclosure of the fantastic phenomenon is conducted by only one focalisor—Vijean. Although another character is reading the diary, we follow what has happened through the eyes of Vijean and in a linear order, a strategy that serves to build the suspense. The events are carefully structured in three almost symmetrical time frames of a month each. These three stages of the phenomenon (landscape—interior—body) correspond with the following moments indicated in the diary: 8th of January, when he notices it, mid-February, when he realises the event, 8th of March when it affects the room and 8th of April, when it gets his body. There are three symbolic spatial forms that follow these time frames: first, the ellipse indicates the movement progressing toward its own interior. Then the circle surrounds the protagonist. Finally, the circle becomes something that resembles an hourglass, a figure irrevocably appealing to the temporal dimension. Note also the similarity between these forms and the shape of the number eight, which is the date on which he records his experiences in the diary. It is in this last stage that the collapse between interior (the character) and exterior (physical body) culminates.

The three frames of reference against which the phenomenon is measured—window, chair and him—are crucial in the story, since they raise doubt about objective distances. This issue of subjective measurement is recurrent and fundamental throughout the whole short story, as the following excerpt shows:

> The possible rapprochement between the shape of the landscape and that of his eye concretises the most feared trap of his observations: subjectivity. (22)

In their efforts to portray a phenomenon in an objective manner, the character and the narrator are at all times aware of the limitations of the observer. Both the narrator and Vijean are conscious of the impact of the observer upon the event observed, an aspect which strongly evokes Heisenberg's uncertainty principle, a theory that in the early twentieth century helped challenge the Positivist conception of scientific knowledge as absolute, neutral and independent from the observer.

Reality as a Subjective System of Boundaries

The fantastic transgression of this text is constructed on a literal correlation between the subject's perception of physical space and the form of that physical space. In other words, the Fantastic arises from an equating of the exterior with the interior apprehension of space. First, the landscape adopts the form of the protagonist's eye, then the room does, and finally the protagonist feels his body taking the shape of a shrinking ellipse, circle or hourglass. The boundary that articulates these spaces, against which they are measured and distinguished from each other and from the observer, is constantly mobile. In the end, the protagonist is incapable of determining any distance (literally) between his body and the physical surroundings.

In an article on architecture in the Quebecois text of the Fantastic, Simone Grossman mentions Yance's short story as an example of subversive architectural constructions. She asserts that, by portraying the built environment as "incapable of organising rationally space" (Grossman 2004:157), this short story attacks the "rationalisation of the real according to the rules fixated by engineers" (156). Built structures, central to the impression of order and fixity explained at the beginning of this chapter, fail here to articulate space in a comprehensive referential system.

However, the question to ask is whether Yance's text deals only with architecture. Underlying the issue of architectural form is a more profound conception of the notion of boundary in the experience of space.

Through the fantastic figure of the 'fluctuating boundary', the author is saying—as the title indicates—that experience can only be attained from an interior point of view and thus will always be subjective. The transgression presented in this short story builds on the idea that a particular point of view shapes the perceived, a notion that can be traced back to the realm of physics with Heisenberg's principle and which became a core principle of postmodern thought. Yance's text questions the very notion of an objective boundary against which to measure and verify what is taking place or to know what is real. Instead, any system of boundaries is necessarily attached to an observer who establishes it.

Vijean's impression of the built environment fluctuates; it lacks consistency and fails to remain articulated and ordered. Vijean describes a progressive loss of physical form, structure and reliable boundaries against which to *locate* himself. This last point is crucial: the notion of boundary that differentiates buildings and dictates distances between them ('here/there', 'outside/inside') is movable, hence the feeling of vertigo in the face of an unstable system of spatial coordinates and references. This results in the negation of a verifiable experience of a real with referential relations of distance and location. Instead, these seemingly objective systems of reference are always conditioned by the observer. At the end, the boundary collapses between observer and observed. This conjunction of interior and exterior space is equated with the fusion of objective/subjective or with the cancellation of the dichotomous 'objective/subjective' perspective. As captured in the title, everything is interior, everything is subjective. With no referential and stable boundary against which to contrast his views, as the title points out, the only reality that is possible for the protagonist is interior. If everything is subjective, everything is only interior and is thus questionable. This thought strongly contrasts with the Renaissance and Positivist view of the boundary as a stable entity in the construction of the real, as presented in the beginning of this chapter. It dismisses the notion of a universal point of view and thus dismisses also the objective validation of perspective and knowledge. By this, every system of thought is then always subject to the perspective from which it is looked at. The following quote from *The Gay Science* (1882) of Nietzsche, visionary philosopher of Postmodernity, captures this viewpoint:

> How far the perspectival character of existence extends, or indeed whether it has any other character; whether an existence without interpretation, without 'sense', doesn't become 'nonsense'; whether, on the other hand, all existence isn't essentially an interpreting of existence [...], the human intellect cannot avoid seeing itself under its perspectival forms, and solely in these. (2001:239–240)

Ultimately, Yance's story offers the following paradox: there is no space without a subject who perceives it, and conversely there is no subject without a referential system of boundaries in which he can locate and define himself. However, as examined in Chapter 2, subject and space are interdependent entities. Deprived of objective boundaries, both space and subject cease to be differentiated from one another. Therefore, this distortion could also be read as a form of 'psychasthenia' (Chapter 2, section 3), in which the body becomes the external physical space it occupied.

I will end this section with an example of elastic boundaries in cinema, provided by *Skhizein* (Clapin 2008), the short film I mentioned in the previous chapter. When Henry is displaced by a meteorite sideways and downwards from everything else, the referential system of coordinates he had, until now, shared with other humans is invalidated, which leads to a profound isolation and depression. He now has to learn to mark new distances with chalk to avoid bumping into objects and people (see Figure 2.1). After his displacement, Henry emphasises how he would like to reverse the slippage, to break his isolation and return to his original 'location': "And all I want is to get back to *where I was*" ("Tout ce que je veux maintenant c'est *retourner à ma place*" in the French original, emphasis mine). All he wants is to return to the shared system of references of bodies in space.

3. THE FANTASTIC RHIZOME

Another work drawing on a relational perspective on space is the next sample text—"Trastornos de carácter" (1989) by Juan José Millás. The relationship between Millás and the Fantastic is perceptible in a large variety of the author's short story volumes and novels, such as *Primavera de luto* (1989)—the collection from which the sample short story is taken—in *Ella imagina* (1998), *Cuentos a la intemperie* (1997), *Los objetos nos llaman* (2008) and *Lo que sé de los hombrecillos* (2010).

In contrast to the scenario in Yance's story, in this text the supernatural interconnection established is not that of 'subject/space' but rather that between different physical spaces that in factual reality are not (or are perceived not to be) adjoining. By interconnecting locations that should be at a distance from each other, this fantastic distortion questions the reliability of how we perceive spatial boundaries. It interconnects (or cancels) spaces that our real world atlases would present as noncontiguous and unrelated, giving rise to a form that I call 'the fantastic rhizome'. This concept is inspired by Deleuze's and Guattari's rhizomatic philosophy (1988), where traditional hierarchies and binary logic are dissolved in favour of multiplicity and interconnectedness. As is well known, Deleuze's and Guattari's conceptualisation of the rhizome derives from organic structures in the natural world, where there is no referential centre or point of origin but there are instead points of contact, with interrelations instead of relations of hierarchy: "in nature, roots are taproots with a more multiple, lateral, and circular system of ramification, rather than a dichotomous one" (2004:12). Drawing from this philosophical approach, the sample short story presents a view of the real as a system of hidden connections rather than as circumscribing boundaries.

This spatial transgression bears strong resemblances to the theme of the multiverse, which originated in theoretical physics and refers to multiple interconnected realities coexisting in time and space. Since the multiverse trope will be dealt with in more detail in Chapter 5, this present section is restricted to the concept of boundary. Therefore, the focus is not on *juxtaposition* or *superimposition* of two or more realities but rather on the *interrelation* between physical spaces belonging to the same plane of reality.

The volume of short stories from which this sample text is taken, *Primavera de luto* (Juan José Millás 1989), is strongly based on the theme of the interconnecting boundary. Although this is a compilation of short stories, there is one aspect that gives it a sense of continuity and allows it to be read almost as a novel. The short stories are elaborated with a very similar structure, always ending with the phrase "ah, well" (*"en fin"*, in the Spanish original) pronounced by a narrator who resigns himself to accepting the odd occurrences in this life. Millás plays on various figures of symmetry and recurrence including character types (e.g., 'the neighbour') and the relationships between lonely and isolated human beings. The short story that best represents the topic of this section is "Trastornos de carácter". It describes the relationship between Vicente Holgado and the narrator, neighbours in a standard, impersonal apartment block in the city of Madrid. In the story, they keep each other company until Vicente Holgado suddenly disappears. The narrator finally reveals that his neighbour had discovered, in his wardrobe, one of the conduits connecting all wardrobes of the world and got lost in it, unable to find his way back to his apartment.

Location: Modern Apartments

From the start, the reader is located in a specific city: Madrid. This particular location is, however, not particularly relevant in itself but is instead significant for its connotations as a big city. In this metropolis, the two main characters live, we are told, in their very small apartments. The trope of the modern urban apartment is a recurrent setting in the fantastic fiction of Millás and very frequently is employed to emphasise the characters' alienation from society as well as to introduce a note of criticism of this type of modern construction, which disrupt the individual and his perception of the surrounding reality. The small, sterile apartment is central, for example, in "La casa vacía" ("The Empty House", Juan José Millás 1994), where a character is deeply affected by his move from a big house to a modern isolated apartment. Bored with his daily life and isolated from human contact, he creates a character that he observes obsessively. It is an image of a woman that he projects onto the empty flat opposite his apartment to the point that he believes her existence to be real.

Similarly, in "Trastornos de carácter" the action takes place in a very ordinary urban landscape with which the reader might easily identify. A mundane setting is essential for Millás' presentation of the Fantastic. While the Fantastic is still perceived as *impossible* according to the laws of logic, it is not unlikely in a place as crazy as the contemporary city, whose inhabitants "have to face numerous strange manifestations that a city like Madrid daily produces" ("Trastornos de carácter", 1989:34). The ending of "Trastornos de carácter" clearly illustrates this understanding of the Fantastic:

> From these pages I would like to issue a call appealing to the kindness of all people, first, to keep their wardrobes clean and presentable, and second, if ever when they open one, they find in it a subject dressed with a fragile pyjama and a sad face as I have described, recognise that it is my friend Vicente Holgado and report his whereabouts as soon as possible.
> Ah, well. (1989:38)

Once the cause of Vicente's disappearance has been revealed, the narrator, who had until then remained sceptical, issues this public appeal to the population, urging them to check their wardrobes in case Vicente is there. This action creates an even stronger aura of everydayness around the impossible element, bringing it closer to the everyday domain of the reader. In the way in which it is presented in the story, all that one needs to become potentially a part of this fantastic network of wardrobes is to have a wardrobe at home.

The wardrobe-net is juxtaposed with the previous state of confinement; Vicente lived in his small apartment, a highly structured domain controlled by routine habits and consisting of barely any interaction with the outside world. In this constricted environment, those interconnected channels expand their living space. The interplay between confinement and extension reflects a critical message about the modern alienated individual who rarely leaves the comfort of his four walls, a situation that necessarily leads to a "personality disorder". In the short story being considered here, the narrator specifically addresses this issue, first by referring to the apartments as "holes" (31) or "boxes" (32) and then by claiming that such apartment living destabilises people's mental well-being:

> I still haven't met anyone living in a carpeted and narrow apartment who hasn't suffered serious personality disorders between the first and second year of entering this sort of attenuated death that living in a box is. (32)

Isolation, routine, impersonal environments and how these affect the individual and his perception of the reality surrounding him are aspects that have already appeared in other texts, notably in J. G. Ballard's notion of the 'privatopia' (Chapter 2, section 4).

Discourse: Reflections

From the very start of the description of the apartment, there are hints of the fantastic event to come. The figure of the "anticipatory metaphorical image" (Casas 2010:12) is a frequent linguistic device of the Fantastic, which I have already mentioned in Chapter 1 in relation to "The Fall of the House of Usher". The strange connection between the two adjoining apartments is described as "a disturbing speculative relation" (31). Both apartments are not only extremely similar but are also increasingly seen, as the story progresses, as replicas of their owners: "The speculative relation I mentioned between his apartment and mine had extended recently to finally reach us" (31).

The wall here, as well as articulating physical spaces, acts as a mirror between the two subjects (see also Faye's glass-window between the two rolling trains in section 4): "[...] when going to bed, I toyed with the idea of my friend doing the exact same things as me, at the same time" (31). This game of mirroring in the construction of the relationship between both apartments becomes particularly important when the neighbour disappears. In a reflection of their similar apartments, Vicente and the other character are almost the same individual. The persistent question that haunts the narrator is "who reflects whom"; who is the "shadow" (35) of the original. Very much in line with the Baudrillardian hyperreality (1981), the logical relation between original and copy, or between subject and his image, is called into question. Vicente's absence triggers a severe crisis of identity for the narrator, who feels orphaned without his counterpart. This is expressed with the figure of a mirror that no longer reflects.

As well as engaging with the visual interplay between image and reflection, the semantic construction of narrative space is also largely based on another sense: that of hearing. When the wall separating both apartments prevents the neighbours from seeing each other, it is sound that connects both physical spaces. In evoking the notion of Vicente's presence and later of his absence, it is the auditory that predominates, reaching its peak with Vicente's permanent disappearance, described as "a scandalous absence" (34). Sound filters through the physical boundary of the wall. We are told that the narrator is only aware of having a new neighbour when he hears him playing music on the other side of this wall. Conversely, Vicente's absence is experienced in the lack of noise through the walls:

> One day, when I returned from work, I could hear neither Vicente's record player nor his TV or any of the other noises he generally made when wandering around in his small apartment. (31)

Another element that extends beyond physical boundaries is the wardrobe. The reader is immediately alerted to the fact that there is something unusual about this piece of furniture when Vicente refers to it for the first time not only as "spacious", an adjective that belongs to the semantic field associated with wardrobes, but also as "comfortable" (36), an adjective that surely clashes with this semantic field (a "semantic impertinence", Erdal Jordan 1998:115; Casas 2010:11–12). On each occasion that Vicente spends time in the wardrobe, his eyes capture "the blurred reflection of cities, villages and people obtained after a long trip" (37). The impossible attribute of this wardrobe is a paradox: its interior confines a space that extends beyond the apartment where this wardrobe is located.

Story: The 'Locked-Room Situation'

The function fulfilled by these narrative spaces points to a classic plot structure of detective fiction: the so-called 'locked-room mystery', consisting, as the narrator himself explains, "of situating the victim of a crime within a room whose possible exits have been sealed from the interior" (34) (cf. "The Murders in the Rue Morgue", E. A. Poe 1841; *Le Mystère de la chambre jaune*, Gaston Leroux 1907; *The Valley of Fear*, S. A. Conan Doyle 1915). The reader is confronted from the start with the following mystery: Vicente disappeared leaving a strange 'crime scene'; no trace or clues are found in his apartment and, what is more, it is locked from the inside. The 'locked-room situation' is an excellent example of spatial frames serving as an active element generating a plot; since all of these walls frame and seal the inside, the logic behind this spatial disposition needs to be solved.

The action that follows the 'locked-room' situation is devoted to finding a logical explanation clarifying these circumstances. But what is the logical revelation at the end? Here the great difference from the classic detective story is present in that the situation is not clarified by means of a rational explanation that ties up all the loose ends. Instead, this text fuses the detective model with the Fantastic. Although there is an explanation for the disappearance in this case, it is one that is impossible according to our realist laws: Vicente has vanished within the (imperceptible to the rest) ramifying structure interconnecting the world. The narrator, forced to accept the extraordinary, expresses his resignation at the end of the story with the formula: "ah, well". These words of resignation vis-à-vis the Fantastic—closing each short story of the volume—emphasise a reversal of the detective story pattern, which usually provides a satisfactory logical end and a sense of closure.

The Network Reality

As shown, the fantastic transgression operated by physical space in this text deals with the boundary as an interconnecting element. A further example of this kind of transgression would be Juan José Millás' "Oraciones metro a metro" (1997), a text in which the author plays with the idea of the metro as a means of transport that compresses physical distances. The fantastic transgression is precisely the literal expression of this; one of the passengers gets on in a station in Madrid and gets off a little later in Paris ("One day I took the metro in Pirámides [Madrid] and exited in Saint-Sulpice, which is in Paris" [2001:30]).

The spatial figure of channels, through which one can quickly transit from one place to another, finds an analogy in the "compression of time-space"—Harvey's famous formula characterising a postmodern paradigm of space (1990).[5] This figure is strongly influenced by the rise of network systems—for instance, the World Wide Web—interconnecting multiple points in space, compressing time and space. In the text, this idea is expressed in a literal compression of distances, as a sort of wormhole. If the right frequency or "conduit" (1989:37) is found, it is possible, for example, "to reach within seconds the wardrobe of a house in Valladolid" (37). The character has only to enter into the wardrobe to be able cover a long distance in a short time. The interesting aspect of this short story is that this spatial figure is equated with the structure of the mind. Vicente says that he discovers these conduits when he realises that they are not a place but a "state of mind" (38). Vicente's capability for appreciating these channels is presented not merely as unusual, but as extraordinary. His disappearance remains unsolved within the rules of the 'ordinary' world. The wardrobe network does not correspond to the way in which humans comprehend spatial structures, hence Vicente's difficulties in returning home through this magma of channels, the spatial form of which is not codified for the human mind. From then on, once he is capable of interconnecting the otherwise disconnected elements, he can travel around this network. On a more abstract level of meaning, it could be said that he can mentally create links with elements that others perceive to be isolated. In contrast with those who "cannot see beyond their noses" (35), Vicente has the capability of discovering these confluences. There is a reference not only to the capability of the mind to transcend material reality but also to material reality being composed of channels that the human mind constantly overlooks. Only some (supernatural) individuals (just like Elba, in "Mi hermana Elba", Chapter 1, section 5) are endowed with the capability to move across channels that others cannot detect.

4. ABSENT BOUNDARIES

Another attempt to destabilise the idea of physical space as objective structure is found in Éric Faye's short story "Tandis que roule le train" (1997). In this case, the notion of boundary is transgressive because it is absent where it is expected to be present. In the selected text, the author draws on the figure of unlimited space, or rather, on a space with no conceivable limit. This presents various similarities with the canonical Borgesian infinite structures (e.g., "The Library of Babel", 1941; "The Book of Sand", 1975), and it touches upon a dislocation of spatial hierarchy by introducing a larger frame within a smaller one; the infinite within a finite reality (see Chapter 4).

Edgeless-ness, however, is not necessarily conceived in this chapter as a form of infinity. French author Éric Faye confronts us with the following anguishing situation: ever since they can remember, a community of people, of which the narrator is part, has been entrapped in a train that is in permanent motion. This train has been rolling for a long time, maybe for eternity. Within, a whole structure of a society has learned to live in a normal fashion. Although the narrator has never been outside, he knows that he is on a train and can imagine what it looks like from the outside because there is another train running parallel to his. His own train is reflected in the windows of the other. There is no certainty as to where the two trains are heading. Many years ago, they were promised a destination, but some of them, discouraged, have given up hope of the train finally stopping. Meanwhile, the train continues to roll onward and its passengers do not question why.

While an allegorical reading of this story would be possible, there are sufficient elements within the text that present this situation as fact within the fictional reality, thus also justifying a 'fantastic reading' of this situation (that is, as impossible and not as allegorical).

The author was awarded the French literary prize Prix des Deux Magots (1998) for the book of short stories—*Je suis le gardien du phare et autres récits fantastiques* (1997)—in which this text is included. And yet, Faye's fantastic fiction remains undiscovered by the vast majority of scholars.

In the introductory note to this collection, the author emphasises that his use of fantastic elements is not a random choice. For Faye, this is the best narrative form to use to express the central concern of the volume, summed up in the question: "[c]an the man of the end of the 20th century still hide from the world, escape from the plural to benefit from the singular and become a free electron?" (1997:3). In all the texts of the volume, the fantastic element plays a central role in interrogating the position of the contemporary man in the late twentieth century, his quest for individuality and his relationship to the globalised environment around him. The existential question—who is the contemporary man?—is translated in spatial terms as 'what is his position in this contemporary world?' Three leitmotifs capture this problem: first, the voyager, main character of every story; second, the image of displacement, what Faye expresses as "the praise of escape" (1997:3), and third, the topos of the no-man's land. This voyager arrives at forgotten places to be confronted with areas populated by communities abandoned and forgotten by the rest of the world. The influence of Kafka is perceptible in the parable-like structure of the stories, which contain very simple plot lines but very rich symbolic imagery, as well in as the recurrence of typically Kafkaian motifs, such as the presence of authority, the unreachable destiny and the perpetual search (for example, the station of "Tandis que roule le train" or the summit of "Frontières").

Location: Trains in a Plain

One aspect that gets the reader's attention from the start is the lack of geographical features determining where the action is emplaced. All spatial information is concentrated on three general zones: the train where the narrator is located, the opposite train and the exterior. The voyager immerses us from the outset in the only world he has known since he was born, that of his train, as clearly expressed in the opening paragraph of the story: "I have never seen what our train is like from the exterior. Like a number of my fellows, I was born in it, grew up there and it is there where my life is (1997:13)".

Despite the awkwardness of this situation, life on this train is, in the broader sense, very similar to our factual reality. Families reside in compartments, and there are marriages, graduations and the same type of societal rituals with which the reader is familiar.

The opposite train that goes parallel at the exact same speed to his allows the narrator, Anton, to imagine what his own train might look like. Anton even has a Platonic love in the opposite train, a female counterpart named Antonia. (I will be returning later to these Platonic figures of symmetry.)

The window separating the interior of the trains from the exterior is a boundary in which is concentrated a great deal of meaning, since almost every action takes place at this boundary. The window connects the everyday of both trains, and yet it is an impenetrable boundary that isolates the realities of both trains from each other and from the outside: "I would love if spring melted the glass windows down" (14).

The lack of spatial referents to provide location is compensated by some guiding temporal allusions. Once more, it is the window that enables the occupants of the train to identify the passing of time. For example, winter is recognised because it obliterates the silhouettes of the people on the other train.

These trains roll on a seemingly endless railway. The exterior is vaguely defined, referred to only as "the plain". This journey would end, the passengers were told, when they reached the promised station, a moment they view as "the decisive moment" (16).

Discourse: Us, Them, Limbo

The three central spatial domains—the narrator's train, the parallel train and the exterior—are constructed using three contrasting semantic fields: the first is the space of the known, the 'us'; the second is the space of 'them'; the third is a state rather than a suspended space, a 'limbo', where no referents or physical characteristics are specified.

In the case of the first of these fields, throughout the text the narrator refers to it with the first person plural pronoun ("our train", "we roll" [13]). It is not only a physical frame but also a whole domain with values of culture and identity attributed to it: "It is here where my life is" (13). Note, also, how the French expression "*chez nous*" (16) locates him in a space of a collectively constructed social reality with which he identifies.

The discourse on boundaries is very significant. The train is a sort of incarceration and is, as the narrator describes it, static despite being in constant movement: "each of us remains in an assigned compartment and we don't feel like checking what is happening at the front or back" (15). It is also characterised by a rigid pattern of social conventions to be followed, as the various expressions of mechanic succession show: "My comrades, by lassitude or conformism, married. One after the other, they resigned themselves and married one of our own women" (15–16).

The parallel train is the space of the other, combining the figures of homology and alterity. The first is represented by expressions that compare: "they too" (14), "to them too" (14): "the other train" (13), "us and them" (14), "Antonia is the love of my life *for* she is on the other train" (15, "*car*" in the original; emphasis mine). Note the implications of this last example. It is only because they are in different trains that they can reflect and complement each other. It is the 'them' that allows the 'us' to be perceived and identified, so the other (train) serves literally as a mirror. This exchange of reflections is, according to the narrator, crucial in keeping the passengers in a balanced state, ("[a]s if our carriage, during those moments, had the clarity of a mirror, we send to our interlocutors the same pieces of information" [14]).

Finally, the construction of the third space, the exterior, is remarkable precisely for its lack of definition. It is only mentioned once, as being a monotone plain (17). Other than that, it remains vague, indefinite, without materialisation. If the other train is the image of self-reassertion, the exterior is constructed upon a doubt: it is the realm of the "perhaps": "Perhaps we will reach the station. Perhaps the landscape will change, maybe we will leave this plain" (17).

An important aspect is how the passengers have dealt with this absent boundary and with the utter impossibility of knowing the location of their ever-moving train. The characters have formulated various hypotheses relating to the moment that will potentially interrupt and alter their situation, the most popular of these being the story of the station. This station is as intangible as all other exterior elements and is located in a remote moment in time. However, the narrator emphasises at all times that the existence of this station as a physical reality might also be in question. It might simply be an invention, a myth originating from popular folklore to explain what they cannot understand or know for certain:

> We, the younger ones, don't know anymore what distinguishes the myth from reality. We soon will doubt the existence of that day to come, and we already doubt the existence of a station. (17)

This station is thus a matter of interpretation. Some of the passengers interpret this final frontier as a utopia, some as a home of sorts, heaven, or Promised Land: "a welcoming station with clumps of flowers" (14), which immediately triggers parallels with the image of the Wandering Jew. In contrast to the undefined exterior space, this wishful thinking about the station as the point of arrival is expressed in verbs that indicate a specific location in space ("to reach *the* station" [17], emphasis mine) and in time (i.e., the day of arrival).

Another legend depicts the end as a cliff over which the train will fall. This contrasts with the collective image of the station as a place of arrival. It is in this evocation of the cliff that, for the first time, the word "void" appears: "we will dive into the void" (17), the final sentence of the short story.

As long as the train keeps moving on, the final point remains, for good or for bad, an open question. Since the end might be worse than being in this ceaseless movement, it is this sense of doubt which keeps them "on board" (14), while it is also this sense of doubt that generates a strong sense of anguish.

Story: The Endless Space

This text is an excellent example of how a restricted spatial frame, presented by a narrator whose focalisation is also restricted, delimits not only a physical space but also, as in this story, a whole ontological domain. And the characters, from the start, are already located in this different ontological domain. This is clearly seen in the opening sentence, where the word 'train' could be replaced by 'world' or 'reality':

> I have never seen what our *train* is like from the exterior. Like a number of my fellows, I was born in it, grew up there and it is there where my life is. (13, emphasis mine)

The train thus is a synonym for the bounded idea of reality of its occupants; a world with its own community of inhabitants, rules, codes and system of beliefs. In this train, our world as readers is recreated. The characters have accommodated the codes of our empirical world in this compressed space of action. Apart from the social rituals, we learn that this microcosm also contains character-types, all of them defined by their attitude toward the end point. There are the spiritual guides ("who will guide them to the frontiers of the spirit" [15]); the anxious ones who wait impatiently, ready to leave at any moment ("ready for something" [16]); the sceptical, the narrator included, who are unsure even about the very existence of this end; and the nihilistic, who think of the end point as an abyss into the void. Reaching the station symbolises reaching an 'end' in the double sense of the English word: as ending and as goal. For some, this end will reveal the purpose of their trip. For others, the final destination is nothing other than a proof of the pointlessness of their trajectory.

One of the astonishing aspects of this short story is that the very nature of the fantastic element is never called into question. The logic of the situation they are in is never challenged: how come this space is never-ending, and how is it possible for the train to keep moving for such a long time? The fantastic element not only fails to elicit surprise but is, from the start, assumed to be an unavoidable, given condition. The physical impossibility of this boundless space thus serves as a background setting against which to bring forth other issues: 'who they are', represented in the symbolic relation of both trains; and 'where they are going to', represented in the various legends on the final limit.

Reality as an Arbitrary System of Boundaries

At this point, we arrive at the core of this fantastic transgression of space, expressed in the figure of space with no conceivable end boundary. The philosophical evocations of Faye's story are manifold. This text could very well be a modern version of Plato's theory of ideas, more specifically as expressed in the parable of the cave. A confined community (cave/train) can catch glimpses of reality only through the exterior silhouettes projected onto the boundary of their world (cave wall/glass window). However, in contrast to Plato's clearly two-fold view of the real, the existence of a higher reality existing outside their confined world of experience is not a certainty. It remains a mere possibility. For the characters of Faye's text, that external reality might be nothing more than a constructed discourse "that ramifies in a delta of nuances, of different versions, it slowly acquires a status of legend" (17). Its origin and purpose might be to alleviate this uncertainty.

The cosmological evocations bear strong similarities to Borges' "The Library of Babel" (1941), the infinite and boundless nature of which is dealt with by structuring it into a number of galleries, corridors and bookshelves, an arbitrary system of boundaries "which, repeated, becomes order: the Order" (Borges [1941] 1999:118).

The existential overtones of the story are also undeniable. The experience of being is equated to the doubt of the boundary, the surpassing of boundaries. An existential fear is provoked by the lack of a conceivable physical dead end. The text, then, captures this experience of the existential vertigo of being exposed to a space with no boundaries. What is more, this spatial image of the void denies teleological time in favour of a cyclical never-ending time, as in a form of eternal recurrence where teleological time is inconceivable.

Most important, however, is the way in which the characters have chosen to deal with this situation. The society of the train shows that this lack of boundary is necessarily compensated by the invention of boundary. This is achieved by creating conventional systems that regulate both the interior of the train, in the form of social rituals, as well as the collective imaginary of the passengers, in the invented "something at the end" (14). Within that ever-moving, boundless and ultimately questioned external frame of reference, which might be called 'reality', the passengers have constructed their ordered and embraceable structure. The text suggests the manner in which humans, when confronted with the endless (both limitless and pointless), might handle this disheartening situation by creating artificial boundaries, structures and compartments, in order to find orientation. Therefore, this text suggests that the conventional, societal, *human* construction of the real counters the idea of no end, no purpose, illustrated here with the metaphorical image of the inexistent train station.

The model of the real that the text portrays can be applied to other fantastic texts. In a shorter and less-developed form, the motif of the never-ending railway is used by Jacques Sternberg in two microstories. "Le Tunnel"

(1974) is centred on the confusion of the passengers in a train yet to leave the tunnel it entered some time ago.

> [...] I remembered all of a sudden, the train crossed in full engine a region of plains and endless fields, without any hill, without any relief. From then on, one single question haunted me: in what direction exactly was the tunnel being crossed? (1998:84)

As this passage describes, this provokes a profound dislocation as to the whereabouts of the train and as to what awaits at the end of this tunnel. Vanishing points are eliminated, and perspective is abolished, thus creating a sense of vertigo and suspension. Bearing much in common with Faye's story, this sense of suspension provoked by homogeneous never-ending surfaces is an aspect that Jorge Luis Borges, in a conversation with Pierre Drieu La Rochelle, once called "horizontal vertigo" (in Vicente 1999:29). When Borges envisaged the Argentinian pampas, this vast extension of flat land where the eye meets no end, he said it provoked in him a sensation of "horizontal vertigo" as he could not determine any spatial end when situated in this endlessly extending landscape in nature. This concept has recently been adopted by some urban sociologists (e.g., Ford 1993 and Villoro 2003) to designate the subject's anguish when confronted with the enormous extension of the contemporary megalopolis, whose boundaries extend beyond what meets the human eye.[6]

Similarly, Sternberg's "La Sanction" (1974), an example of flash fiction that combines the Fantastic with the absurd, tells of the punishment of being placed in a never-ending railway in a tunnel. The condemned, in anguish, run toward an end that never arrives. Once more, this text captures the idea of how the lack of an embraceable end is a sort of existential punishment, as the title indicates. Another example is "La escalera de Sarto" (1980) by Spanish author Ricardo Doménech. A professor of art history discovers a very peculiar architectural piece: some stairs that "serve only to go up" (1980:36). These stairs have no final point, since they keep ascending infinitely. Once the subject accesses it, this "evil" (1980:32), "unheard-of" (32) structure invalidates the opposition of up/down, as well as that of inside/outside.

Finally, it is worth remembering that if space can be understood and used as a boundary to structure our (otherwise boundless) physical experience, so too can time. Two texts are representative of this: the canonical "The Highway of the South" (1964) by Julio Cortázar, and "Ignición" (2007) by the Spanish author Ángel Olgoso. In the latter, Olgoso captures very well the fantastic distortion that is provoked by the image of being suspended while in movement. The plot is simple: a man is entrapped with an attendant in a lift that does not seem to move or to stop. In this situation, the suspension of the temporal and spatial is expressed with images to reference-lessness: "the trip becomes never-ending" (2007:110). "I don't know how much time has passed. [...] Will it still be Friday?" (2007:110) "My fingers are light years away from the alarm button" (111), in a moment of suspension in space where time too "has lost its appearance and purpose" (112). Most clearly, the oxymoronic expressions "Still hours/Motionless disorientations" (110) once more serve to annihilate both time and space as articulating elements. Furthermore, Cortázar's text builds upon the idea of the lack of suspension not only in and through space but also in time. He constructs a scenario where millions of cars are trapped in a literally endless traffic jam near Paris. The end cannot be envisaged and they remain there during the rapidly succeeding seasons. As in Faye's train, the lack of spatial vanishing points is rapidly compensated for by the characters through their construction of invented structures and roles that generate a societal tissue to function within this extraordinary situation.

* * *

Having established that the 'boundary' is a crucial device for humans in in our experience of space and apprehension of reality, it is not surprising to find that it is also a key realistic device in fiction. The impression of realism created by a set of spatial frames is precisely that which the transgressions presented in this chapter destabilise.

The three transgressions examined in this chapter disrupt this realistic effect by showing ways in which the expected logical frames are obliterated. Elastic boundaries present shifting distances between buildings. This prevents the subject from finding any absolute position in space. Rhizome structures present a reality that is interconnected but whose actual connections only some characters can perceive. Last, the notion of an absent boundary plays on the metaphysical *angst* experienced when facing a limitless structure. There is one aspect that is characteristic of all three thematic lines: the models they present lack the reassuring, stable and universal consistency provided by an objective system of referential boundaries. The abolition of a fixed referential point of view (what Warf calls the elimination of "Cartesian ocularcentrism", 2009:60) leads to a relational system of boundaries that is always subjected to the individual regarding it—a conception of space, and with it of the real that, as in Chapter 2, is always constructed by the subject with no reference beyond himself.

Apart from the notions of distance and definition, there is a second aspect that derives from the relational system of boundaries, one that makes reference to how spaces are organised in hierarchical order. How this expected hierarchy can be transgressed will be the subject of the next chapter.

NOTES

1. The Platonic *chorismos* is the separation between the world of ideas and the world of the senses. For Aristotle, the *chorismos* divides the *Physis* (that which

is seen) and *Metaphysics* (that which cannot be seen). Beyond that *chorismos*, scientific knowledge is impossible. Therefore, knowledge is equated and dependent upon this *chorismos*. There is no science beyond and without that boundary (*Le Problème de l'être chez Aristote*, Pierre Abuenque 1962).

2. Bal explicitly refers to spatial frames as a 'stabilising' device in which the reader can locate the action: "[...] information concerning space is often repeated, to stress the stability of the frame, [...] as opposed to the transitory nature of the events which occur within it" (Bal 2009:140).

3. Since no official English translations were found, all short story translations of titles and quotes in this chapter are mine.

4. A large variety of anthologies and critical studies demonstrate the consolidation of the Fantastic in Quebec at present. For further anthologies, see *Anthologie de la nouvelle et du conte fantastiques québécois au XXe siècle* (Eamond 1987) and for critical overviews specifically on the postmodern Fantastic in the Quebecois literary tradition, see "L'écriture fantastique au Québec depuis 1980" (Lord 1995/1993), *Récits fantastiques québécois contemporains* (Laflamme 2009) and "Le postmodernisme dans le fantastique québécois" (Grossman 2010).

5. As well as Manuel Castells' work on the sociological aspect of this topic (*The Rise of the Network Society*, 1996), another illustrative text on the figure of the network as contemporary paradigm of space is "From Surfaces to Networks" (Warf in Warf and Arias [eds.], 2008:59–76).

6. This metaphor in relation to the Borgesian poetics of the infinite has been explored by Henry Vicente in *El vértigo horizontal* (1999). In the socio-urban context, see Richard T. Ford ("The vertigo one feels in LA comes not from vertical but from horizontal distances: the multiplication of boundaries [...] makes it impossible to conceive of any absolute boundary, any sense of place. Centre and periphery become meaningless in a sweeping map of topography" ("Spaced Out in L.A.", 1993:88), and Juan Villoro's "El vértigo horizontal. La ciudad de México como texto" (2003).

4   Hierarchy

Spaces Inside-Out

"I was astonished that such narrow courtyards, little more than long entryways, could have contained such numbers of people."

‐("The Man on the Threshold", J. L. Borges)

1. CONTAINMENT AND REFERENCE

In the last chapter, I referred to Ryan's perspective on spatial frames within narrative spaces. These spatial frames included spatial boundaries and hierarchical relationships (Ryan 2014:6). Given the relevance and complexity of these two elements in the narratives of the Fantastic, they are treated separately in this book. While Chapter 3 dealt with boundaries—those material structures that define and articulate the spatial dimension—this chapter is focused on the second element: the notion of spatial hierarchies. Just as was the case for the interdependence between body and space explored in Chapter 2, the principle of containment is a basic relational notion of space. Therefore, the transgressions examined in this chapter modify the spatial principle of the container and the contained in that they violate the rules of hierarchical order which we abide by in our everyday reality.

Logically, although perhaps not remarked upon enough, the order that classifies spatial frames hierarchically is fundamental to generating the reality effect within the literary text. When presenting or presented with a literary world that follows realistic conventions, the author or reader performs this process almost automatically, in that it is recognised or assumed that, for example, Raskolnikov's garret (*Crime and Punishment*, 1866) is contained within a larger structure (the guesthouse). This garret is at the same time part of a larger frame (the city of St. Petersburg), which also belongs to a broader space, etc. Note how narrative space, in particular the various embedded spatial frames, is employed in the opening of *Crime and Punishment* to locate the reader in a verisimilar space:

> On an exceptionally hot evening early in July a young man *came out of the garret* in which he lodged *in S. place* and walked slowly, as though in hesitation, towards K. bridge. He had successfully avoided

meeting his landlady on the staircase. His garret was *under the roof of a high, five-storied house* and was more like a cupboard than a room.
(Dostoyevsky 2000:3, emphasis added)

The same applies to fantastic narratives, where the principle of spatial hierarchy—when it is not being violated—reinforces the realistic setting that the impossible element will disrupt. Kafka's *Metamorphosis* (1915), to quote a canonical example, is one of the many texts in which spatial frames are not transgressed and yet are meaningful. Most of the action unfolds within the house, where Gregor Samsa is confined after his transformation.

The interplay between the logical dialectic of container/contained is frequently found in ancient folklore, by making—as P. M. Schuhl puts it in his study of the theme of containment in the Marvellous—"the large fit into the small" (1952:69). An example is the genie of the lamp in *The Book of One Thousand and One Nights*, or the world within the world, the microcosm, as in "Le Diamant" (*Feu de braise*, André Pieyre de Mandiargues 1959), in which the princess-protagonist falls into a little diamond while looking through it. The impossible relationship between the bigger and the smaller in those two narratives of the Marvellous is, however, not presented as impossible within the logical rules of the fictional world. Instead, this inversion of hierarchies is the catalyst for the various subsequent adventures of Aladdin or of the princess within the diamond.

Tangled Hierarchies of Postmodernism

While the inversion of spatial hierarchies is an ancient motif, it has never before received as much critical attention as paid to it in the context of postmodern narrative. This context saw an unprecedented rise in the number of critical works addressing two techniques in particular: those of metafiction and metalepsis (Waugh 1984; McHale 1987; Hutcheon 1988). The work of Douglas Hofstadter (*Gödel, Escher, Bach: An Eternal Golden Braid*, 1979)—which connects Bach's canons, Escher's loop structures and Gödel's logic theorems, all of which are regarded as paradigmatic for what Hofstadter calls "Tangled Hierarchies" (1999:668–742)—was to provide inspiration for subsequent academic analysis. The author begins his research by reminding us of the hierarchical nature of our perceptive processes and then goes on to analyse various ways of representing a distortion of the expected logical hierarchies. As a result, various spatial forms arise where the laws of physics and mathematics are violated in one way or another to produce an incomprehensible total system. Hofstadter's concept of "strange loop" ("tangled hierarchies")—occurring "whenever, by movement upwards (or downwards) through the levels of some hierarchical system, we unexpectedly find ourselves right back where we started" (1999:10)—was later applied by Brian McHale to the postmodern literary text (1987). Jumps, loops, recursion, infinite regress and self-references among the interplay between fictional levels are, he argues, strategies employed in postmodern narratives to foreground the problematic ontological status of fiction that characterises this literary period (1987:113). A key implication of this ontological question is that by disrupting the principle of hierarchy in the text, particularly the hierarchy of embedded fictional levels, two of the most ancient questions of literary theory are brought to the fore: mimesis and referentiality.

Elaborating on the interrelation between literary space and extratextual reference, Bertrand Westphal dedicates an entire chapter in *Geocriticism* (2007 [2011a]) to the issue of referentiality. Westphal starts by contesting a common view in postmodern criticism that negates the dichotomy between the real and the fictional and denies the relationship—traditionally regarded as hierarchical—of fiction as part of, and stemming from, what is our factual reality. Fiction, according to the view that Westphal seeks to challenge, should not be regarded as being the reproduction of the real; quite the contrary, our extratextual reality should be viewed as being produced by (and thus a product of) fictional discourses. In this sense, the hierarchical relationship between referent and representation is altered: the copy cannot derive from the referent (the extratextual real), since the copy is even more real or authentic than its referent or is even, as Jean Baudrillard claims, the only possibility: "Simulation is no longer that of a territory, a referential being, or a substance. It is the generation by models of a real without origin or reality: a hyperreal" (Baudrillard 1994:1).

In a contemporary context, everyday experience is heavily influenced by fictional discourses, as Baudrillard (1994) and Augé (2000), among many other postmodern thinkers, have recurrently emphasised. However, the approach of this book supports Westphal's idea (2007/2011a) in stating that there is a reality that can be transmitted through the literary work, although it should be noted that the notion of reality is more contrived in postmodern narrative. My assumption here is that any fictional product derives from reality and that fiction—not considered as an exact copy of its referent but rather as an extension to or complement of this referent—is still a representation deriving from the extratextual real. This is a fundamental premise required for the Fantastic to operate, both in its traditional and postmodern manifestations. The Fantastic needs the mimetic contract until a breach occurs, thus the referential illusion is maintained until the impossible irrupts. Therefore, although postmodern approaches seek to place the idea of reality and fiction on the same level, the reader still contrasts what is read in the text with his/her idea of the extratextual real. During the reading act, the distinction between reality/fiction prevails.[1]

However, within the fictional realm (both in fantastic fiction and in other genres) this hierarchical relation can be called into question. The inversions of hierarchy are, as McHale and Westphal among others have claimed, a strategy particularly present in postmodern narratives.

The strategies of metalepsis and metafiction have been the subject of attention among scholars of the Fantastic (Brooke-Rose 1981; Erdal Jordan

1998; Horstkotte 2004; Rodríguez Hernández 2010), who have pointed out that these strategies represent the fracture between language and reality after the Language Turn or, as Erdal Jordan puts it, they "impose the linguistic reality as option over the empirical one" (Erdal Jordan 1998:123).

In a fantastic mode, the strategies of metalepsis and metafiction have been explored in texts such as "Lost in the Funhouse" (John Barth 1968), now a paradigm of the postmodern in literature. In this story, the protagonist is entrapped in a funhouse which is equiparated with the space of a book that never ends (see section 3). Similarly, in "Continuity of Parks" (Julio Cortázar 1956), what the character reads has an effect upon the space from which he is reading. The same strategies and plot line have been employed in more recent short stories, like "En el hemisferio sur" (Cristina Fernández Cubas 2009), "El caso del traductor infiel" (José María Merino 1994) and "El purgatorio" (Ángel Olgoso 2009). These are but a few of the large number of texts in the plots of which Derridean ideas concerning the autonomy of the text in relation to the real, the pure self-reflexivity of language and the absence of all implication of the text in the world are embedded.

An interesting variation on the traditional metalepsis is one that replaces the embedded fictional level with virtual space. The jumps across hierarchical levels take place between the realistic domain and the virtual one. This leads to plots where, for example, cybernetic creatures trespass into the realistic domain within the text, such as the artificial monster of "Intimidad cibernética" (José María Merino 2002), a creature that one day replaces his creator. Conversely, the real becomes part of the virtual in texts like "El dominio" (Fernando Iwasaki 2004), a short story juxtaposing the traditional sense of 'domain' as physical territory with its contemporary application to virtual space.

McHale not only sets forth the strategies of metalepsis and metafiction but also outlines various distortions of the traditional notion of referentiality in which, within the textual world, referential spaces are combined with imagined ones. Among these, he mentions the strategies of interpolation, juxtaposition, superimposition, misattribution and transworld migration. To this list, Westphal adds the strategy of transnomination, which he regards as "a way to fight against the saturation—here the ideological saturation—of the protoworld" (Westphal 2011a:108), so that referential space "saturated with names and reprehensible realemes [... can] find a new purity" (2011a:108). Another strategy that Westphal mentions is that of anachronism, where a referential space is integrated within a different temporal context than what is allocated in extratextual history. All the aforementioned strategies explore how a combination of referential and non-referential spaces are fused within one single text to portray a narrative world that is neither fully referential nor fully invented: this corresponds with Westphal's category of "Heterotopic Interference" (2011a:104), which is neither "Homotopic Consensus" (referential, 2011a:102) nor "Utopian Excursus" (non-referential, 2011a:108). Since the aim of both McHale and Westphal is to systematise the strategies concerning these games of spatial reference, they do not explore how these incursions are presented within the text (i.e., whether they are portrayed as conflictive and impossible or as an integrated element within the story-world). This explains why their examples embrace short stories of the Fantastic (e.g., Borges' "Tlön, Uqbar, Orbis Tertius", 1944; Cortázar's "The Other Heaven", 1966) as well as other texts which are good examples of postmodern narratives but which are not fantastic (e.g., Calvino's *Invisible Cities*, 1972 and Pynchon's *Gravity's Rainbow*, 1973).

The aspect with which this chapter is concerned is not how spatial hierarchies *construct* the impression of reality in the text (realist literature), nor how they *deny* the notion of the mimetic contract (like postmodern narratives); instead, my focus here is on how the changes in spatial hierarchies de-automatise the reader's relationship with space, *transgressing* the illusion of verisimilitude. This always presupposes a previously constructed textual reality that imitates our extratextual reality and which is conceived as realistic by the reader who constantly contrasts it with his referential reality.

Therefore, this chapter seeks to present games of hierarchy that go beyond the techniques of fantastic metalepsis and fantastic metafiction. The three sample texts analysed disrupt automatic associations of spatial relationships of containment, not those of embedded fictional levels but exclusively those of architectural space. Nonetheless, the ontological question and the notion of spatial reference are also clearly present in the analysed corpus.

As in the previous chapters, parallels with the metaphors of these transgressions are found outside the literary domain. The disruption of hierarchy and containment has also been an area of greatest scholarly concentration among contemporary human geographers. As will be shown, this fact once more highlights the importance of engaging, in any geocritical study, with the interrelation between narrative and extratextual spaces.

The first theme, based on the text "La casa de muñecas" (Fernando Iwasaki 2004), alternates the roles of the container space and the contained, the part and the whole. This principle presents similarities with Edward S. Soja's concept of the "Cosmopolis" (2000) and Fredric Jameson's analysis of the Westin Bonaventure Hotel, as an all-embracing all-integrating space that is not part of the city "but rather its equivalent and replacement or substitute" (Jameson 1990:40). The best metaphor for these urban phenomena, Soja argues, is found in literature and is Borges' "The Aleph" (1949), a precursor to this transgression, which I will call 'the container-contained'.

Marc Augé's theory of the non-place (1992), which concentrates on the absence of relationship between a place and its surroundings, is taken to the extreme in the second sample short story. "Dejen salir" (José Ferrer-Bermejo 1982) presents a cancellation of hierarchies by interlocking various spatial frames. This turns into a Möbius effect, a self-referential structure—a metro station—where inside and outside lose their polarity. Parallels are also to be found with De Certeau's metaphor of carceral space and the automatisation of spatial practices in our everyday (1988).

The last short story, "La Brume" (Jacques Sternberg 1974), is an excellent example of how the logical assumptions of spatial hierarchies can be literally suspended. It juxtaposes the subjective impression of space with its objective representation, an aspect that coincides with the contrast that Bollnow (1963) establishes between lived and mapped-out spaces ("hodological" versus "mathematical" space), as well as with Lefebvre's categories of perceived and conceived space (1974).

2. INVERSIONS OF HIERARCHY

What Gilbert Durand labelled in his *Anthropological Structures of the Imaginary* as "the archetype of the *container* and the *contained* (1999:208)" refers to a trope that inverts the basic spatial relation of embedded spaces. The same phenomenon has been tagged in the realm of fantasy narrative as "the little-big trope" (*The Encyclopaedia of Fantasy*, 1999:586), named after the eponymous fantasy novel (*Little, Big* by John Crowley 1981): "In fantasy almost anything that can be entered—a body, book, rabbit hole or other portal, garden shop, labyrinth, underground cavern, edifice liner, forest, island, polder or otherworld—may well be bigger inside than out" (1999:586). However, once again, in narratives of fantasy and the Marvellous—narratives that are removed from our model of extratextual reality—this spatial paradox is not (re)presented as a transgressive element, in the sense that it does not arouse a logical conflict within the storyworld. For example, in the aforementioned text by de Mandiargues, "Le Diamant", the dramatic and thematic focus is not placed on the (illogical and impossible) confinement of a human being within a tiny object.

Returning to the confines of fantastic narratives, a precursor to this trope is the egg-shaped object of "The Crystal Egg", by H. G. Wells (1897). This transparent egg transgresses the logical principle of spatial hierarchies; despite its relatively small dimensions, it contains a whole society of Martians. What's more, not only are the roles of the container and contained inverted but so too are those of the observer and the observed, a characteristic that is also found in Fernando Iwasaki's short story. The main character of "The Crystal Egg", Mr Cave, initially assumes he is an omniscient observer of the whole society contained in the egg, so that he has a 'panoptical view' over the totality of what is taking place within the egg. However, in the last paragraphs of the story, the position as an absolute observer is displaced to the condition of being observed. This crystal egg in which he thinks he is observing the Martians is in fact nothing but a medium for the Martians to gain a close view over the Earth.

Inspired by this short story, as Borges himself states in the epilogue of his compilation *The Aleph*, is the short story "The Aleph" (Jorge Luis Borges 1949), an early example of the postmodern Fantastic and one that is indispensable for comprehending the type of spatial transgression considered in this chapter. The narrator of "The Aleph" discovers in the basement a point in space in which is contained all possible angles of the world: "Each thing (a mirror's face, let us say) was infinite things, since I distinctly saw it from every angle of the universe" (1999:192). This sort of (key)hole enables a total view of space and time; it contains the world, accessible through an absolute gaze. The transgression of the physical laws of space that Borges presents is thus based on the following two paradoxes:

The first paradox is the same as that exemplified by the crystal egg. The aleph, physically speaking, has constricted specific dimensions—like a keyhole, we imagine—but at the same time it is the container of a space larger than itself. Second, the contained is not only larger but is also total and absolute, representing the paradox of containing the infinite within the finite. This is the logical problem encountered by the narrator when he has to describe the aleph: how can he express an infinite image within the finite extension of words and the limited dimensions of the page?

> [...] the central problem—the enumeration, even partial enumeration, of infinity—is irresolvable. In that unbounded moment, I saw millions of delightful and horrible acts; none amazed me so much as the fact that all occupied the same point, without superposition and without transparency. What my eyes saw was *simultaneous;* what I shall write is *successive,* because language is successive. Something of it, though, I will capture.
>
> ("The Aleph", 1999:282–283, emphasis added)

The figure of the aleph confronts the narrator and reader with a vision where all spatial (and temporal) tools (e.g., orientation, reference and selection) that human beings possess to make sense of physical space and to represent it are eradicated. To express this impossible vision, the narrator employs different rhetorical devices: disjointed reiterations, lists of enumerations of what he sees simultaneously ("I saw"), absolute quantifiers, ("each", "every", "all") and, most interestingly for this analysis, a juxtaposition of the relationships of containment: the part and the whole are placed in the same hierarchy: "a copy of the first English translation of Pliny [...] and all at the same time saw each letter on each page" (1999:193).

"The Aleph" condenses three pillars of Borges' fiction: the word—and its limitations in transmitting and representing true knowledge, time—the unreliability of memory and the artificiality of our constructed categories of present, past and future—and space—in this particular story, illustrated by the transgression of the container in the contained. The aleph is an image of a totality, an absolute that serves to portray the limitations of man facing the infinite. This is done by creating a spatial form that reflects a view of space (and time) that the human mind cannot embrace nor codify. The One and the All are fused within one single image, "one of the points in space that contains all other points", the central theme in the philosophical universe of the author. More examples of the same principle are found in passages such as: "Each part of the house occurs many times; any particular place is another place. [...] The house is as big as the world—or rather, it is the world" ("The House of Asterion", 1999:221) and "There is a saying, you know—that India is larger than the world" ("The Man on the Threshold", 1999:270). "The Library of Babel" (1941) and "The Book of Sand" are further examples of structures that play upon the principle of container-contained, finite in their physical dimensions and infinite in what they contain, where each part contains the whole and the whole is simultaneously part of itself.

The cosmic view of the Aleph that Borges proposes has not only generated enormous literary scholarship dealing with the Borgesian figures of the infinite and other spatial figures but the Aleph has also proven to be fruitful outside the literary text.[2] Edward S. Soja (1989) has appropriated it as a metaphor to refer to a postmodern conception of urban space containing and hybridising multiple languages, symbols and identities. "[T]he place where, without admixture or confusion, all the places of the world, seen from every angle, coexist" (Borges 1999:280) is for Soja a paradigmatic metaphor for Los Angeles, an all-integrating space with no discrimination, and no segregation:

> Los Angeles, like Borges' Aleph, is exceedingly tough-to-track, peculiarly resistant to conventional description [...]. Los Angeles is everywhere. It is global in the fullest sense of the word [...]. Everywhere seems also to be in Los Angeles.
>
> (Soja 1989:222–223)

A lesser-known and much more recent text that also borrows and modifies a traditional motif in the Fantastic is Fernando Iwasaki's "La casa de muñecas" ("The Dolls' House", 2004). Peruvian-born Iwasaki has a very varied creative production, ranging from humorous essays and novels to micro-short fiction. His volume of short stories *Ajuar funerario* (2004)—from which "La casa de muñecas" is taken—is the richest for studying contemporary manifestations of the Fantastic.

In this short narrative of just over a page, the author merges the motifs of the doomed place and the animation of the inanimate, crystallising in the spatial transgression of the container and the contained. The concise form of this short story makes it ideal for analysing how narrative spaces intervene to generate the fantastic transgression, since in its 24 lines of text every single word is important in the construction of the Fantastic.

The main character and narrator of "La casa de muñecas" tells us how in an antique shop he is captivated by a miniature house, in particular by the intricate representation of its life inside—which includes another even more miniaturised dolls' house. He buys it and places it in his room. During the night, he is awakened by a light shining in the dolls' house. When he approaches it, he realises that it is the miniature house within the dolls' house that is producing this light. But the narrator's surprise is double: the figurines of the bigger dolls' house not only move as if they were alive but they are as surprised as him by this light and run to the room where the embedded miniature is located. In the next scene, the body of the narrator is found in his room and even though the police search for clarification, no explanation is provided. The clue resides within the dolls' house, however. A new room and figurine have now been incorporated: the narrator's room, and all its contents including himself, are now part of the furniture in the dolls' house.

This story is reminiscent of the well-known short story by M. R. James: "The Haunted Dolls' House" (1923). In this story also, the protagonist acquires a dolls' house in an antique shop and brings it home. Just as in "La casa de muñecas", at night, the figurines come alive but in this case they reproduce the scene of an ancient family drama, the facts of which become clearer after some research is carried out by the protagonist. As will be shown, despite being based on the motif of the doomed dolls' house, Iwasaki's story presents significant differences in the function and representation of this fantastic element that distance it from the traditional ghost story.

Location: Embedded Houses

In Iwasaki's short story, there are three houses—three crucial spatial frames that are embedded within each other, like Russian dolls, until finally this hierarchy is transgressed. The first of these is the narrator's house. It is in the bedroom of this first house that the second frame is found: the newly acquired dolls' house, placed on his mahogany table. The architectural characteristics of this miniature building present an important initial difference from M. R. James' dolls' house, which displayed intricate Gothic features and conformed to the Victorian tradition of dolls' houses, designed to reflect an immaculate order and a grandiosity of wealth. These Victorian miniatures did not aim to convey the impression of everyday life but rather were built as perfect museum houses or as historical testimonies of wealthy families. While being extremely detailed, there is nothing Gothic, ostentatious or museum-like about the dolls' house of Iwasaki's story. In fact, its "appearance of being lived", to borrow Merino's phrase from "El museo" (1982:150, see Chapter 2, section 3), captures the narrator's attention. What makes this house so disturbingly realistic for the narrator is that it reproduces a casual everyday environment, as captured in elements of messiness or untidiness, such as open toothpaste tubes and notebooks with scrawled entries on the tables. Finally, within this dolls' house, there is the miniature replica that becomes illuminated on that night.

The descriptive attention devoted to the three houses differs noticeably. While very few characteristics of the narrator's house and bedroom are given, the description of the dolls' house is very rich in details, as the following excerpt shows:

> [...] on the tables the pages of notebooks filled with scrawls in minuscule characters were spread, and in the kitchen I perceived a cupboard full of tins and preserves with labels miniaturised by a demented artist (2004:42).[3]

And while this dolls' house is itself one of "an obsessive richness" (2004:42), the miniature replica within it is even more "meticulously decorated, like a nightmare" (2004:42). Therefore, the lower we go in this embedded spatial hierarchy the richer the details, a strategy that coincides perfectly with that "excessive ambition for the miniature" (2004:42) that captivates the narrator, as he recounts in the very first sentence of the story.

Discourse: 'Threshold Sentence'

As Ana Casas has shown in her article "Transgresión lingüística y microrrelato fantástico" ("Linguistic Transgression in Micro-Fiction of the Fantastic", 2010:10–13), micro-fictions provide very rich material for the analysis of rhetorical devices that configure the fantastic transgression. Casas herself uses many of the texts of Iwasaki's book *Ajuar funerario* to illustrate this. "La casa de muñecas", in just over one page of text, also provides an excellent example of the linguistic configuration of this fantastic transgression of space. To illustrate this, let us focus on two sentences. The first of these appears just after the narrator acquires the dolls' house:

> The only thing that shocked me was the infinite sadness of the figurines that *inhabited it* (2004:42, emphasis mine).

The verb "inhabit" condenses that which Ana Casas calls "linguistic resignification", where "a metaphorical value is substituted by a literal one" (2010:12), a rhetorical device based on the Todorovian literalisation of the metaphor (1975:79). The author plays upon the various meanings of this verb: the figurines are not only placed there but they literally *live* there. As a result, the expression "the figurines that inhabited it" foregrounds the imminent night animation, which happens in the next paragraph.

A fundamental device employed here to transgress the natural hierarchy of spaces is "polyvalence of deictics" (Casas 2010:13), a strategy which plays upon the referent that deictics necessarily imply. There are two clear examples in the text: first, the polyvalence of the pronoun "it" ("*la*") of the previous sentence, referring to the house but playing upon the ambiguity of *which* miniature house. The same can be applied to "the" ("*la*") in the following passage: "every figurine of *the* house ran towards *the* doomed room" (42, emphasis added). The same holds for the title; "*The* Dolls' House" (emphasis mine) is not restricted to one single referent but to multiple ones: it could be referring to either of the two dolls' houses or even, considering the final transgression when his room is incorporated into the miniature, to the narrator's house itself.

The second sentence to be highlighted appears after the narrator approaches the illuminated dolls' house at night and just before his body is found:

I don't know when *they* entered *my room*. (42, emphasis added)

This passage is very interesting from a structural, linguistic and spatial point of view. First, it functions as a turning point within the plot. Second, the deictics ("they", "my room") of the subordinate clause capture a crucial ambiguity regarding the location of the subject. Nothing is specified— neither who enters (the police or the figurines) nor what room is being entered. Furthermore, this room could be either his normal room or his dormitory newly incorporated into the dolls' house. Therefore, he could be located in one space or the other, or yet again in between both.

This rhetorical phenomenon is a remarkable device in the configuration of the fantastic effect because it combines the Fantastic as a phenomenon of language (Erdal Jordan 1998; Campra 2001; Casas 2010; Rodríguez Hernández 2010) with the subject of this thesis; the Fantastic as a phenomenon of space. This phrase, which I call a 'threshold sentence' (see García 2013a), is ambiguous, spatially speaking: it suggests that the protagonist could have already crossed into the fantastic domain or that he is instead in between two differentiated frames, which are also two domains. Furthermore, this liminal moment is happening not only in the textual world, but it also affects what Campra calls "the reading time" (Campra 2001:186), since the reader is unable to determine where the narrator or subject of the fantastic event is located.

Finally, the change of spatial frames also affects the perspective, as is expressed by a shift in the verb tenses. Whereas the first two paragraphs of the story are told in simple past tense ("I bought", "I ran", "I saw" [42]), after the 'threshold sentence', there is a shift to the present perfect and indicative present: "The police have removed the body and search for hints on the floor. [...] The figurine does not do justice to me but the mahogany table is exactly identical" (43). From where is the narrator speaking in this final sentence? Is he now located inside the dolls' house, watching the scene from a position within it? How is his voice reaching us? These questions remain unanswered but what the reader does know is that the narrator has left the domain of reality and is now speaking from the domain of the Fantastic. This loop in hierarchical spaces also entails a change in ontological status. The protagonist is now telling and seeing from the angle of the Fantastic, a recurrent strategy used by Iwasaki in the volume *Ajuar funerario* (2004), as in for example "La cueva"

("The Cave"), "Monsieur le révenant", "Hasta en la sopa" ("Absolutely Everywhere") and "El salón antiguo" ("The Old Living-Room"), all of which present the impossible element from the angle of he who is already in the fantastic domain: ghost, revenant, figurine or any other fantastic creature. As Roas has remarked (section "Voces del Otro lado", 2011:168–171), this is a general and recurrent feature of the postmodern Fantastic, in that giving voice to the impossible is a radical transgression, as well as a new perspective, of the traditional human voice that narrates the fantastic event.

Story: *Mise en Abyme* of the Fantastic

The function of the dolls' house within the story highlights important differences with the previously mentioned short story by M. R. James. Half way through Iwasaki's telling, any reader familiar with James' short story—or even with the traditional motif of the animated replica (of a house in this case)—might think that the author is reproducing a conventional plot line: the protagonist acquires a doomed object that comes to life at night to represent some unresolved event of the past, as is the case of James' haunted dolls' house. This has been previously presented as characteristic of the model of the Fantastic of Place (Chapter 1), where a particular place provides the frame for the apparition of the fantastic ghost (framing function). It is left to the protagonist to clarify some tragedy related to the alluring past that is embedded within those four walls (time-condensing function). However, whereas Iwasaki's short story might initially seem conventional, it is in fact far from being so, as it presents significant differences from the traditional ghost story.

The animation of the houses' figurines is not the only fantastic intervention in the story. When the miniature house is illuminated, an important detail is that the figurines inhabiting the bigger dolls' house are, like the narrator, puzzled by it. They witness an impossible event: their miniature house becomes alive at night too. This is extraordinarily a double animation of the dolls' house and the mini-dolls' house within the dolls' house. This double animation is, therefore, a multiple apparition of the Fantastic at different levels, or what we could call a *mise en abyme* of the fantastic effect. To express this, the actions of the narrator are mirrored in perfect symmetry by the actions of the inhabitants of the dolls' house: "I *ran* towards the mahogany table and terrified, I contemplated the interior of the tiny dolls' house shining, *while* all the figurines of the house *ran* towards the doomed room" (42, emphasis added).

The fantastic effect appears again in the final scene, when the narrator's room changes from being the container of the dolls' house to being a part of it, with all its details, mahogany table and himself, included. Iwasaki proposes a disturbing inversion between hierarchically contained spaces where the replica—the contained, the dolls' house—integrates its referent—the container, the narrator's room. And what is more, in this hierarchical inversion, the narrator becomes a miniature replica of himself.

The Referent-Replica

Many of the motifs developed in this section are found in other short stories that play upon a similar transgression between referent space and its miniature or, as Durand puts it, based on "the theme of the doubled container, of the container contained [...] the theme of the swallower swallowed" (1999:208). An example is "El proyecto" (2009) by Spanish author Ángel Olgoso, where the scale model that a boy builds as a school project gains life. Also transgressing the relation between the container and contained is "Ecosistema" (José María Merino 2002). There the narrator gets as a present a bonsai, which starts growing its own ecosystem, with miniature birds, plants and people. As in "La casa de muñecas", there is a further impossible occurrence in this story: when the narrator disappears, his family is incapable of explaining this disappearance and never finds his new emplacement because the narrator is now part of this bonsai ecosystem. Another text by this same author worth introducing here is "Nacimiento en el desván" (José María Merino 1982), a title containing the double sense of the Spanish word '*nacimiento*', birth and crib. The motif of a space that simultaneously acts as referent-replica is, in this text, exploited in an even more literal manner: the character builds a detailed miniature scale model of his village, which he keeps in his attic. The situation gets complicated when, as in the case of the dolls' house, the miniature gains life. To complicate things even more, there is a connection between replica and referent— whatever affects the scale model also affects his 'real' village, and vice versa. This is the first transgression of ontological hierarchy, where referent and replica are enclosed in an entangled interdependence. The creator of the miniature discovers that the strange deaths in the 'real' village were caused by his cat, which had destroyed some figurines and houses with his paws. This fantastic interconnection between the two hierarchically different planes, ontologically and spatially, is very clearly seen in this passage, where the narrator recalls what he witnesses in his real village after the cat attack:

> The inhabitants, an elderly married couple, were among the remains of crockery and wood like forgotten figurines after a long afternoon of playing, and only the blood, covering everything, imprinted upon the scene the true stamp of the real. [...], they reminded him of the frailty of the little objects that he himself had carved, and that only a little effort of his fingers crumbled and broke into pieces. (1982:23)

This immediately triggers a dilemma in the protagonist, who starts questioning what space—container village or contained model—is more real: "the horrendous suspicion the appearance of life had suggested to him: that the crib was the real and him only a lifeless figurine carved from the wood chip of some skilled hands" (1982:21). It is then that the word 'real' appears for the first time but, noticeably, related only to the scale model:

> With the rhythm of real life, men and women crossed the streets, entered and left their houses, [...]. He observed the crib petrified: in the centre of the attic, the mountains, the houses, the water currents, the poplar grove, seemed to beat with an undeniable reality. (1982:21)

After this second fantastic appearance, where the referent and the model seem to have exchanged roles, there is a third transgression, which is the most interesting in relation to the theme of the inversions of hierarchy. Just as in "La casa de muñecas", there is a *mise en abyme* of the fantastic effect. The protagonist goes to the attic and discovers that it was his cat that had caused all the destruction. The cat "[l]ooked at the small figurine, from whose neck hung a shredded scarf" (24), and this sentence follows immediately after:

> *The figurine* then ran towards the attic, arrived at the edge of the crib, caught the cat with his hand, went with him to the door and kicked him downstairs. (24, emphasis added)

This crucial passage works as Iwasaki's 'threshold sentence'. The question of 'Who is the figurine?' can only be answered by determining where this figurine is located. That figurine could be either an inhabitant of the crib or the artisan himself. This last hypothesis would imply a shift of perspective from the artisan—who was the focalisor up to this point—to a narrator who reveals that the artisan was, himself too, just a *figurine* of someone else's model. He is the inhabitant of the miniature dolls' house within the dolls' house.

While in "La casa de muñecas" the exchange of roles between replica and referent takes place through the incorporation of the hierarchically superior space—the narrator's room—into the hierarchically inferior space—the dolls' house—in Merino's text the narrator at the very end adds another (superior) hierarchical frame to the reality of the protagonist. The village, until then presented as real within the storyworld and as referential for the scale model, is itself just a replica of another village.

The subject too, while keeping a panoptical view of his model, is at the same time observed by some other artisan. His (assumed) omniscient panoramic view turns out to be an illusion. The reality of the protagonist is in fact nothing more than part of a broader space that contains it and treats it as a copy: a figurine in someone else's scale model, a room in a dolls' house.

These two texts play with the issue of the transgression of scale, going against the initial presumptions of how container and contained relate, and in so doing challenge what the protagonist and reader assumed: that the space where the character is located was the 'real' referent to the copy. The idea of the replica that gains ontological dominance over its referent echoes the Baudrillardian notion of hyperreality, where spaces (like Disneyland, or any miniaturising model) stand out as copies without their model. For Baudrillard, the only possible reality is a copy without the substance or qualities of the original. The question to ask is whether this mirroring interplay between embedded structures implies that there is no such thing as referential real, as Baudrillard argues. Whereas there is an underlying challenge to our preconception of the relationship between reality and referent, the major transgression that these short stories suggest distances itself from the loss-of-the-real view. Through the interchange of the container and contained, the exchange of their roles as referent and replica, the notion of referential space is not *invalidated* but *relativised*.

The complex metaphor arising from this transgression of the container-contained could be read as a metaphysical question. What these embedded spaces suggest is anguishing: there could be further (spatial and ontological) levels, in either direction. There could be hierarchically inferior levels—more dolls' houses within the miniature one—or, worse still, that which was presented as referential reality at the start, that domain where the narrator observed the dolls' house, could just as well be a 'room' in a house contained in a larger frame where another individual witnesses another animation. This recalls very much the character of "The Circular Ruins" (Jorge Luis Borges 1941), who while trying to dream of a man discovers he is nothing but the dream of another man.

If the miniature dolls' house is a replica of a bigger dolls' house, if this bigger dolls' house is a copy of the ordinary reality represented in the text and if this (realistic) domain is itself a replica of the reader's extraliterary space, could the same line of thought be continued to infinity? The question that this text raises is that the space of the reader—what we call everyday reality—although believed to be the referent to artistic representation, could also be just a replica of a hierarchically higher space containing it.

These texts present a complex model of realities, all embedded within each other and all (falsely, naively) seeing themselves as the absolute referent while being nothing other than a figurine in a scale model. The view of a central, absolute, ontologically dominant referential reality is dismantled with this fantastic transgression of the container-contained.

3. THE MÖBIUS EFFECT

Where the transgression of section 2 was based on the possibility of leaping between hierarchically embedded spaces, this section concentrates on a transgression which is, to some extent, its opposite: it deals with the impossibility of accessing otherwise interconnected spaces. The character of the sample short story—"Dejen salir" ("Exit", José Ferrer-Bermejo 1982)—gets into a subway station and can never find his way back outside.[4] By moving upwards through the levels of some hierarchical system, the protagonist unexpectedly finds himself right back where he started. The result is that the principles of container and contained are cancelled by what could be called a 'Möbius effect', giving rise to a self-contained space where outside and inside cease to be oppositional categories. "Dejen salir" has been included in *La realidad oculta: cuentos fantásticos del siglo XX* (2008) as a representative text of the Spanish consolidation of the fantastic short story during the 1980s. My analysis will look more specifically at the distortion of spatial coordinates, namely the hierarchy of built spaces and the resultant generated metaphorical significance.

An earlier text based on this motif is "A Subway Named Möbius" by A. J. Deutsch (1950). The Möbius effect of the title is found in the mysterious disappearance of a train, a disappearance attributed to a fold in space; a sort of fourth dimension, as the mathematician protagonist asserts, "of amazing topological complexity" (1968:160) and "of a high order of connectivity" (1968:160). Another canonical literary example of the Möbius strip is John Barth's *Lost in the Funhouse* (1968). Barth plays with this topological figure and with the physical space of the page to capture the self-referentiality of language, which is a central point of his volume of short stories. The most explicit example is his "Frame-Tale", composed of two single lines of text— "Once upon a time there/was a story that began" (1969:1–2)—in which the reader is instructed to fold in the shape of a Möbius strip. The title story is an excellent example of postmodern metafiction combined with the Fantastic. Ambrose, the protagonist, ends up confined for good in the funhouse of an amusement park. This disorienting maze works as a metaphorical space for the self-enclosed nature of the work of art and as a reflection on the creative process, as clearly articulated at the end of the story, "[...] he will construct funhouses for others and be their secret operator" (1969:94). This short story, one of the most widely studied examples of the device of postmodern metalepsis, applies the figure of the Möbius strip to fictional embedded structures as a means of questioning the duality 'fiction/reality'.

"Dejen salir" is remarkable in this respect, since the self-referential element does not refer to fictional layers but exclusively to architectural frames. This shifts the focus from the metafictional overtones to an idea that touches upon material space itself.

The story tells of the following event: the character and focalisor of "Dejen salir" is confined within a metro station in Madrid. There seems to be no way out, as the title indicates, since he is constantly drawn back to his point of departure. Already trapped in this looping space when the narration starts, he finally surrenders and accepts that his situation is not due to a lapse of concentration on his side but is instead a fact: no matter how many tunnels he goes across and stairs he goes up and down, he always ends up at the same point of departure, with the same scenes repeating over and over again. There is no access back to the street and the city, which would be the higher level in the spatial hierarchy: there is no outside or inside, since it is all one single self-referential surface.

Location: A Subway Station

This short story is an excellent example of how narrative space can be used to recreate the impression of verisimilitude in fiction. Of the whole corpus examined in this book, this text possesses the most detailed referential descriptions. The locations where the event takes place are carefully described, all of them having an equivalent in extratextual space. Even a reader unfamiliar with the topography of the metro of the city of Madrid could easily follow the character's journey on a real map. After buying some tissues "in the corner Princesa-Alberto Aguilera" (1982:81), the protagonist gets on the train at the station of Argüelles, travelling through the stops of Ventura Rodríguez, Plaza de España, Callao and, finally Sol, the stop where he gets off (yellow line 3). Once at the station of Sol, he goes through the passageway to the "Mayor" exit. This considerable number of specific real references contributes to enhancing the reality effect of an everyday scene in a big city. Gullón explicitly reminds us how the "accumulation of details— is carried so that—the reader feels himself on familiar ground" (1980:19). "[This] procedure carried out by writers of realistic fiction [...] reduces the distance between the reader and the narrated, so that the reader can move naturally among the characters whose existence does not impose any suspension of incredulity" (1980:19).

Further details that are part of the everyday urban environment include advertisements (for shoes, an airline, a drink), vending machines containing chocolates and chewing gum, benches and bins. All these objects both enhance this reality effect and act as orientation landmarks for the character. Once the loop starts, they will keep reappearing and repeating themselves as the story evolves. This is how the protagonist knows he is back at the same spot again.

The emplacement of the Fantastic in the station of Sol is interesting, since geographically it is a neuralgic point of Madrid, the so-called 'Km Zero' of the Spanish radial network of roads. As for the type of enclave itself, what is remarkable is that the impossible event is linked to a common metro station. This ordinary urban location—seldom exploited in traditional fantastic narratives—enhances the surprise effect for the protagonist, who cannot understand how it has taken place in a journey that he has undertaken countless times before.

Discourse: Literalisation of Habit

The short story opens *in medias res*: "He surprisingly is back at the platform, now empty again, and he takes a seat on one of the benches" (1982:81). From the very first sentence, the reader is immersed in the fantastic event.

The character is already within this impossible self-referential structure and this is conveyed through expressions of repetition ("back", "again"), the deictic "the" (platform), implying a previous presence, and the adverb "surprisingly", clearly establishing that this occurrence is not treated as natural within the storyworld.

As in Adolph's "La casa" (Chapter 2, section 2), in which a character enters an extraordinary house during his everyday journey to work, the first part of the short story emphasises how everything was unfolding as it would on a usual day in the character's life. He is absolutely familiar with the space that his journey covers, he knows "by heart the name of each and every station" (1982:84) since he has been "using the metro service all his life" (84). This force of habit will become the central element in the construction of the fantastic effect. The expressions of frequency will become literalised. Note in the following paragraph, in which he is referring to the very start of the loop, how the phrases emphasised signal the imminent fantastic transgression:

> [...], the train arrived *as normal* and then the stations followed each other with no incident [...]. He had gotten off calmly/confidently ("*con toda tranquilidad*") when the doors opened, being *as always* careful not to introduce his foot into the gap between the train and the platform. (81, emphasis added)

That "as normal", which could also be translated as "as usual" or "as always" ("*como siempre*" [81]), becomes literally an eternal recurrence. The same applies to later passages referring to "the same platform", "the same ads for the same shoe brand", "the same benches", "the same vending machines" (82).

The literal effect of routine actions becomes even more explicit toward the end, where an analogy is drawn between his situation and a "carousel horse" that mechanically "starts his path again" (85). He is compared to a "soulless puppet on the everyday platform, that platform of all eternity" (85). If these passages were decontextualised from the self-referential structure in which he is now confined, they could easily be rhetorical phrases referring to the way in which the character experiences his repetitive routine. The fantastic hyperbole—an "exaggeration to the impossible" (Casas 2010:12)—is what converts these otherwise normal reiterated actions in the character's routine into fantastic recurrences. His only exit in the end is to leap out of this circular sequence by going toward the rails as the same train is, once more, approaching.

The final aspect of the discursive construction of the fantastic effect is found in the verb tenses. The cancellation of spatial levels between outside and inside is ultimately a distortion of time: the character is suspended in an eternal present. The events prior to his enclosure are told in the past tense ("he took the metro [...] he had lost some time buying tissues" [81]).

However, once the circular loop starts there is a shift to the present tense, a tense that predominates throughout the story. This tense is only momentarily interrupted by a future tense, when he describes the elements out there that he knows he will see if he leaves, which serves to recreate the impression of a stagnant present.

Story: Cancellation of Coordinates

As the story evolves, the character's anguish over this situation grows. This is portrayed through an acceleration of movement, which leads to an acceleration of the Möbius strip: "he is in a hurry, he is in a terrible hurry, increasingly more terrible hurry" (83), "he goes down some stairs, goes up other ones, again, and again, and again" (84). This crystallises toward the end where all the signs "form a sort of strip with no end: EXITEXITEXITEXIT" (84). This is another literal resignification of the well-known phrase of the story's title, which is displayed in the metro requesting that exiting passengers be let out first.

The transgression in this short story parallels the conception of 'space' captured by the German word '*Raum*'—a dimension or 'room' for bodies to move around in. The three coordinates of height, length, and depth are invalidated in order to suggest that there is neither distance nor extension. The protagonist goes up and down a few stairs and across some corridors and yet he is back to the same point of origin. Up and down, across and through, instead of creating a sense of space—of '*Raum*'—where the character can move around, these directions always return the character back to the one same single position. The character is stuck in one fixed point with no possible displacement away from it.

Furthermore, the character's perception of the impossible element should be noted. While the impossible element is never naturalised by or for the protagonist—as indicated in the "surprisingly" of the very first sentence— the character initially attributes this occurrence to himself, in particular to being under pressure caused by stress and work: "There are days in which one's head is acting mad and things like that do happen, particularly if one takes into account some problems, a lot of things on one's mind [...]" (82). This is a phenomenon similar to the one noted in texts like "L'Érreur" by Jacques Sternberg (Chapter 1, section 5), where the fantastic event is perceived as a human mistake. The protagonist of this story also knows the limitations of his perceptual abilities and is aware that his mind can play tricks on him, since "everyone can make a mistake, even if he had been travelling all his life by metro" (82). Of course, this justification is illogical. The first attempt of rationalisation is followed by a second, equally irrational effort. Those to blame for this "unbearable event" (84), according to him, are those who built this structure: "those cretin architects, or engineers or whatever the fuck they are called, who made of that metro an immense labyrinth where even the most clever individual could get lost"

(84). Therefore, although perceived and described as impossible, the character first attempts to rationalise the fantastic essence of this self-referential structure as being the product of his hectic everyday life. However, no matter how absent-minded someone might be, it is of course impossible to pass through a corridor and find oneself back on the spot from which one left, regardless of how intricately the structure was built by engineers.

The Self-Enclosed Referent

The fantastic texts enumerated in the first section of this chapter use the devices of metalepsis and metafiction to foreground the self-referential essence of language in the construction of reality. By establishing continuity between different fictional levels, the Derridian formula "*Il n'y a rien en dehors du texte*" ("there is no such thing as out-of-the text") appears in a literal manner.

"Dejen salir" is an exception since the notion of self-referentiality does not necessarily refer to language (although this could be a possible interpretation) but is rather employed in the context of everyday material spaces. The impossible architectural form that this text presents is that of a self-contained, self-referential structure, and it does not entail jumps between hierarchically different narrative levels. The discourse of routine provides the basis for creating a tissue of locations—the platform, the corridor, the stairs—that appear in succession while the character always returns to the same point of departure. The 'here' and 'there', 'inside' and 'outside' and the notion of extension are invalidated. Why this shift from textual to architectural spaces? A possible answer can be found in the way in which De Certeau (1988) and Augé (2008) have employed the same metaphor of the carceral self-enclosed space in the context of everyday sites of transition; for instance, the metro.

De Certeau regards urban transitional space as a domain of imprisonment for the individual, in that material space is turned into carceral space precisely by force of habit, this habit being that produced by underlying power relations. De Certeau's theory of everyday spatial practices describes how power and social discipline interact in pedestrian automatisations in ordinary built spaces. In a chapter entitled "Railway Navigation and Incarceration", he argues that the monotony of public transport regarding social habits and architectural space turns the citizen into an automaton "pigeonholed, numbered, and regulated in the grid of the railway car" (1988:111). Very much influenced by Foucault's take on architectural space and disciplinary practices, De Certeau regards the metro as "[a] bubble of panoptic and classifying power, a module of imprisonment that makes possible the production of an order, *a closed and autonomous insularity*" (1988:111, emphasis added). Even more striking are the parallels between "Dejen salir" and the following passage: "A travelling incarceration. Immobile inside the train, seeing immobile things slip by. What is happening? Nothing is moving inside or outside the train" (1988:111). Although it does not explicitly discuss issues of power relations embedded in everyday spaces, the short story of "Dejen salir" also deals with automatisation through forces of habit.

Furthermore, the metaphorical isolation from the exterior found in the trope of the carceral place appears in Augé's theorisation of the non-place, those "spaces which are not themselves anthropological places and which, unlike in Baudelairean modernity, do not integrate the earlier places" (2008:63). According to Augé, a fundamental characteristic of the non-place is its lack of integration into its surroundings, an aspect exploited literally in "Dejen salir".

Another ordinary non-place that plays host to a fantastic scene is the airport of Barajas (Madrid), where "Los viajeros perdidos" (José María Merino 2002) is set. This disorienting gigantic space literally captures within it many hurrying passengers, who try in vain to find the ever-changing departure gate and so end up stranded there for good, lost and "going adrift, absent-minded and beaten" in its corridors (2002:64).

Finally, another short story based on a circular enclosure is "L'Examen" (1988) by Quebecois writer Jean-Paul Beaumier. The nightmarish structure of the strange school of the story forces the character to return to the examination room each time he tries to leave after finishing the exam. As in "Dejen salir, the scene is looped interminably": "I know that I don't have another option but to surrender, go and open that door: 'Hurry up! The exam is going to start soon'" (42). As in José Ferrer-Bermejo's story, the narrative opens *in medias res*: the character is already immersed in this anguishing situation where the exterior—the open air, from which the title of the volume of the short stories (*L'Air libre*) is derived—is unreachable.

4. HIERARCHY SUSPENDED

In the last transgression to be considered here, two contradictory pieces of information can be found regarding the way in which container space (in the text: a region, coastal area) and contained space (a hotel) relate to each other. An excellent short story though which to analyse this spatial transgression is "La Brume" (1974) by Jacques Sternberg 1974. Sternberg's country of origin, Belgium, has a long tradition of the Fantastic, tagged as *l'École belge de l'étrange* (cf. *La Belgique fantastique*, Baronian [ed.] 1975). Sternberg is a leading Belgian figure of the micro-story, of science fiction (as seen in his volume *188 Contes à régler*, 1988) and of the Fantastic, particularly in the volume *Contes glacés*, 1974. *Contes glacés* is composed in its entirety of stories that seldom exceed two pages in length and in which the metamorphosis of space, time and body are thematic constants.

The restricted length of the stories results in a vivid sketching of the fantastic occurrence, concentrating the focus on a single disruptive element and on the effect that this provokes. The limited spatial extension of the text, already mentioned in relation to Fernando Iwasaki's very short story, makes it ideal for the analysis of the construction, function and meaning of the spatial transgression. In "La Brume", the narrator recalls his arrival at a hotel on the coast in the middle of the night. His insomnia leads him to take a stroll out to the sea. After exiting through one of the entrances of the hotel, he ends up as he expected on the shore. He then decides to explore the other side of the hotel where, in theory, the road that led him to the hotel should be. However, passing through the opposite entrance of the hotel, he surprisingly finds himself once again directly on the shore. The next morning, the fog prevents him from finding the road leading down to the sea and this situation continues for a long time. Even though the map and his previous topological memory of the area tell him that the road should be there, the hotel seems now to be floating on the sea. Although initially determined to wait for the sky to clear up, he begins to accept that the fog will never dissipate and neither will he discover his location and thus his way out. Therefore, it seems that this hotel had been accessible by a road, as such as road is featured on the map. However, the hotel also seems to be segregated from the ground like an island. The crucial unresolved question is then which of the two spatial dispositions is the 'true' one and will he be able to go back.

Location: The Lost Hotel

In his situating of the story, Sternberg revisits a traditional trope of horror and fantastic narratives: the character's arrival at a lost hotel in an isolated region in the middle of the night. "I did not see anything anymore: the night and the fog blurred it. I took a room in the only hotel of the region. A dreary hotel, big and pale, that clung to a promontory of cliffs" (1974:85). The fog, the ocean ("the sea and the sky fused together in form of a chasm" [1974:85]) and the hotel on the cliff—these are all elements that generate the atmospheric description that opens this story, very much in line with the Romantic foggy, isolated, tempestuous *locus amoenus*.

However, the actual function of narrative space in the story is far from merely providing an atmospheric frame for the action. This setting will instead be the subject of the transgression, while in the traditional use of this motif, as mentioned in Chapter 2, the hotel serves as the stage for a mystery or an apparition—as a building that contains and hosts the Fantastic. In this short story, the hotel of this foggy region itself transgresses the laws of space because, as the story develops, this hotel seems to be not only figuratively but also literally lost somewhere in space, suspended on a cliff, surrounded by sea on both sides.

Discourse: Figures of the Void

The visual is prioritised in the construction of the environment in this short story. And it is limitations of sight that prevent the reader from achieving a thorough understanding of the area: "I couldn't see anything else from the landscape", "I could only see the ocean", "the misty sky" (85), "[t]he next day, the fog still diluted the landscape" (86). The imprecision of sight is evoked numerous times to imply that no orientation references can be attained. The boundaries defining the topological features are blurred; "the sea and the sky fused together in form of a chasm" (85), the colours of the landscape are indistinct, faded. Whereas the hotel is a solid material structure, it is surrounded by nothing but fog. Various references to elements that have no visible limits are employed to emphasise this contrast ("behind a window which led to the void" [85]).

The metaphorical images of the abyss that the narrator employs to describe the area become literal in the second half of the short story. These descriptions of his sensations therefore prefigure the subsequent action (see "anticipatory metaphorical image", Casas 2010:12) in that they become transposed into the actual features of this space. "I had never had with such a certitude the feeling of having reached the edge of the world" (85). "What's more, I must have been on one of the extreme points of the country" (85). The clearest literalisation of the subjective experience of space is captured in the sensation that the narrator experiences of being in a place outside the real world, in a void "beyond time, beyond everything" (85). This initially seems to be nothing more than an impression on the part of the narrator, but it transpires that, in fact, this desolate hotel is literally suspended.

Story: The Floating Space

As indicated in the first part of this section, narrative spaces in "La Brume" serve two central functions. Initially, it is the atmospheric mystery, gloom and isolation that are highlighted. This extends through the first half of the text and is very much centred upon the description of how the character experiences his arrival to this area. Hence, the predominant adjectivisation ("A dreary hotel, big and pale, that clung to a promontory of cliffs" [85], "the small pier" [86]) and the use of verbs belonging to the domain of perception ("the sensation of having reached" [85], "[...] captivated, fascinated" [85]).

This atmospheric function of narrative space is abruptly modified almost exactly half way through the story, with the appearance of the Fantastic. The descriptions of space in the first part of the narrative are interrupted by a short and concise factual sentence: "But there was no path" (86). This is how the character expresses his surprise when he exits the hotel from the far side of the hotel, where he expects the path to be. It is then that the stage of the action becomes the subject that transgresses the expected spatial dispositions: does the hotel belong to the region where he had arrived last night? From then on, the descriptive elements of the area become less important and the focus of the narrative shifts to a succession of actions that relate how the narrator tries in vain to find his way back ("In the hotel, I have found a map [...], "[...] I have tried to locate the regional route" [86]). There is also a shift in the verb tenses: it is in this second part of the story that the indicative present and the present perfect appear for the first time ("It has already been ten days" [86]), denoting that the character is still in that lost space. The final abnegation of the character who suffers the fantastic event is transmitted in the last sentence ("But I begin to lose all hope. Sometimes I have the impression that the fog will never dissipate" [87]).

The essence of the impossible element here—the changeable emplacement of this hotel—coincides with the classic Todorovian theorisation of the Fantastic (1970), based on the hesitation between a rational and irrational explanation of the event. Either the reader accepts a natural explanation—the fog is the cause of this disorientation—or a supernatural one: the narrator is now in a place the topographical features of which have metamorphosed. Both interpretations are facilitated within the text. The fog is to blame for his disorientation, "It would be necessary for the fog to clear up for me to know exactly where I am" (87) and/or the hotel is now not accessible by road anymore, and it is no longer located in the region that the map shows: "In the hotel, I have found a detailed map of the region. I have found on this map the national road on which I had arrived [...]. But it is in vain that I have tried to locate the regional route that I had taken to this hotel" (86–87).

Either way, the character is left with no points of reference indicating precisely where he is. Or, and as would be worse again, he does have reference points but they are useless because they are contradictory: the true location of this hotel either corresponds to the coordinates indicated by the map—and thus a realistic reading—or the hotel is surrounded completely by the sea, all this represented by the metaphor of a lost space floating without determinable coordinates for the character, and by inference for the reader too.

The Ghost Referent

"La Brume" proposes a transgression based on a space that does not seem to have the expected relation with the domain that contains it. As mentioned, the motif of the fog offers a double reading that oscillates between (a) having a realistic referential equivalent, and so being located in our mental maps of extratextual reality (a hotel by the sea), or (b) on the contrary, being located in a domain that shares no similarities with our real extratextual geography: an impossible island on a road.

As was also true of the other sample texts, this fantastic transgression serves to generate a metaphor that destabilises the relationship between referent and representation. In this case, the representation of space, the "map" of the region, does not correspond with how the subject experiences the space represented by the map. It is a disjunction between Lefebvre's (1974) categories of the "perceived" (spatial practices as experienced) and the "conceived" (representations of space), which in this case do not seem to point to the same referent, the same space. These aspects coincide with Bollnow's conceptual distinction between hodological and mathematical space (1963).

The former—deriving from the Greek *hodos*, path-making—corresponds to the human perception of movement between two different points on a map: it is the subjective experience of space. The latter is the objective, the mapped geometrical representation of space, with constant measurable distances. While Bollnow emphasises that it is fundamental to keep in mind that the mathematical and human senses of space differ, in "La Brume" the transgression is constructed upon the literal disjunction between hodological and geometrical distances. "La Brume" also exposes the unreliability of maps as a valid epistemological tool with which knowledge about reality can be gained and represented objectively. This metaphor recalls Philippe Vasset's conclusion in *Un livre blanc* (2007) (see Chapter 1, section 5). Vasset's sociogeographical research, applied to the blank spaces in a contemporary map of Paris, leads to a conclusion that alerts the reader to the limitations of maps as accurate and reliable mirrors of our reality.

Further textual examples in which the same transgression is found are "Dérapage" (1988) and "Retour" (1988), both from Quebecois Jean-Paul Beaumier. In both short stories, the protagonists who witness the event are on a road with which they are familiar. However, on this occasion its topography seems to have metamorphosed and the road signs do not correspond to the distance that the character thinks he has covered, as this passage from "Dérapage" illustrates:

> [...], the driver focuses on the road that disappears immediately after them, without leaving trace of them. Then he scrutinises the night without being certain that Liliane will be there when he arrives, he does not know where. (1988:20)

The village of Brumal operates in a very similar manner in "Los altillos de Brumal" (Cristina Fernández Cubas 1983).[5] This little village is where the protagonist grew up and where she returns to in order to recall her childhood. When she arrives in the region, no one seems to know of the existence of such a village, neither does any village figure under that name in the council register of towns. Whereas the village's description is very detailed (the main square, the church, the attic), its location is vague. Once more, the story offers a double reading, coinciding with the Todorovian Fantastic: (a) a realistic explanation—Brumal is one of the "few lost villages on the hills and practically abandoned by its inhabitants" (2008:130), or (b) an impossible one: "[...] neither the name of Brumal, nor any other village that would correspond with its geographical situation, figured in the lists of parishes of any diocese" (2008:139). The degree of referentiality of those spaces is unresolved in both texts and the uncertain, contradictory position of the foggy hotel in "La Brume" and of the village of Brumal in "Los altillos de Brumal" questions how these spaces relate to the storyworld that contains them, which goes back to the hierarchical principle of how the part relates to the rest.

* * *

The spatial transgressions of this chapter deal with the interplay between spatial hierarchies or, in another articulation of the same relationship, with the logical connection—that expected in accordance with our extratextual reality—between container frame and contained space. These transgressions challenge the logical assumptions of the hierarchical principle of a space 'being part of' or 'being in' another. "La casa de muñecas" inverts the hierarchy between the container and the contained; what is relativised is the notion of absolute referent. Spatial hierarchies are nullified in the Möbius-strip motif, a self-contained and self-referential structure disengaged from the framing space containing it. "La Brume" is centred on a place whose position and integration within the larger frame are not determined. Since its representations—maps, road signs—do not seem to correspond with what the character encounters, the experience of space and the graphic representation of it are not only disengaged from but also contradictory to each other. Thus, their referent—the nature and emplacement of the space in question—is also indiscernible.

The first transgression analysed in this chapter inverted the relationship between container and contained, the second cancelled this relationship out and the third invalidated them by providing various contradictory possibilities. What all of these examples have in common is that while they do not refer to a transgression of fictional realities, as would be the case in metalepsis and metafiction, the notion of spatial referentiality is to the fore in all cases.

The next chapter also draws on the issue of referentiality. Textual/factual referentiality necessarily implies an ontological reflection on questions such as 'what is the original and what is the referent?' or 'what is real and what is a copy?' Extrapolating this to a higher level of abstraction, the following chapter is dedicated to the examination of the idea of a problematic plurality of realistic worlds within the literary universe, a strategy that challenges the notion of a single referential reality.

NOTES

1. Possible Worlds Theory, in particular in Doležel (1998), offers a clear explanation of the distinction between fictional and factual reality. Fictional worlds differ ontologically from the real world because of their incomplete nature. Since it is impossible for the human mind to think up an object (much less a world) in all of its properties, every fictional world presents areas of radical indeterminacy (or 'ontological gaps'). For example, the favourite book of a particular fictional character can never be known if this is not specified in the fictional world.
2. On spatiality in the fiction of this author, see *El vértigo horizontal* (Henry 1999), *Figments of Space: Space as Metaphor in Jorge Luis Borges, with particular Emphasis on 'Ficciones' and 'El Aleph'* (Medina 2006), *Place and Displacement in the Narrative Worlds of Jorge Luis Borges and Julio Cortázar* (Tcherepashenets 2008) and *Borges and Space* (Richardson 2012).

3. Since no official translation was found, all translations from the Spanish stories analysed in this chapter are mine.

4. The title of this short story, which has no official translation to date, loses some of its connotations when translated into English. The Spanish expression "Dejen salir" is based on a well-known formula of politeness in the metro, similar to "Exiting passengers first". However, implicit in the Spanish title is a voice requesting a way out of a situation; hence, "Exit" seemed the most appropriate solution.

5. Note that '*Brumal*' implies foggy in Spanish, thus indicating a space of blurry confines and location. '*Brumal*' is also an anagram for 'umbral', i.e., 'threshold', liminal space between referents and thus, with no identifiable referent. For these reasons, '*Brumal*' was chosen as the name for the academic journal *Brumal: Research Journal on the Fantastic* (Universidad Autònoma de Barcelona).

5 World

Ontological Plurality

"Le monde est longtemps resté un. Pour mieux dire, il s'est longtemps voulu un."

(Bertrand Westphal)

1. POSTMODERN MULTIVERSES AND THE LOSS OF CENTRALITY

In the previous chapters, narrative space was discussed in relation to the different elements that construct (and transgress) the textual physical reality. 'Body', 'boundary' and 'hierarchy' are, as shown, principles fundamental to narrative space and to the effect of textual realism. They provide a consistent, defined and ordered impression of the physical dimension in which characters move and the action takes place. However, narrative space also embraces a higher level of abstraction, which relates to the different laws and possible constituents that give coherence to a fictional world. As the proponents of the theory of possible worlds have demonstrated (e.g., Pavel 1986; Eco 1994; Ryan 1991; Doležel 1998), narratives can be conceived in terms of storyworlds. This idea is of the utmost importance since it signals a shift of focus from narrative space as 'physical dimension' to it as 'world'. Therefore, narrative space is not only the sum of that which exists within the story; it is also the 'container' of this totality. It is not, however, a 'passive' or 'neutral' container of existing matter: it is endowed with physical and logical laws, which determine what can happen inside. From this angle, space is a frame of constraints regulating that which is contained, best captured by Irish writer Flann O'Brien in his novel *The Third Policeman* in the following sentence: "Anything can be said in this place and it will be true and will have to be believed" (2007:88).

In order to elaborate on this fantastic transgression of narrative space conceived of as world, some principles of Possible Worlds Theory (PWT), when carefully engaged with critically, are useful. Deriving from Leibniz's *Monadology* (1714)—which views our actual world as the realised possibility of many other possible worlds—combined with modal logics, the proponents of PWT have identified the need to develop an approach to narrative that prioritises the ontology of fictional worlds. In so doing, they have moved away from regarding the fictional text as a temporal sequence to a perspective of literature as space, as a universe of multiple worlds.

One of the core theoretical principles of this perspective is that any fictional text derives from the actual material world and is always engaged with it. Based on our extratextual world ("actual actual world", or "actual proto-world"), fictional texts are structured like a solar system (Ryan's "fictional universe", 2006; Doležel's "Heterocosm", 1998), sometimes referred to as fictional universe, fictional world or storyworld interchangeably. At the centre, a fictional world (or "textual actual world" or "textual proto-world") is realised as an actuality within the text. This happens by providing enough information in relation to actions and characters, which confirms that what happens in the fictional world is an actual fact (within the fictional universe, of course). Many other possible worlds spring out as satellites from this centre: these are possible (sub)worlds, which differ from the proto-world of this fictional system because they are not actual. Instead, they embrace wishes and dreams of the characters and designate hypothetical courses of events. For my study on the Fantastic, these possible (sub) worlds and their hypothetical situations will be left aside to concentrate on the nature of the world central to the system. To simplify, this will be referred to as the 'central world'.

The whole system, central world and derivate subworlds, is regulated by modal constraints, such as the alethic (possible/impossible), deontic (allowed/prohibited), axiological (good/bad) and epistemic (known/unknown). Of these constraints, the most relevant to this research are the alethic ones. Three possible models have been outlined by PWT scholars concerning the ontological nature of the central world. The reader is the key figure in distinguishing these three models: "Having reconstructed the fictional world as a mental image, the reader can ponder it and make it a part of his experience, just as he experientially appropriates the actual world" (Doležel 1998:21). More categorically, he later proclaims: "the semantics of narrative is, at its core, the semantics of interaction" (1998:97).

First, this world can be 'natural', as in the case of realistic texts. Once more, it is the reader who identifies the world as being natural, according to the physical characteristics of his extratextual world: it "overlaps the world of a reader's encyclopaedia" (Eco 1979:221). These views converge not only with the reader-oriented theorisation of literary realism (see Villanueva's "The Realist Reading", 1997:121–147) but also with the theoretical perspective of the Fantastic adopted in this book. The Fantastic cannot exist without the collaboration of the reader. It is the reader who constantly compares the information he obtains with his mental model of reality. In so doing, the reader identifies, through a constant referential reading, that the reality created in the text is very similar to the factual extratextual one. Only then can the fantastic transgression be perceived as impossible within that realistic frame.

Second, a 'supernatural' storyworld is characterised as thus in that its ontological centre opposes what is possible in our real world. If the characters of natural worlds are physically possible counterparts of humans, supernatural worlds violate the laws of the actual world.

Third, both the natural and supernatural can be combined. These fictional universes are dyadic systems (Pavel's "dual structures", 1986:54–57), constructed as in opposition by the alethic constraints: what is possible in one of the worlds is impossible in the other. The structure of the mythological worlds is mentioned as the paradigmatic example of dyadic structures of the alethic modality (Doležel 1998:129).[1]

Another way of approaching these dual ontologies has been provided by Ryan in an article entitled "From Parallel Universes to Possible Worlds: Ontological Pluralism in Physics, Narratology, and Narrative" (2006). In this article, she draws an overview of narratives that contain more than one ontological centre and combines the theory of Possible Worlds with contentions deriving from quantum physics to outline different versions of the 'multiverse'. These multiple-world cosmologies are, as Ryan points out, recurrent features of fantasy and science fiction writing, in that they have two coexisting worlds realised as actual: one is realistic and the other one is not.

While the supporters of PWT acknowledge the possibility of various ontologies within one fictional text, none of them explore how the natural and supernatural interact within the text. In failing to do so, they disregard the Fantastic as a form distinct from fantasy and science fiction, where this distinctiveness is specifically due to the *conflictive* coexistence of the natural and supernatural. In Ryan's plural cosmologies of fantasy, science fiction and historical metafictional texts, as well as in Doležel's mythical structures, the coexistence of ontological heterogeneity is not conflictive. The characters that populate these worlds do not reflect upon, nor problematise, this ontological plurality. As repeated on various occasions throughout this book, it is in fact exactly the opposite that happens in fantastic narratives.

For the purpose of this chapter, it is important to address two issues arising from these theoretical perspectives:

First: what is the difference, if any, between Doležel's 'dyadic structures', composed by two domains, and Ryan's 'multiverses'? That which distinguishes a domain from a world is tackled by neither Doležel nor Ryan and it seems that these two concepts are used interchangeably, particularly by Doležel.

And second: is it the opposition between a physically possible/physically impossible world that sets the duality of natural/supernatural, as Pavel, Doležel and Ryan seem to suggest? Put differently: is a physical impossibility the only constraint that defines the supernatural in fiction?

Let us start with the first question. As to the distinction between domains and worlds, I argue that any fantastic text presents a system composed of two domains (real and supernatural) but does not necessarily present two worlds. All the sample short stories that have appeared in this book up to this point coincide with Ryan's "single-world cosmology" (2006)—with the exception of "Mi hermana Elba", where the holes could be seen as worlds. There are two domains in these stories (realistic/fantastic), but the fantastic domain is contained within a central realistic world: it is an (impossible) element within it. In contrast to the rules of this realistic central world, the reader identifies the fantastic domain as a supernatural exception. The house of "La casa" (Chapter 2) is an exceptional domain within the general realistic world, as is, for example, the magnetic museum of "El museo" (Chapter 2), Ballard's house of "The Enormous Space" (Chapter 2), Iwasaki's dolls' house (Chapter 4) and Ferrer-Bermejo's Möbius metro station (Chapter 4). What is crucial is that even if the character's (and by extension the reader's) perception of the central realistic world is weakened by these impossible elements, this realistic world is at all times the *only* ontological central referent, the only world.

However, in the sample short stories of this chapter, the impossible is not a part within the world (such as a house, a dolls' house, railway, or island). This is when the distinction between domain and world becomes important. The supernatural is not a domain within this world, but it affects the idea of world as a whole.

Regarding the second question, the three sample short stories will also contest the duality of physical possibility/impossibility in narratives of more than one world. As mentioned before, 'natural' is traditionally viewed as that which is physically possible ("a possible world in which the physical laws of the actual world are valid", Doležel 1998:281). 'Supernatural' is, in contrast, physically impossible. This definition is applicable to many fantastic stories, including the ones analysed in the previous chapters. All those stories presented physically impossible places, whether due to their topological features or the agency they exert upon the human character. The man-eating house of "La casa", the physical force exerted on the subject by the museum-house of "El museo", the never-ending railway of "Tandis que roule le train" or the island on land of "La Brume" were all supernatural elements based on the notion of physical impossibility with regard to the laws ruling a realistic world.

However, as the analysis of the following sample texts demonstrates, multiple-world texts do not have to be composed of a physically possible and physically impossible world. That is but one of the many possibilities of fantastic transgression. All narratives examined in this chapter provide physically possible models of our extratextual world. There is nothing physically impossible about them except the fact that they coexist; a coexistence that in the case of fantastic narratives is presented as problematic. All of these texts are linked in that the transgression in each case is effectuated by the apparition of another world, a fact that displaces the univocal position of the central world.

The multiplication of centres is now widely recognised as the essence of postmodern thought. The idea of multiplicity of worlds and referents provides the grounding for Westphal's geocritical method in Comparative Literature: "The world of modernity, supporting an 'objective' real, is fragmented in a constellation of possible worlds whose representation constitutes just an approximation. Possible worlds are postmodern" (Westphal 2011b:12). It is in this work, entitled *Le Monde plausible* (2011b), where Westphal develops this thought:

> After 1942, after 1945, after the massive diffusion of the *nouvelle* of horror, the excessively peremptory nature of a world declined in singular became evident to those who did not want to see, nor to listen or understand.
>
> (Westphal 2011b:12)

As this quote expresses, the conception of the world as unique was superseded by the idea of a multiplicity of possible worlds, of angles, constructions and representations of these worlds, each of them hierarchically equal. The same thought is captured in the opening quote of this chapter, which is also the opening sentence of *Le Monde plausible*. As Westphal reminds us, fundamental to this shift is the concept of space as 'world', in its most abstract dimension: "To talk about the world in singular or plural is to talk about space, a space that has indissoluble links with time" (2011b:13). As will be shown, in postmodern narratives of the Fantastic this change in the way of viewing the world will be expressed by a problematic shift from one fictional world to multiple versions of it.[2]

2. FANTASTIC THIRDSPACE

The short story "Das Kapital" (2010) by Spanish author David Roas is a representative example of how the traditional motif in fantastic narrative of two juxtaposed realities can be much more than a literary commonplace. The author, awarded the Premio Setenil in 2011 for *Distorsiones* (2010), the book from which this text is taken, is one of the leading theorists of the Fantastic today (see *Teorías de lo fantástico*, 2001 and *Tras los límites de lo real*, 2011). In his two collections of short stories, *Horrores cotidianos* (2007) and *Distorsiones,* the fantastic element is omnipresent, frequently combined with humour or the grotesque and, almost with no exception, starting from a mundane situation that becomes distorted into the impossible. This is the case of "Das Kapital", a short story that combines political content and humour with the Fantastic.

The narrator relates that, because his flight was overbooked, he is placed for the first time in his life in first class. His excitement and curiosity are centred on how things are experienced in this other "world" (2011:40), as he says, in particular on how the tourist class is viewed from the other side of the curtain. It is from this other side of the curtain that he is confronted with the fantastic event: while the second-class passengers are heavily shaken by turbulence, the area of first class remains literally immune to it. The Fantastic is thus built on a juxtaposition of two realities—turbulence and its absence—within the one space of the plane.

Leaving the political implications of this short story aside, of interest here is the space that comprises both possible realities. In this space of synthesis between the affirmative and the negative, two physically possible and yet mutually excluding worlds coexist. This complex concept is present here in a simple form: an ordinary plane of which only one-half is affected by turbulence. Bearing strong resemblance to the theory of the multiverse, which originated in theoretical physics and refers to multiple interconnected realities coexisting in time and space (see Greene 1999, Tegmark 2003, Kaku 1994; 2005), this short story provides the basis for what I will refer to as 'fantastic Thirdspace'. This term is borrowed from Edward S. Soja (1996) and will be employed here to refer to a physical space—in the sample story, the plane—that blends two differentiated realities.

In his volume *Thirdspace: Journeys to Los Angeles and Other Real-and-Imagined Places* (1996), Soja defends what he calls "critical thirding" (cf. Bhabha 1994) beyond traditional Hegelian dialectics. This concept provides a different way of understanding social relations—between history and geography, male and female, etc.—when they are inscribed in space. Thirdspace merges:

> [...] subjectivity and objectivity, the abstract and the concrete, the real and the imagined, the knowable and the unimaginable, the repetitive and the differential, structure and agency, mind and body, consciousness and the unconscious, the disciplined and the transdisciplinary, everyday life and unending history (1996:56–57).[3]

Although resembling it, Soja's Thirdspace is not exactly a synonym for liminal space. Whereas a liminal space is that which articulates the 'here' and 'there', simultaneously joining and separating, Thirdspace designates a larger frame, hierarchically superior to 'here' and 'there' because both are integrated in it. It is the space that merges oppositional logics and integrates polarities. Taking the figure of the Aleph as the paradigm, Thirdspace is for Soja a synthesis without diffusion of its elements. The inversion of the relationships of part/whole, also present in "The Aleph" (1949), already considered in the previous chapter, is of interest here because of the idea of impossible synthesis.

Leaving aside the political tongue-in-cheek of this short story, my focus will be on the configuration of the worlds in this Thirdspace. Following the same structure of analysis adopted in the previous chapters, I set out to explore how the trialectics are configured, where two (physical and logical) worlds are juxtaposed forming a space that is impossible according to the laws of physics and logic.

Location: The Plane

The story develops in two main locations: the first part takes place on land, at an airport in Switzerland, where the character is told that his flight is overbooked and that, as a result, he has been upgraded to first class. This domain of action helps the reader locate the story in a mundane setting.

The second and central frame of action is the plane. Inside, as with any ordinary flight, first class and second class are separated by a curtain. This last element—of symbolic meaning in extratextual reality, since it segregates two socioeconomic spaces—will play an important role in the construction of the fantastic effect.

There is, therefore, nothing extraordinary in terms of the location of the action. As was the case in many of the previously analysed short stories, the domestic, everyday setting enhances the sudden apparition of the Fantastic in those spaces where it is least expected. Remarkable, however, is that one of Augé's 'non-places' has been selected as emplacement of the action. Both airport and plane fall into the category of non-places. To recall, Augé's main thesis is that with the advance of Postmodernity (what he calls Supermodernity), the citizen spends more and more time in transit, whether shopping, travelling or surfing the Internet. This has caused the proliferation of areas whose function is to facilitate the transit from one point to another: such as airports, railways, motorway routes and hotel chains. A second characteristic of non-places concerns the issue of individuality; according to Augé "[a] person entering the space of non-place is relieved of his usual determinants. [...] The space of non-place creates neither singular identity nor relations; only solitude, and similitude" (2008:103). Augé regards the non-place as a space where differences between individuals are blurred to produce one single sample: the passenger.

In this short story, however, the approach to the non-place diverges to some extent from Augé's definition. First, while the plane is a functional space of transit, neither its origin nor its destination is of relevance to the plot. The entire action is concentrated in the plane as the domain of action, which leads to the second point: is this plane really a space where identities are homogenised? The two different classes in the plane are highlighted constantly from the start of the story. This is achieved not only by emphasising the difference in the customer service that the first-class and second-class passengers receive but is further accentuated with the fantastic transgression of space. The story is thus a reminder that these non-places are not melting pots, where everyone is reduced to a single condition of 'passenger' as Augé claims. Instead, they are areas where socioeconomic differences are still sharply differentiated.

Discourse: First- and Second-Class Worlds

The two sections of the plane are constructed in opposition: what one has, the other one lacks. However, this schema does apply for physical possibility/

impossibility. Both halves of the plane, considered separately, are completely ordinary and physically possible. The importance lies in how they relate to each other.

Both halves are sharply differentiated by the facilities therein, goods served and treatment received. The world of first class (of the first-class world, as the author writes) is constructed with superlatives that exaggerate this abundance. The seat is "enormous" (32); the food "exquisite" (33) and "sublime"; the wine "marvellous" (33) and "even the coffee is excellent" (33). All these positive attributes are presented in close succession and are condensed into a single paragraph. To enhance the impression of excess, on various occasions the author reiterates the characteristics of objects that had already been referenced in the text. For example, in the end, the protagonist does not just return to his seat but to his "grey leather seat" (32/34).[4]

Once the character has finished his copious meal, he has the "irrepressible temptation" (33) to approach the curtain and view the other side from this new, previously unexperienced, angle; "a matter of perspective" (33). It is then he sees the area of second class shaking violently, the passengers and hostesses in panic are "holding tight to the armrests" (33), screaming, while things fall from the overhead compartments. Even "the crew, sitting at the end of the aircraft, cannot repress their panic" (33). And then there is the other half: the world of first class. This area is immersed in a lethargic atmosphere and remains quiet. The protagonist sees the passengers reading and dozing off. The staff, too, seems to be drawn into this pleasant atmosphere and, in contrast with the panicking staff in second class, they carry out their duties with a "placid smile" (33). To intensify the effect, these two scenes are juxtaposed employing a cinematographic technique: the author rapidly shifts from one frame to the other on three occasions, which coincide with three paragraphs. In the first one, "[he] move[s] the curtain a bit and looks through it. The scenario that appears before [his] eyes is horrific" (34). This is immediately followed by him casting a look behind, to "realise that in first class everything is as calm as the start" (33), and then, once more, he "stick[s] [his] head through the curtain again and see[s] the same hair-raising scene" (34).

Story: Entanglement

The narrator is the only person who can access and join both realities: neither the staff members nor the other passengers cross the boundary of the curtain. While the other first-class passengers doze in comfort, only he witnesses the other reality. Therefore, the protagonist is the element allowing "entanglement" (Ryan 2006) between the two realities separated by the curtain. His function is to activate both realities and trigger this impossible coexistence. At the very end, however, he adopts the same attitude as his "comrades" (34) and returns to his comfortable seat in the calm first class and pretends that he is "thinking about the revolution" (34). This depicts an attitude toward the fantastic element that has already been seen in "La casa" (Chapter 2) and in "Trastornos de carácter" (Chapter 3). The reaction of the protagonist to the impossible event, while initially one of horror and surprise, ends up as one of acceptance or denial. In this short story, this last point is even particularly present in the final paragraphs, where the denial of the fantastic element is also a denial of a whole social reality of shaken second-class citizens. The protagonist, a second-class citizen himself who, as he confesses, is flying first class for the first time, ends up succumbing to the passivity of first class, "sprawled" (34) on his seat, "intoxicated with the taste of the malt" (34) and, what is more, not even thinking about the revolution but just "pretending" (34) to do so.

The second element that interwines both realities is the curtain. As the reader will recognise, in flights this curtain isolates the first-class area from second class, an act that the narrator had "always perceived, from [his] second class seat, as an insult" (33). However, this curtain is not only a liminal entity that segregates two physical spaces as well as two classes; in the text, it also articulates the dual reality present within the plane. This aspect had already been anticipated in the sentence uttered by the character as he entered the plane: "A new *world* [...] opens up to me" (32) (see "anticipatory metaphorical image", Casas 2010:12). The motif of threshold in this case is an unusual one in the sense that this curtain, normally just a symbolic boundary between two classes in a plane, becomes an ontological boundary of two differentiated realities. Similarly, first class and second class are not only two physical and social spaces of the plane; their division through the duality of turbulence/non-turbulence reflects two realities where different laws operate. In isolation, both of them are possible according to factual reality but what constitutes the Fantastic in this story is that they are both present within one single space: the plane.

The World as Impossible Synthesis of Realities

This plane is thus an impossible space that brings together two verisimilar and yet contradictory realities. Roas' dual plane encapsulates the concept of Thirdspace discussed above, since it incorporates the positive and the negative at once. It is a space that unites two incompatible versions of reality.

This Thirdspace does not find classification according to the contentions of Possible Worlds Theory. It is not composed by the natural and the supernatural, be these domains (Doležel's dyadic structures) or worlds (Ryan's multiverses). In the plane of "Das Kapital", two 'natural' worlds are present. As argued above, the Fantastic resides in the plane as the frame in which these two worlds exist at the same time.

A further characteristic of the fantastic Thirdspace is that it challenges the very notion of referentiality. Generally in literature, parallel worlds are connected by a character that shifts from his referential reality to another reality, with this second reality presenting a version of facts contradictory to the referential one. However, in this text, which of the two realities (or worlds) is the real one? The one with turbulence, or the one without? It is impossible to answer this question. Both worlds are presented as actual and possess the same referential and ontological status. They are both real and possible: what is impossible is precisely that they are *both* real.

Further versions of the fantastic Thirdspace are seen in, for example, "The Other Heaven" (1966), by Julio Cortázar. In this story, the temporal and spatial distance between the Paris of the late nineteenth century and the Buenos Aires of the mid-twentieth century is cancelled out in a city that acts as Thirdspace. It joins two space-times: it is neither Paris nor Buenos Aires, while being both at the same time.

Another example is Jorge Luis Borges' "The Other" (1972), which tells of an encounter between two Borges: one from 1918 and one from 1969. This triggers a conversation about who is dreaming of whom; who is subject and who is other. This fantastic encounter is not only based on the symbiosis of two temporal moments in one instant, but it also takes place in an impossible space. What makes this space of encounter impossible is that it merges two existing places in an extratextual reality. In this, the notion of the fantastic Thirdspace is condensed in the motif of the bench where they sit next to each other. This bench is simultaneously (in) Cambridge and Geneva ("We are in 1969, in the city of Cambridge. / No, […] I am here in Geneva, on a bench, a few steps from the Rhône."):

> I replied that the supernatural, if it happens twice, is no longer terrifying; I suggested that we meet again the next day, on that same bench that existed in two times and two places (1999:416).

An interesting variation of fantastic Thirdspace is present in the story "La casa de los dos portales" (1982) by José María Merino. The abandoned house where the protagonists go to play provides access to a decaying version of their city located in a remote past. The abandoned house, a portal that joins both representations of the city, is the equivalent of Roas' curtain in the plane. The city works as a fantastic Thirdspace in that it 'is' various contradictory versions of itself at the same time: "And when I go out onto the street, after opening the only door of my house, I am often afraid of finding myself in that immobile, corroded, infinitely sad city, which accompanies the other one like an invisible shadow" (1982:95).

Yet, contrasting with the aforementioned narratives by Cortázar, Borges and Merino, "Das Kapital" is unique since it plays with the idea of Thirdspace without necessarily alluding to jumps within the temporal line. In this respect, it is worth introducing another short story by the same author: "Duplicados" (2010). An aspect that emerges even more clearly in this short story than in the previous is the parallelism with quantum superposition, a contention of quantum mechanics that establishes that a single quantum particle has the ability to simultaneously exist in multiple differential states.

Whereas it is not the aim here to go further into the complex realm of quantum mechanics, the philosophical implications of this premise are quite extraordinary: a singularity can 'be' two or more contradictory states at the same time. This is illustrated by Schröedinger's paradox, where a cat in a black box is alive and dead at the same time until the observer opens the box. This is explored in "Duplicados", where a physics teacher who is about to carry out Schröedinger's thought experiment is puzzled to realise that the hypothetical experiment has become an actuality. The cat in the box is duplicated: one of it is alive, the other is dead. He then exclaims: "Quantum superposition in all its splendour. / And then—I can't find a way to express it any better—the tissue of space has split" (2010:61). The dichotomy of alive/dead is invalidated, just as was the turbulence/non-turbulence of the flight. The event in this case takes place in a box, a further representation of fantastic Thirdspace, where—like the plane—exclusive and irreconcilable worlds are real simultaneously. Later on in the story, the physicist from "Duplicados" extends what has happened inside the box to serve as a reflection of his own ontology as an individual: "And I have started to imagine what my other me will do in that other reality" (63). This leads in to the next theme of this chapter, where the idea of doubling the single is further explored.[5]

3. DUPLICATES

Another text that presents two versions of a similar reality is the short story "Une dure journée" ("A Hard Day", 1988) by Jean-Paul Beaumier. There is an important difference between the motif of Duplicates, as typified in this story, and that of Thirdspace, as present in section 2. While in Thirdspace the notion of referentiality is indiscernible due to the co-presence of antithetical oppositions (e.g., turbulence/non-turbulence), in this section the referent is called into question by several doublings of itself. Touching also upon issues of identity, this theme parallels the classic motif of the *Doppelgänger*. However, in this case these issues are centred not on the physical doubling of the subject but on the *space* of the subject. Therefore, the emphasis is on how the physical reality of the character is suddenly doubled, hence providing multiplications of the original idea of one reality or world. These versions of his world are not only copies but are equally referential and possess the same ontological status.

Before proceeding to the analysis, it might be worth introducing further the author of the story, who is relatively unknown beyond the confines of Quebec and yet who is key to the contemporary Fantastic. Quebecois author Jean-Paul Beaumier has cultivated the Fantastic in various compilations of short stories, such as *L'Air libre* (1988)—from which "Une dure journée" is taken—and *Petites lâchetés* (1991). Beaumier is a one of a leading group of authors, the work of whom testifies to the vitality of fantastic narrative in Quebec; with others including Bertrand Bergeron (e.g., *Parcours improbables*, 1986; *Transits*, 1990), Jean-Pierre Girard (e.g., *Espaces à occuper*, 1992), Michel Dufour (e.g., *Circuit fermé*, 1989; *Passé la frontière*, 1991), Claude Mathieu (*La mort exquise*, 1989), Gilles Pellerin (e.g., *Ni le lieu ni l'heure*, 1987; *Principe d'extorsion*, 1991), Maria-José Thériault (*La cérémonie*, 1978) and the aforementioned Claude-Emmanuelle Yance (*Mourir comme un chat*, 1987) (for further critical perspectives on the Quebecois tradition of the Fantastic, refer to endnote 4 in Chapter 3).

"Une dure journée" is built upon the disturbing idea of being in (at least) two worlds, the two of these almost identical, with only a slight detail—a postcard—allowing the character to identify that he is not in his everyday reality. As the protagonist returns home from a long day, he follows his usual sequence of actions: he opens the post-box, enjoys a glass of whiskey on the couch, and exchanges a few words with his wife Catherine, who he can hear working in the kitchen. He first notices that the furniture in his house has been rearranged, as his wife periodically does. He then discovers a postcard on the table. It is signed by Michel, a name he does not recognise, and it is addressed to M. and Mme Paul Boulard, who are also unknown to him. All these details indicate that, although they are extremely similar to his own, he is now in someone else's house and life—he has shifted to an almost identical parallel world. The story ends abruptly at that point, with no indication as to how the two realities have been interchanged, where his original house is or if he can ever return to it.

Location: The Housing Estate

Jean-Paul Beaumier has chosen to emplace the action in a setting which has already appeared in other short stories analysed in this book: the housing estate (see "privatopia", Chapter 2, section 4). The main emplacement of the action is the narrator's house, or at least what he believes is his house. Everything indicates that this house is part of a housing estate composed of identical looking houses: "a bungalow looking like the other dozens of them on this street" (1988:95). All the neighbouring houses receive the same commercial mail, all these, as he says, targeted at the same type of person ("last Thursday the office stank of the shaving lotion *Old Spice:* guess why" [97]).

While this impersonal, standardised suburb—which could well be taken from a text by J. G. Ballard—might initially seem unremarkable, it is a key element for interpreting the story. In an environment where the houses and inhabitants are scarcely distinguishable from each other, the author seems to suggest that slipping into the neighbour's life is almost natural. This idea, which will be further elaborated in the following sections, presents an interesting inversion of the traditional Gothic enclave. In Chapter 1 (section 3), I pointed to the importance of the setting within the Gothic-Romantic tradition of the Fantastic. Isolated and remote castles and mansions, atmospheres of decay and gloom were favourite locations for invoking the supernatural.

This was understood in relation to Burke's theory of the sublime, which was very influential at the time and which suggested that the aesthetic characteristics of certain places (the Gothic enclave) facilitated the perception of extraordinary events beyond the boundaries of human reason.

However, the place of the fantastic event in "Une dure journée" is far removed from these conventions. The narrator's house is not remote and isolated from civilisation; quite the opposite, it is at the heart of it. Furthermore, in contrast with the rich architectural features of the Gothic site, Otranto's castle being a good example, there is nothing peculiar about the character's house in "Une dure journée". It is just one of the many identical looking prefabricated houses. Nonetheless, the thought underlying the selection of this setting for the Fantastic seems to converge to some extent with the nineteenth century Gothic ideals: namely that certain types of places facilitate the apparition of the extraordinary. In this late twentieth century version of Burke's aesthetic philosophy, it is not the remoteness and complex architecture of the sites that calls up supernatural experiences but instead precisely the opposite: just as Ballard's short story suggested, the unremarkable, homogeneous features of buildings in large residential areas seem to provide 'suitable surroundings' in which the ordinary can unexpectedly turn into the extraordinary. Converging also with the Ballardian ethos, Beaumier seems to imply that these types of spaces synthesise a form of social numbness, which the sociologist Paul Virilio expressed as "uniformity breeds conformity" (1998:47).

Discourse: Anticipations

The homogenisation characteristic of the housing estate is paralleled in the homogenisation of its residents. Instead of being portrayed as individuals, they are presented as 'types' of individuals or, even worse, as 'a' type of individual. The sameness of lifestyles is best illustrated by the objects and goods sent by post to the inhabitants of the housing estate. The main character views this with indignation, repeating syntax and reiterating the expression "the same" in a sequence of sentences:

> [...] are you going to brush your teeth with the same toothpaste as Mme Plourde? Gargle with the same mouth-rinse as M. Bertrand? Wash your hair with the same shampoo as your neighbour? Drink the same beer brand because you are more or less of the same age? (97)

Another important aspect is the way in which the protagonist's arrival 'home' is presented. The story starts abruptly with what is almost an everyday set phrase—"Finally! You got home. You thought that this damn day would never finish" (95)—and, immediately after, the protagonist recalls situations that irritated him at work: "a first class nuisance (*"emmerdeuse"* in original) would not stop calling my phone [...] You know it is *very* important that

I know *immediately* if there will be any delays" (95, emphasis in the original). This diverts the reader's attention away from the first sentence, which in fact is already anticipating the fantastic event. His wife's words when he enters the house are also anticipatory: "Is that you?" to which he replies upset: "Evidently, who does she want it to be? But if you were Catherine, you say to yourself leaving your briefcase next to the entrance, you would prefer that it was anyone else (*n'importe qui d'autre*) today" (98).

All this seems to indicate that he is so absorbed from his hard day at work, as described in the title, that he disregards the small details around him. These details gradually disclose—if not to him then at least to the reader—that he is not in the place he thinks he is.

A scene in which this is very clearly portrayed is when he opens the mailbox. There he sees only what he expects to see, "Evidently, there is nothing but bills and commercial mail" (96), and laconically establishes:

> After such a day at work, it is comforting to learn that a bag of ten kilos of potatoes is less expensive at Steinberg than at Provigo [...] yesterday you found toothpaste when you put your hand into the narrow mailbox. The other day you received a new brand of tampons, which were suspended on the door-handle since the mailbox was full. With a little luck, you will receive condoms soon (96–97).

His anger prevents him from noticing the impossible elements that are already present among the commercial mail, all of which are quickly rationalised by him once he does notice them. A new telephone bill—which he thought he had paid already—the electricity bill—nothing but an annoying mistake since they have oil heating—and two misdirected letters. As he puts this post into the bins, his thoughts, which appear in brackets, already anticipate the fantastic exchange of identities: "[...] the telephone bill (you thought that you had sent a cheque to these people last week)" (97). The same process is repeated throughout his progressive encounter with this other reality that he has slipped into: he rationalises what is different and out of place by describing how irritated it makes him. His door is "for once not bolted" (98), the telephone "(is never even where it should be)" (98), and if things are misplaced it is because of Catherine's "bad habit of changing periodically the disposition of furniture" (99).

The next aspect concerning the textual construction of the Fantastic is related to focalisation. It is the character himself who sees and relates the events but he does so as if addressing himself. Although following the actions from the protagonist's perspective, the reader gradually comes to discern the character's incapability of appreciating that there is something wrong. This is quite an unusual strategy of constructing the fantastic tension, and is based on the character's self-absorption, which blinds him from seeing beyond his "very bad day at work" (98). This element of irritation also anticipates the supernatural from the start, as the following passage shows: "All that is now behind you, you have closed the door, left your problems in the office (what would you not give so that this was true)" (96). Therefore, even when at home, his "hard day" is not left outside the door.

Story: Ascending Structure

All this serves in the gradual construction of the fantastic effect. The character is initially confronted with a normal situation with a few things out of place until, at the very end, a final element (the letter) breaks this process of rationalisation and reveals its impossibility: "Paul Boulard? But [...] but [...]" (99), definitive moment of realisation, followed by the wife's words: "Paul? Are you ready to sit at the table? Paul? Paul?" (99).

The linear construction of the impossible follows the Todorovian description of fantastic narratives. In Todorov's view, a structural characteristic of the Fantastic is that it is graduated toward a final culmination, an aspect that also forces a linear, unbroken reading from beginning to end if the story is to make sense (1975:87). However, although this story corresponds to Todorov's characterisation of the Fantastic, it should be stressed that, as attested to by that fact that several of the sample texts considered in this book started in medias res (e.g., "Dejen salir" and "Tandis que roule le train"), this graduation toward a final culmination is not in fact a necessary structural characteristic of fantastic narratives.

In this short story, the ascending structure of events is worth remarking— it features an aspect that is also encountered in the other sample short stories in this book. This aspect is related to the motif of the threshold, but with a distinctly postmodern take. As previously argued, a characteristic of the Fantastic of Place (Chapter 1) was that this physical division between spaces—for example, a window or a door—also marked the access into the domain of the supernatural. A theme particularly recurrent in the traditional forms of the Fantastic was that the crossing of a threshold entailed accessing a new space with new codes. Furthermore, the physical threshold played an important role in the disclosure of events: crossing this threshold was the turning point in the story. None of these characteristics are present in "Une dure journée". As was the case of the structure in "La casa", "Habitante" or "The Enormous Space", there is no explicit moment that marks either the access into the fantastic domain or the start of the fantastic transgression. The fantastic transgression seems to be taking place gradually, without preparation or warning. The Fantastic is only confirmed once the character realises it. Where then is the 'impossible' located? The effect is that the reader—just as is the case for the protagonist—is unable to confine the supernatural to a precise temporal or spatial frame (note the contrast with the Fantastic of Place). The classic correlation between a physical threshold and a temporal one in the action (turning point) is diffused.

As can be seen best in "Une dure journée", it is impossible to determine when the shift of houses and identities, and so the doubling of realities, has taken place. Did it happen when he entered the building, as that initial "Finally! You got home" (95) sarcastically anticipated? Or as he performed his routine actions, such as reading the post, greeting his wife and having a whiskey on his couch? The sentence which opens the story in the original French version—"*Vous voilà arrivé à la maison*" ("You have just arrived home", 95), a common expression in French but still constructed with the defined article "la",—reflects the ambiguity as to where the character is located. Perhaps the entanglement between the two realities took place at that first point, and thus this sentence would correspond with the previously introduced concept of 'threshold sentence' (Chapter 4, section 2).

The abrupt ending confirms that the impossible has at some stage seeped into the possible. Another commonly occurring characteristic in postmodern narrative is the fact that this is revealed by an unremarkable everyday object: here, it is a simple postcard addressed to someone other than him. This confirms that the space does not correspond either with his house nor with his life. After finding the postcard, he does not recognise himself in this new space and there is no sign as to where his referential 'home' was or should be. And yet both worlds are presented as equally real: his house and this other house; his life and this other life. Has he become a counterpart of himself, under another name? It is important to bear in mind that the character's personal name is never mentioned. All we know is that he is not Paul Boulard: he has never been, or he is not anymore, depending on which way the story is read. Stressing the strong bond between space and identity, subject and emplacement, as examined in Chapter 2, both interpretations would lead to the same outcome: he is not the one he was or should be, which the story translates as 'he is not *where* he should be'.

The World Cloned

The spatial transgression presented in this chapter points to an erasure of the notion of one 'reality' in favour of 'realities' that coexist and are, at times, perceived in their simultaneity by someone who shifts from one to the other. Parallels of this transgression can be found in the theory of multiverses, which posits that our universe is composed of multiple simultaneous realities and yet the human being can tune into only one of them. From this point of view, what this short story presents is a character who intersects with another, one very similar to himself and yet different. Embedded within this idea is the notion that what the human being perceives is only one of multiple possibilities: our perception of reality is, thus, limited. Whereas what we think is 'the' reality, is just 'a' reality.

The occurrences in Beaumier's short story also evoke the previously mentioned contention of quantum physics—quantum superposition—which states that a quantum particle can be in two states at the same time. To make things more complicated, another phenomenon of quantum physics— that of quantum entanglement—shows that two distant particles can react similarly to a fact or an event. Even though these phenomena belong to quantum cosmology and as such are not perceptible to us in our everyday physical reality, the challenge that they pose to our system of logic is enormous. Of particular interest to this short story is the challenge concerning the dualism of singularity/place: if one element can simultaneously *be* in two different locations, is this particle still to be considered as a *single* particle or instead as multiple ones? This relates back to the motif of the *Doppelgänger* in that it indicates the disintegration of a—singular, individual—identity. Therefore, similarly to the doubling of a subject, this transgression of doubling of worlds suggests that what was thought of as univocal is in fact but one of many copies of the same referent. This multiplication affects the idea of single entity, and in doing so reveals the frailty and constructed essence of the notion of individuality. Moreover, even more gravely, it attacks the whole notion of world or, in other words, of a 'single reality', whose central position in the fictional cosmology is displaced by multiple, equally possible counterparts.

Another recent short story that exploited this theme is "Venco a la molinera" ("Venco, molinera-style", 1998) by Spanish author Félix J. Palma. In this text, the character, returning from a flight, realises that he has slipped into another reality. This other reality is absolutely identical to his, with one exception: the word 'chicken' ('pollo' in the original) has been randomly replaced by the word '*venco*', with no meaning in Spanish. This generates a crisis in the protagonist, who wonders what other things might be different in this other reality. It opens up a whole new world that differs from his now lost referential world in only this simple detail (so far, this is the only one he is aware of). In so doing, the text suggests that, in our everyday environment, a multiplicity of very similar worlds (almost identical to each other) springs up from the least expected places.

In another short story, "La Banlieue" (Jacques Sternberg 1988), the protagonist goes to a café where he is supposed to meet a date but when he arrives he realises that that café has multiplied and is now situated at every street corner: there are an infinity of cafés, one at every corner. There is even a Nicole (the name of his date) present in each one:

> Every woman living in this neither poor nor posh suburb looked like the Nicole I had met in town. All of them were called Nicole Moreau. And they could not be elsewhere than in the *Café au Coin*, on the junction of the *rue de la République* and *rue du Général-de-Gaulle*, since all cafés and all streets bore those names, never any another (1998:45).

As a result, he does not know where to find the right café nor who is the right Nicole whom he is supposed to meet. These multiple doublings of space coexist in the present and so the temporal line is not altered. Every singularity (the *Café au Coin*, the corner, his date Nicole) is by the end of the short story conceived as not one but as multiple, all very similar. All differences and specific references (the *Café au Coin*, the *rue de la Répub-lique*) lose their specificity and become general categories (a café in a corner, a street like any other).

In "Une dure journée", this disintegration of the classic notion of the 'individual' is foreshadowed by the location of the action. The homogeneous colony of identical-looking houses, all of which seem to contain similar life-styles, is an ideal background which, exaggerated to the extreme, gives rise to the metaphor of cloned realities with barely any distinctive features.

4. REPLACEMENTS

Time, which was set aside in order to focus on space instead, also plays a key role in the two sample texts analysed so far. The conflictive coexis-tence of two worlds supposes an impossible alteration of the temporal line. To take the example of "Das Kapital", a plane could be affected or not by turbulence but the two options (turbulence and non-turbulence) cannot occur at the same time. In presenting the two as occurring simultaneously, the normal course of events, which human beings have structured in the—artificial but necessary—notion of linear time, is challenged. In the final text to be analysed, time and space operate jointly to produce the Fantastic "Los palafitos" (2007) by Spanish writer Ángel Olgoso is an excellent illustra-tion of how the traditional fantastic motif of jumps within the space-time continuum can be adopted not only to deconstruct the notion of linear time but also to annihilate all presumptions concerning the concept of 'world'. A large number of Ángel Olgoso's works take the form of the fantastic short story, as in *Cuentos de otro mundo* (2003), *Los demonios del lugar* (2007), *Astrolabio* (2007), *La máquina de languidecer* (2009) and *Las frutas de la luna* (2013). "Los palafitos" was recently selected for inclusion in the compi-lation *Perturbaciones: Antología del relato fantástico español actual* (2009) as an exemplar of Olgoso's treatment of the Fantastic.

Let us return now to the subject of worlds. If, as Davies writes (1996:254), the universe can be taken as the totality of space and the totality of time, then history, space and time in their most abstract manifestation are trans-gressed in "Los palafitos". When confronted by another physically possible version of the world, the certainty of the character's learnt facts about his world crumble. Therefore, it is this short story that most directly illustrates how notions of space and of time are two intrinsic references in the con-struction of reality, as physical dimension within a historical line.

The plot is the following: the protagonist and narrator, an expert in botany, recalls how he gets lost during one of his frequent excursions in the countryside. On his way, he finds a fisherman "with an ancient look" (2007:45), who invites him to rest in his small village by the lake. This fact already surprises the narrator, since he knows the area very well and is cer-tain that there are no lakes around. His arrival at the village is even more shocking: its inhabitants live in *palafitos*, those primitive wooden constructions on water. The longer he spends there, the more he realises this village has remained in the past. As night suddenly falls, the fisherman shows him a world map. This is a crucial moment in which the strange turns into the impossible. The map shows a world with the same geography as the narrator's world, except for one aspect: it is exclusively populated by *palafitos*, even—and this last detail is crucial—where there were never any in the past. Confronted with this new version of the world, the protagonist sees all the certainties about his world crumble like all those historical constructions that the map omits. This village is not the past; it contradicts History as he had known until then. As in "Une dure journée", there is no mention as to where the narrator's world is now, or if he will ever be able to return to it. In "Los palafitos", the response to the newly introduced reality is more developed: the short story ends with him accepting without much resistance and adapting himself to this new world of *palafitos*.

Location: The Modern City versus the Fisherman's Village

There are two central spaces in the story, as will be shown, that not only act as locations but at the end are also revealed to be two different ontological domains.

One of these is the narrator's world, with cities, concrete, and other modern elements that indicate that it corresponds with the reader's world. The other is the fisherman's village. In contrast to the narrator's world, this space is portrayed as archaic, with *palafitos* on the water instead of "buildings on the ground" (2007:53), ancient traditions (barter, burials under the dolmen), materials and food (skins, tapioca, dry fish) and superstitions (the night as the moment of the supernatural), all of which indicates it is distanced in time from the referential space of the narrator. If the narrator is shocked by the villager's old-fashioned culture, in the village of *palafitos* the words concrete, brick and glass provoke a similar bewilderment. This is clearly seen in a conversation where the narrator tells the fisherman that he lives in a concrete building of twelve floors and the fisherman replies: "I don't know those things of which you are telling me, they don't even fit into a human's mind" (2007:53), and later:

> Sir, what speaks from your mouth is not natural reason. There are many things that one does not know, but an old man like me is certain of what he knows. Twelve bodies, you say? (2007:53)

In terms of their configuration, the two locations are composed by a scheme of inversion: that which is found in one is absent in the other. And yet, and this is very important, neither of them is physically impossible. They do not even have different ontological qualities. Once more, as in the other texts, their coexistence is what constitutes the impossibility. The fishermen's village and the narrator's city are contradictory domains that cannot coexist in the same larger frame that contains them, whether this be a region or—as later will be confirmed with the map—within the same world. The key, however, is how they relate to each other, a relationship that alters throughout the story.

Discourse: Dwelling into the Fantastic

In considering the previous short story, "Une dure journée", I indicated how the motif of the threshold as a marker into the fantastic domain was absent. "Los palafitos" is another illustrative example of how the access into the other world is not rendered explicit with a physical boundary to be crossed but is instead a smooth transition.

A transition is present in this short story, but it is almost as imperceptible for the reader as it is for the character. There are two important rhetorical strategies used in constructing this, both related to narrative space. The first of these is a poly-sensorial construction of the narrated space, which turns the protagonist's walk into an absentminded lingering, and the second concerns the local fauna, flora and topography.

The narrator tells us that he is strolling in nature, looking at all sort of plants, "carried by the delicious breeze that lapped against the hills" (45). He recalls not only what he sees but also what he hears ("the exultant song of the trumpeter", *aligrís* [45]), the textures he feels ("the insect-catcher leave" [45]) and the various aromas he smells ("the aroma of hawthorn" [45]). Fully immersed in this sensory appreciation of the landscape, the character, as well as the reader, has already crossed into the other world without perceiving it. In his description of flora, fauna and topography of the area, the narrator is already located in an impossible space by the end of the first paragraph. Significantly, the end of this paragraph is succeeded by the first intervention of the fisherman, who asks "Are you lost?" (45).

Story: Demolition of Universal History

The configuration of the two worlds and how they relate to each other evolves during the short story. This is what, borrowing from Ryan (2006), I will call the cosmology of this short story. As the story progresses, the narrator provides different hypotheses on the existence of this village of *palafitos* in relation to the world he knows (his referential world). This notion of referential world is what will be contested in the ending. Although the narrator progressively begins to realise that this situation is impossible, it is not until the map is displayed that it is confirmed. In this way, the various dispositions of these two worlds across the story—the different 'cosmologies'—can be distinguished in three different phases:

At first, the narrator—as well as the reader—thinks he has encountered a strange hidden area within his world, a black hole where different rules abide. The village of *palafitos* is perceived as an exceptional place where, in contrast to the dry region in which it should be located, there are lakes. This is clearly articulated by the narrator: "you are the exception [...] A very picturesque and impossible exception within these latitudes" (59). The village is at this point regarded as a fantastic interpolation into the narrator's idea of reality, as the house of "La casa" or "Habitante" or "El museo" or many other impossible places that have been mentioned in this research might be. Important, however, is that the narrator's idea of world still remains referential. Applying Possible Worlds Theory, the narrator's world (which the reader recognises as realistic) would be the actual textual world and would still maintain the central position of the narrator in the ontological system of the text. In such a case, we would be dealing with a classical ontology, or single-world cosmology, which concerns texts "centred around one, and only one, actual world" (Ryan 2006:652). In this one single actual world, an "uncertain region" (51)—the village—appears interpolated ("a Neolithic cottage stuck in a short distance of the city" [52]).

However, as the narration progresses, there appear an overwhelming number of clues contradicting this first hypothesis. This leads to a second ontological cosmology. The lake is not the only thing that does not correspond to the narrator's referential space. In the village, the elements of modernity are as yet undiscovered, as seen, in particular, in a lack of evolution of architectural constructions. When the narrator exclaims that there have not been any *palafitos* in his country for centuries, the fisherman replies:

> You know perfectly well that there has never been in the world any constructions other than these, whether on water, on the shore, or on firm ground. Has it not always been so and will it not always be? (50–51)

This confirms that the lake village is not only a strange topographical exception in the region. The entire village reflects a regression to the past. Where the narrator finds himself is in fact his same world but he has jumped across its historical line. Two temporal versions of the same idea of world are thus juxtaposed. However, even in this case his idea of world is still referential. As he describes his experience in the fisherman's *palafito*, it is clear that he retains his spatio-temporal referent: "light of an archaic yellow", "a millenary cavern" (56). In terms of Possible Worlds Theory, this is a double-world cosmology, where the *same* world coexists in two versions: present and past.

This collapses when the map appears in front of his eyes, showing a world of *palafitos*, even in those regions in which there would not have been any *palafitos* in Antiquity. Through this archaic architectural construction that spreads around the continents, another idea of world is introduced. The fisherman's world imposes itself as actual, whereas the narrator's idea of world is displaced into some lost position. The narrator's world is completely displaced from its unique position in the cosmology of the short story by the introduction of this second world of *palafitos*, in which the history of humanity has followed a different fate. The realisation of this fact generates in the narrator a "totalising fear that abruptly appears, under our feet, the ground of certitudes" (57). To illustrate this loss of ontological centrality, the author dedicates more than three pages to the development of a metaphor on the downfall of the narrator's referents. The architectural constructions that have shaped the history of humanity crumble in his mind: pyramids, amphitheatres and temples, castles and palaces, churches and cathedrals. This is the clearest evidence given to show that the narrator has not leaped into a past version of his own world. The world of *palafitos* is irrefutable evidence that both worlds—the narrator's and the fishermen—are real; and their coexistence, impossible. A new History is a new Reality. With surprising ease, the narrator adapts himself to it. The short story closes with him saying that he would like to spend the night with his wife "dressed in jute, her arms adorned with bracelets and shells, sheltered here from the open and from darkness, mutually comforted, leaning on [their] *palafito*" (62).

The World as *Arché*

The interrelation between architecture and human history is reflected through the symbolic association between 'construction' and 'evolution'. The buildings that have constructed the chronicles of humanity are silenced by this unexpected world solely populated by *palafitos*. As the author indicates in an interview (in *El síndrome Chéjov*, 2009), the effect sought after was "the progressive demolition of universal history". The finding of the map represents a moment of absolute loss of the referential frame retained by the narrator till then. The metaphor that the text raises echoes Vattimo's thesis (1985), in which it is argued that Modernity comes to an end when it is no longer possible to speak of History as something unitary or singular. This thought also parallels Lyotard's philosophy of incredulity toward metanarratives, as stated in his book *The Postmodern Condition* (1979). There is not one version of History but there are instead *histories* (or *stories*), all equally valid and dependant on the point of view from which they are articulated—the narrator's world and the world of the *palafitos* are two co-existing and yet incompatible—hence the fantastic effect—versions of history of humanity.

Finally, to close the analytical chapters of this book, it is worth noting how this metaphor refers back to the etymological origin of the word architecture, mentioned in the Introduction to this book. The architect was originally he who constructed the *arché*, who transformed the unknown into the known, chaos into cosmos. The lack of architecture, therefore, the architectural void, is equated with the end of certainties: it is an epistemological crumbling. René Descartes, in his *Discourse on the Method* (1637), employed a similar image to indicate the necessary test of 'solid foundations' for every certainty.[6] For the philosopher, reason is something that man needs to construct to shelter himself from uncertainty and chaos. Tearing down the foundations is equivalent to being in the open—unprotected, homeless— and yet this demolition is a fundamental step to constructing any solid and rational system of thought. This can only be achieved and a new system of thought constructed by first returning to the *arché*.

The narrator of "Los palafitos" also describes this collapse of the known using the metaphor of a descent into a void ("dissipating as collective spectres into the void" [58]), which at the same time is a return to the origin, to the *arché*, waiting to be constructed by the skilled craftsman, the *tekton*. Note also the use of images indicating a regression to a zero point in scientific and historical knowledge:

> Ages, tides, planetary orbits, Northern and Southern skies, devouring each other, return to the fresh start, to their original seed, to their intact womb. I realised that it was increasingly difficult to invoke my memory, to imagine that which I could not see, to establish analogies between the evident and that which was becoming remote, to recover that which had not even happened. [...] The sun never browned superb domes, [...] the wind never made windmills spin around [...]. [...] calendar pages were falling like withered petals and sepals, as ashes of an inexistent time, a prelude to a type of sudden and atrocious extinction, of abysmal uncertainty, and of forgetfulness (59).

This quote reflects how the narrator experiences the discarding of his referential frame, of his foundations based on geography and history. His original idea of the world is demolished. Considering this, it is understandable that his adaptation into this new world is in the end as smooth and unexpected as the access had been. This seems to imply that once all referents have been destroyed, once architecture has failed to provide the epistemological and ontological foundations of *a* world, a new *arché* arises. This *arché*, or pure origin, remains to be constructed and articulated by centuries of history, and as such it is to be embraced as one of many possible potential versions of the world.

***

The fantastic transgressions of space explored in this chapter were related to the idea of space as world. Based on some contingencies of Possible Worlds Theory, it was observed how this technique affects the macrostructure (Doležel 1998) or cosmology (Ryan 2006) of the fictional text. Whereas realistic texts, as well as many traditional fantastic texts, present one central world around which other possible ones (character's beliefs, dreams, etc.) orbit, this type of transgression presents more than one ontological centre. The fantastic transgression of the multiverse as explored in this chapter finds analogies with Possible Worlds Theory, in particular with Ryan's parallel between ontological plurality in Physics and Narrative (2006). However, an important difference with PWT is that dyadic structures or multiverses have been restricted to a natural and supernatural domain, the latter being configured in opposition to the physical laws of the former. In the constellation of worlds identified in the three sample texts, not a single one is physically impossible according to our reality. All of them offer a plurality of physically possible worlds; the impossible is their coexistence.

Also important to note is that the proponents of PWT do not recognise the Fantastic as a narrative form different from other neighbouring forms, such as fantasy and science fiction. Their category of multiverse (Doležel's dyadic structures, 1998) embraces all narratives of the supernatural equally and does not analyse whether or not this multiplicity of worlds is presented as problematic within the text. Fantastic narratives are the only narratives within the supernatural modes that present this coexistence as conflictive: or, put differently, they are the only ones in which the character is aware of the (impossible) multiple ontologies offered. This leads to the following questions: to what conflicts do these multiple ontologies give rise? What themes are the authors exploring through this type of fantastic transgression? What are the philosophical implications?

Although the motifs of juxtaposed and parallel worlds in space and/or time are not new in fantastic narrative, it is the way they are presented in the sample texts that makes them innovative. The plane of "Das Kapital" offered a space of dichotomies. The simultaneous existence was as impossible as that strange turbulence affecting only one side of the plane. Neither of the two worlds, in isolation, broke our physical laws of nature or of logic. What was impossible was, instead, that they were inscribed in the same space. This is what I called Thirdspace, a space which synthesises two worlds whose harmony is unattainable. This plane is itself the space of opposed logical actions, a fantastic space par excellence.

The next transgression, with "Une dure journée" as prototype, presented the doubling of the single. A second version of the character's world, extremely similar except for one feature, rendered it evident to him that he had shifted into a different reality, one coexisting with his.

Jumping across spatial and temporal realities, "Los palafitos" offered a disturbing telling of how history and territory combined to delete the preconceived certainties regarding the idea of world and thus illustrated a return to the *arché*. History was dismantled in favour of *histories*, an aspect that parallels Lyotard's theory and Fredric Jameson's thinking on this subject matter: "In faithful conformity to poststructuralist linguistic theory, the past as 'referent' finds itself gradually bracketed, and then effaced altogether, leaving us with nothing but texts" (Jameson 1991:18).

In conclusion, the ontological plurality offered in the three thematic lines of this chapter expresses a view that greatly differs from the nineteenth century idea of reality as something 'objective' containing set points of reference that is perforated by an element or event. As summarised by Teresa Bridgeman:

> Space in the nineteenth-century realist novels emerges as a concrete and stable phenomenon, while in modernist fiction it is filtered, like time, through the perceptions of protagonists. In postmodernist fiction, the idea of a "world" is itself destabilised, and different spaces multiply and merge (2007:56).

Deeply influenced by poststructuralist views on language, which regard language as something having not one but many referents, these texts reiterate that there are as many realities as there are possible constructions of reality, as there are stories, perspectives and mediations on it. The metaphor of the loss of the model of one single world shows the fracture or displacement of a central point of view, as the opening quote by Bertrand Westphal reflected. A singular ontology is atomised by plural ones. This is the feature found in the three sample short stories: the world as a single entity was displaced by introducing more versions of it. This made the protagonists realise that their stable and univocal idea of world, until then believed to be 'the' reality, was in fact just one of many coexisting realities. This is traceable back to the classic figure of the double in the Fantastic, and alludes to a disintegration of the singular and referential (identity, in the case of the double; reality, in the case of space as world). In the examples considered in this chapter, a new vision of the singular is provided: 'the' subject and 'the' reality are now inextricably formed by multiple different versions of themselves. This is precisely what triggers the unsettling fantastic effect.

NOTES

1. Westphal exposes the weakness of this theory, since Doležel oversimplifies the ontological construction of the central world without much elaboration on the notion of referentiality. As mentioned in Chapter 4, Westphal also proposes three categories (homotopic, utopic and heterotopic worlds) that coincide with Doležel's ontological categories. However, Westphal provides expanded variations for each of these according to the issue of referentiality (2011:99–110).
2. Martin Horstkotte has also noted this in his study on the British postmodern Fantastic. He dedicates a chapter to the issue of incompatible worlds, a feature that he establishes as being central among postmodern fantastic fictions: "a theory of binary structures, whether of time or of space, is bound to fall short of explaining the parallel worlds of the postmodern fantastic which sometimes offer three or more parallel worlds" (2004:72). His analysis, though, is less focused on spaces as 'worlds' and more oriented toward the transgression of time and history (historiographical metafiction) and of literary genres (fairy tales, for example).
3. A different take on Thirdspace can be seen in Westphal's *Geocriticism* (2007/2011a), in which he borrows this idea to apply it to the study of space in

literature. Literary space is thus an example of Thirdspace, since it is always a synthesis between the real and the imagined. Conversely, any perception of real space is also affected by fictional discourses and the literatures around it (e.g., Dublin or Lisbon).

4. All translations from short stories quoted in this chapter are mine.

5. A further insight into how the contingencies of quantum physics have modified the paradigm of the real is provided by David Roas in the section "¿Hay literatura fantástica después de la mecánica cuántica?" (2011:21–27). In it, he draws from the theories by Goodman (1984), Feynman (1995), Kaku (2005) and Damasio (2007), among others, to illustrate how the discoveries of quantum mechanics and neuroscience have produced a new way of understanding what is possible and impossible. This new paradigm, however, does not mean that the 'impossible' is irrepresentable within the literary text: the Fantastic survives as literary form, proof given by the many short stories quoted in this book.

6. "[...] it often happens that a private individual takes down his own [house] with the view of erecting it anew, and that people are even sometimes constrained to this when their houses are in danger of falling from age, or when the foundations are insecure" (Descartes 2008:18). "And, just as in pulling down an old house, we usually reserve the ruins to contribute towards the erection, so, in destroying such of my opinions as I judged to be ill-founded, I made a variety of observations and acquired an amount of experience of which I availed myself in the establishment" (2008:27).

Conclusion
The Fantastic Dimension of Space

This book has sought to demonstrate the relevance and productiveness of the question of space within the postmodern Fantastic. By highlighting the potential of narrative space to dismantle the effect of textual realism, this phenomenon reveals precisely what it transgresses: the importance of the spatial dimension within the human construction of the factual and textual real. This idea, although central to the Spatial Turn in the Human Sciences, had not been explicitly acknowledged in relation to the fantastic text. This book, therefore, is aimed at addressing this existing gap in literary criticism: while the importance of narrative space in the construction of textual verisimilitude has been emphasised and, while the relation between space and *mimetic effect* has received considerable scholarly attention, the relation between space and *fantastic effect* has to date not been appropriately explored, neither within the emerging field of Geocriticism nor in theoretical and thematic studies on the Fantastic. As a result, in addition to the four dimensions (location, discourse, story and context) of the spatial sign, the theoretical contribution of this study relies on a fifth dimension: the fantastic function of narrative space, which instead of intervening in the construction of textual realism is in fact that which provokes its transgression.

The corpus of texts analysed here reflects that the Fantastic in the postmodern context is by no means debilitated or extinct, as Todorov's thesis asserted (1975:150–175). And neither did other forms such as science fiction replace it, as Caillois (1975) and Bozzetto (2005:31) anticipated, nor did it succumb to the clichés of the classic horror story as Finné's study on the American Fantastic suggested (2006:7–9; indeed it is for this reason that Finné's study stops in 1985). On the contrary, the variety of authors presented in this book confirms that the postmodern Fantastic today possesses a significant vitality, despite the fact that has been subject to limited academic attention. This vitality is particularly evident from the late seventies onwards, when the popularity of the Fantastic began to converge at the level of authors, readers, critics and editorial interest within different narrative traditions.

It is also true that the treatment of the Fantastic in the corpus analysed here reveals what could be said to be a less 'pure' Fantastic. This Fantastic hybridises with other narrative forms; bringing together the absurd in

"La casa" (José B. Adolph 1975), borrowing from the detective story in "Trastornos de carácter" (Juan José Millás 1989), merging with humour in "Das Kapital" (David Roas 2010) or bordering on the allegorical in "Tandis que roule le train" (Éric Faye 1997). Nonetheless, the basic trait of the Fantastic since its origins is maintained: an impossible element manifests itself within a realistic context. Also, as observed in the selected corpus, it is a Fantastic that shares common elements beyond geographical frontiers. This is the reason why a comparative study is of particular relevance within the postmodern context.

Returning to the issue of space as impossible agent, a comparative approach has enabled the identification of various points of intersection within the corpus in relation to the theme at stake. These points (outlined below), grouped according to the four dimensions of the spatial sign, show continuity with, as well as a renewal of, traditional motifs of the Fantastic. Finally, the observations will conclude with a summary of the new dimension that this book explores: the fantastic dimension of narrative space.

Situational Dimension: The Inversion of the Sublime Topos

In relation to space as setting of the action, a characteristic that recurs throughout the corpus of texts analysed in this book is that of the mundane, domestic—and thus unremarkable—topos. Very often, the settings of the postmodern Fantastic are not only realistic but are deliberately banal. This is transmitted through descriptions that emphasise the codes of routine marking these spaces, whether the space be an ordinary house or a metro station.

Paradoxically, this phenomenon demonstrates an interesting parallel with the Gothic topos, typical of the Fantastic in its origins. As mentioned in Chapter 1, the Gothic topos feeds from the philosophy and aesthetics of the Sublime. When applied to the issue of space, this can be summarised as a place that acts as an ideal medium for experiencing the extraordinary. This correlation between place and event is also present in contemporary texts such as "The Enormous Space" (J. G. Ballard 1989), "Trastornos de carácter" (Juan José Millás 1989) and "Une dure journée" (Jean-Paul Beaumier 1988). These texts suggest that the location of action is directly related to what will happen in this location. In other words, the place of action, its ambiance, predisposes the subject to the supernatural. However, even more interesting is the fact that the contemporary location of the Fantastic is also the absolute inversion of the Gothic ideal: in contrast to those remote, isolated and, in a way, unique architectures, the places that appeared in our corpus were suburban colonies, cloned residential areas and minuscule apartments at the centre of an overcrowded megalopolis. There is a common denominator in these settings: a serial fabrication of homogeneity, which instead of enhancing the sense of individuality—as was the case with the Romantic *locus amoenus*—deletes any trace of it. As mentioned, this coincides with Augé's concept of the non-place (1992): those sites devoid of identity and history built for the subject to go unnoticed.

The fact that these types of spaces have become favourite sites for the fantastic apparition can be interpreted as a translation of the fears of our postindustrial society. These fears relate to a de-individualisation that the proliferation of these non-places entails, an aspect that has been on the agenda of sociologists such as De Certeau and Augé. Ballard is one of the writers in the corpus who shows most sensitivity toward this issue. In "The Enormous Space", for example, he creates an agoraphobic character who constructs his own personal cocoon within an impersonal neighbourhood. This entrenchment seems to be the only possible way of securing individual experience. However, the author also warns of the possible consequences: fortified spaces breed fortressed individuals and that individual space ends up being their only possible reality, leading potentially to madness. In other texts, as seen very clearly in "Dejen salir" (José Ferrer-Bermejo 1982), this threat is translated into the metaphor of becoming a robot of one's own routine. The character becomes one of the many automatons traversing daily the same metro stations, repeating the marked codes of conduct denounced by De Certeau.

These observations confirm that the settings of the postmodern Fantastic reflect and explore the fears deriving from the studied context and point to the convergence between the Fantastic and contemporary sociological theories, an area that undoubtedly deserves further academic exploration.

Linguistic Dimension: Threshold Devices

At the level of the rhetorical construction of the Fantastic of Space, this book has drawn attention to classic techniques of this narrative form, applied to the transgression of space. An example of this is 'semantic impertinence', a technique that merges two distinct and incompatible semantic fields as in the 'comfortable' fantastic wardrobe of "Trastornos de carácter" (Juan José Millás 1989), as well as those holes that "never fail" and make invisible he who finds them in "Mi hermana Elba" (Cristina Fernández Cubas 1980).

A strategy to be highlighted in relation to the spatial transgression is that of the 'fantastic polyvalence of spatial deictics', with a paradigmatic sentence featuring in this last-mentioned short story: "we were there but we weren't". The illogical concatenation of the two statements invalidates the reference of the adverb of place 'there'. Where is 'there'? The reader cannot establish the specific emplacement of the character, which might be in the realistic domain or might have already crossed into the Fantastic. This device has led to the formulation of another: the 'threshold sentence'. The best example of this is found in "La casa de muñecas" (Fernando Iwasaki 2004), but it also appears in other texts, such as "Une dure journée" (Jean-Paul Beaumier 1988). As indicated, this phenomenon combines linguistic and spatial elements and refers to a sentence that is ambiguous regarding the character's position. After this sentence, it becomes evident that the character has already crossed into the fantastic domain. The 'threshold sentence' is thus a moment of suspension, in the classic Todorovian sense. And this 'fantastic' sentence also replaces the traditional motif of the architectural threshold into the Fantastic.

On other occasions, as occurs in "Los palafitos" (Ángel Olgoso 2007), the lack of a physical threshold determining the shift of spaces—and of onto-logical domains—is fundamental. Instead of a recognisable access into the Fantastic, a progressive and—more importantly—imperceptible transition is generated. In order to achieve this, the sensorial potential of narrative space is exploited by the author; the five senses are engrossed during the walk while, distracted, character and reader wander into an impossible zone.

As shown, again in the linguistic dimension, classical rhetorical strategies of the Fantastic are adopted, while new rhetorical devices are integrated. This attest to the double force (maintaining-breaking with tradition) drives the newer voices of this narrative mode.

Semantic-Actant Dimension: The Subject as Architect of the Fantastic

With regard to the structure of events, this book has remarked upon the fact that a variety of short stories break with the classical ascending linear-ity that culminated with the fantastic revelation, a structure that Todorov identified as a structural characteristic of the Fantastic. In "Dejen salir" (José Ferrer-Bermejo 1982), "La casa de muñecas" (Fernando Iwasaki 2004) or "Los palafitos" (Ángel Olgoso 2007), the short story opens directly from within the fantastic domain, the events are narrated by a character who is already situated "on the other side" (see "Voces del Otro lado", Roas 2011:168–171). And yet the experience is recounted in retrospective. Where is the narrator at the moment of the narrating act? Should we suppose that he is still located in the fantastic domain? This disorients the reader: once again, the lack of transition-thresholds reveals an architectural void to structure the story.

In terms of how the Fantastic is received within the storyworld, there is a trend common to almost all the short stories analysed here: the new real-ity to which the characters are exposed is quickly accepted by them with resignation, as if this shift of realities were foreseeable or unavoidable. The clearest expression of this resignation is found in the words that close each short story of Juan José Millás' collection *Primavera de luto*: "ah, well" ("*en fin*" in the Spanish original, 1989).

This leads to a peculiar means of dealing with the impossible element: the character tries to justify the fantastic event by blaming it on him-self. This is the case of, for example, the narrator of "Dejen salir" (José Ferrer-Bermejo 1982), who initially blames his stressful life for the situ-ation in which he finds himself. Similarly, in a story significantly entitled

"L'Érreur" (Jacques Sternberg 1974), the narrator attributes the disappearance of his house to a 'mistake' of his memory. This notion of the individual as source of the Fantastic differs from other narratives where the supernatural is of the external kind, such as a ghost or a vampire. As mentioned previously, this presentation of the Fantastic is not new. It is inherited from a trend in the late nineteenth century, one of the most revolutionary figures Guy de Maupassant. Maupassant's Fantastic sets the individual at the heart of the supernatural experience, as a source of uncertainty and victim of existentialist terror by continuously questioning the boundaries of madness. With Maupassant, the Fantastic emerged from within. However, what characterises the texts analysed in the previous chapters is that there is no hint at a mental pathology—with the exception of the borderline case of "The Enormous Space". The receptor of the Fantastic is a normal subject who does not trust his/her eyes and memory to register correctly what he/she sees. Characters are more aware than ever of the limitations of their abilities of perception and, as a consequence, are also conscious of the possibility that they themselves are 'fabricating' the fantastic experience to which they are being exposed.

Pragmatic Dimension: The Postmodern Fantastic as Continuation and Regeneration

How is the Fantastic read today? How does our context contribute to its meaning? It has to be kept in mind that the contemporary reader inherits one and a half centuries of fantastic commonplaces. Therefore, and as is illustrated by the corpus of texts considered in this study, there is a renewal at the thematic level in order to maintain the ability to surprise the reader. Classic motifs are integrated with substantial modifications. These indicate a thematic evolution very much linked to the prominence of space as theme. Some examples of this encountered in this book are as follows:

The motif of the cursed or haunted place (as seen in "The Haunted Dolls' House", M.R. James 1923; *The Haunting of Hill House*, Shirley Jackson, 1959) is transformed into a supernatural space without evil qualities or historical tragedy in "La casa" (José B. Adolph 1975) and "La casa de muñecas" (Fernando Iwasaki 2004). The sway these spaces exert over the individual lacks finality or causality, potentially further disorienting the intra- and extratextual receiver.

The Romantic ideal of being at one with the natural environment is translated into a physical abdication of the subject who dissolves into his own constructed microcosm, for example in "The Enormous Space" (J. G. Ballard 1989).

The classic motif of the exchange of identities (e.g., "Lejana", Julio Cortázar 1951) now displaces the attention from the subject undergoing this change to the space that produces it. Out of this motif another one arises: the 'magnet space', which always retains a keeper, a figure to be continuously replaced by further victims who will perform the same function (e.g., "El museo", José María Merino 1982; "Habitante", Patricia Esteban Erlés 2008).

The double (e.g., "Le Horla", 1887) leads to the motif of 'double space'. Cloned spaces, such as the residential area of "Une dure journée" (Jean-Paul Beaumier 1988), produce cloned individuals.

Finally, in "Los palafitos" (Ángel Olgoso 2007), the classic motif of jumps in the space-time continuum is not centred on displacements across diverse historical periods. Instead, the narrator is confronted with a new history of the world, a new spatio-temporal reality that shakes the foundations of his world and sends him back to a zero point, to the *arché*. Once again, the thematic treatment of the postmodern Fantastic presents a continuity with the fantastic tradition, while also representing a regeneration of classic motifs. Precisely for this reason, "postmodern Fantastic" seems a more accurate term to describe this phenomenon than that of the "neo-fantastic" (cf. Alazraki 1983). Apart from discourse, story, reading time and the implications of space at the level of location, there is a fifth dimension in which these observations are reflected with most clarity, a dimension that I sought to unravel in this book: the fantastic function of space.

Fantastic Dimension: The Fracture Space/Reality

The four pillars of space explored here—body, boundary, hierarchy and world—transmit the weakening character of the notion of 'reality', a leitmotif for the postmodern Fantastic. With regard to the relationship between body and space, and the derivative interrelation between position and being, the transgressions of Chapter 2 demonstrated that the loss of physical place in space is a metaphor for a dissolution that is not only physical but also existential.

As was seen in Chapter 3, the obliteration in the texts of the physical boundaries that differentiate the material environment made tracing any referential system of distances impossible. At the same time, by transgressing the spatial hierarchy dictated by the relation of container and contained (Chapter 4), characters witnessed how reality became unstructured and disorganised. This rendered the adverbs of place—'here', 'there' and 'in'—obsolete, devoid of meaning. The last chapter entailed a frontal attack on the question of the real. In Chapter 5, the idea of real world multiplied, diversified, lost its central univocal position within the fictional universe. Not only was reality less *solid* (Chapter 2), less *defined* (Chapter 3) and less *structured* (Chapter 4), it was also not *unique* (Chapter 5).

With this, I arrive at the final conclusions. The question motivating this book was: why is the narrative of the Fantastic the optimal means by which to study the relationship between space and the literary text?

To answer this question, it is necessary to bear in mind the bi-directionality of the factual and fictional: the literary and the extraliterary dimensions are mutually influencing entities. Following this, it can be established that:

On the one hand, the study of the transgressions of narrative space within the postmodern Fantastic allows us to observe with clarity the interdependence between the literary text and the various contemporary conceptions of space. Examples of this can be seen in the multiple parallelisms established between literature and other perspectives of space originating outside the field of literary theory, such as the heterotopia (Foucault—"Mi hermana Elba"), the disjunction between body and postmodern space (Jameson, Vidler—"La casa"), the non-place (Augé—"The Enormous Space", "Dejen salir", "Une dure journée"), the loss of the existential position of the subject in space (Heidegger—"El museo", "Habitante", "The Enormous Space"), time-space compression (Harvey—"Trastornos de carácter"), the rhizome (Deleuze, Guattari—"Trastornos de carácter"), the liquefaction of the physical environment (Virilio, Tschumi—"Rien n'a de sens sinon intérieur"), horizontal vertigo (Borges, T. Ford, Villoro—"Tandis que roule le train"), the *simulacra* (Baudrillard—"La casa de muñecas"), the carceral space (De Certeau—"Dejen salir"), the disjunction between the mathematical and the human experiences of space (Bollnow, Lefebvre—"La brume"), Thirdspace (Soja—"Das Kapital"), quantum entanglement ("Das Kapital" and "Une dure journée"), the theory of the multiverse ("Une dure journée") and the end of a single version of History (Lyotard—"Los palafitos").

Yet, on the other hand, the ontological *transgression* of the spatial concepts that humans have established to organise their reality is a phenomenon that can take place only in fantastic fiction. By examining the spatial metaphors appearing in the fantastic text, it is possible to reach a better understanding of the importance of space in the construction of reality, in particular in the way it provides a consistent surface where the body rests (Chapter 2), in how it delimits the physical environment (Chapter 3), and in how it provides hierarchical order (Chapter 4) and ontological certitude (Chapter 5).

The study of narrative space in the Fantastic is by no means complete. There are several emergent areas with potential for academic investigation in the future, which were beyond the scope of this book. One of these is the development of new media and its repercussions for textual space within fantastic narratives (e.g., hypertext and the Fantastic). Furthermore, while this book has been centred on the specific historical parameters of the Postmodern, a complementary study could deal with this topic from a diachronical perspective. As with language and time—this latter being another dimension in need of further scholarly attention in the fantastic narrative—conceptions of space function as ideological elements that promote change within literary periods. Since the concept of space has evolved together with different philosophical, physical and aesthetic ideas, a history of the Fantastic in relation to the different concepts of space across time remains to be written. A better grasp of the evolutions of the idea of space would translate into a better understanding of the evolutionary traits of the Fantastic.

While much remains to be said about the relationship between the spatial dimension and the Fantastic, this book attempted to cast some light on the phenomenon of narrative space as transgressor of the real, which was labelled here the Fantastic of Space. As shown, this phenomenon is of particular relevance within the postmodern context. It is true that the Fantastic of Space pursues the same aim as any text of the Fantastic has done since the origins of the genre; the postmodern Fantastic, too, wants to reveal the frailty of the human being's model of reality. As in any fantastic text, this disarticulation is transmitted through the fantastic metaphor. However, in the phenomenon studied here, this metaphor did not arise from unusual beings or objects; it was instead space that was presented as extraordinary. Because it has been pivotal throughout the entire book, I will, to conclude, proceed to synthesise why the Fantastic of Space is fundamentally a postmodern phenomenon.

The structural and thematic constant behind the Fantastic of Space is the relativisation of the notion of reality by pointing to the *constructive* role space performs in this reality. Once again, this refers back to the etymology of 'architecture' and 'architect'. Space, a primary organising principle of the real, is also the principle through which it is revealed that reality is not objective and given but is constructed by the human being. We, as architects of our own reality, have built a system of boundaries, references, distances, volumes and spatial hierarchies to orientate ourselves in this reality. Space is thus undoubtedly a fundamental tool for constructing both fictional as well as empirical reality. Therefore, it comes as no surprise that within the ontological questioning haunting Postmodernity, space becomes a faithful accomplice in dismantling our certainties about the real.

The transgressions of the dimension of space studied here suggest that if there is an 'ordered' reality, if there is 'an architecture' to it, as Borges expressed it, this is necessarily an artifice. By destabilising the natural relationship between the real and space, the postmodern text of the Fantastic exposes space as *human* reality, a reality we have tailor-made; a work in constant motion—just as with Bachelard's nest-world of the quote opening this book—that we never stop remodelling.

Bibliography

LITERARY WORKS AND FILMS

Adolph, J. B. 2009. "La casa", in Portals Zubiate, G. (ed.) *La estirpe del ensueño*. Lima: El lampero alucinado ediciones.

———. 1975. "La casa", in *Mañana fuimos felices*. Lima: Instituto Nacional de Cultura.

Andersen, H. C. 2010. *Hans Andersen's Fairy Tales*. London: Puffin.

Augustine, S. 2009. *The City of God*. Peabody, Mass.: Hendrickson Publishers.

Ballard, J. G. 2008. *Concrete Island*. London: Harper Perennial.

———. 2008. *Crash*. London: Harper Perennial.

———. 2008. *Empire of the Sun*. London: Harper Perennial.

———. 2008. *Miracles of Life: Shanghai to Shepperton: An Autobiography*. London: Fourth Estate.

———. 2007. *Kingdom Come*. London: Harper Perennial.

———. 2006. "Motel Architecture", in *The Complete Short Stories*. London: Harper Perennial.

———. 2006. "Having a Wonderful Time", in *The Complete Short Stories*. London: Harper Perennial.

———. 2006. "The Enormous Space", in *The Complete Short Stories*. London: Harper Perennial.

———. 2006. "The Giocconda of the Twilight Moon", in *The Complete Short Stories*. London: Harper Perennial.

———. 2006. "The Terminal Beach", in *The Complete Short Stories*. London: Harper Perennial.

———. 2000. *Super-Cannes*. London: Flamingo.

———. 1996. *Cocaine Nights*. London: Flamingo.

———. 1993. *High-Rise*. London: Flamingo.

———. 1992. *The Kindness of Women*. London: Grafton.

Barth, J. 1969. *Lost in the Funhouse: Fiction for Print, Tape, Live Voice*. London: Secker & Warburg.

Beaumier, J. 1991. *Petites lâchetés*. Quebec: L'Instant Même.

———. 1988. "Dérapage", in *L'Air libre*. Quebec: L'Instant Même.

———. 1988. "L'Examen", in *L'Air libre*. Quebec: L'Instant Même.

———. 1988. "Retour", in *L'Air libre*. Quebec: L'Instant Même.

———. 1988. "Une dure journée", in *L'Air libre*. Quebec: L'Instant Même.

Bergeron, B. 1986. *Parcours improbables*. Quebec: L'Instant Même.

———. 1990. *Transits: nouvelles*. Quebec: L'Instant Même.

Bierce, A. 2004. "The Boarded Window", in Blume, T. Donald (ed.) *Tales of Soldiers and Civilians and other Stories*. New York; London: Penguin.

————. "The Suitable Surroundings", in Blume, T. Donald (ed.) *Tales of Soldiers and Civilians and other Stories*. New York; London: Penguin.

Borges, J. L. 1999. "The Aleph", in *Collected Fictions*. London: Allen Lane.

————. 1999. "The Book of Sand", in *Collected Fictions*. London: Allen Lane.

————. 1999. "The Circular Ruins", in *Collected Fictions*. London: Allen Lane.

————. 1999. "The House of Asterion", in *Collected Fictions*. London: Allen Lane.

————. 1999. "The Immortal", in *Collected Fictions*. London: Allen Lane.

————. 1999. "The Library of Babel", in *Collected Fictions*. London: Allen Lane.

————. 1999. "The Man on the Threshold", in *Collected Fictions*. London: Allen Lane.

————. 1999. "The Other", in *Collected Fictions*. London: Allen Lane.

————. 1999. "Tlön, Uqbar, Orbis Tertius", in *Collected Fictions*. London: Allen Lane.

Calvino, I. 1974. *Invisible Cities*. London: Secker and Warburg.

Card, O. S. 1991. "Lost Boys", in *Maps in a Mirror*. London: Legend.

Carroll, J. 1995. "The Jane Fonda Room", in *The Panic Hand*. London: HarperCollins.

Clapin, J. 2008. *Skhizein*. Dark Prince Productions, France [short film].

Connolly, J. 2004. "The Inn at Shillingford", in *Nocturnes*. London: Hodder & Stoughton.

Cortázar, J. 1970. "Casa tomada", in *Relatos. Bestiario, 1951. Las armas secretas, 1959. Final del juego, 1964. Todos los fuegos el fuego, 1966*. Buenos Aires: Editorial Sudamericana.

————. 1970. "La puerta condenada", in *Relatos. Bestiario, 1951. Las armas secretas, 1959. Final del juego, 1964. Todos los fuegos el fuego, 1966*. Buenos Aires: Editorial Sudamericana.

————. 1970. "Continuidad de los parques", in *Relatos. Bestiario, 1951. Las armas secretas, 1959. Final del juego, 1964. Todos los fuegos el fuego, 1966*. Buenos Aires: Editorial Sudamericana.

————. 1970. "El otro cielo", in *Relatos. Bestiario, 1951. Las armas secretas, 1959. Final del juego, 1964. Todos los fuegos el fuego, 1966*. Buenos Aires: Editorial Sudamericana.

————. 1970. "La autopista del Sur", in *Relatos. Bestiario, 1951. Las armas secretas, 1959. Final del juego, 1964. Todos los fuegos el fuego, 1966*. Buenos Aires: Editorial Sudamericana.

————. 1970. "Lejana", in *Relatos. Bestiario, 1951. Las armas secretas, 1959. Final del juego, 1964. Todos los fuegos el fuego, 1966*. Buenos Aires: Editorial Sudamericana.

Crowley, J. 1983. *Little, Big*. London: Methuen.

Defoe, D. 2010. *Robinson Crusoe*. London: Harper Press.

Deutsch, A. J. 1968. "A Subway Named Mobius", in: Knight, D. (ed.) *One Hundred Years of Science Fiction*. London: Simon and Schuster.

Doménech, R. 1980. "La escalera de Sarto", in *La pirámide de Kheops*. Madrid: E.M.E.S.a.

Dostoyevsky, F. 2000. *Crime and Punishment*. London: Wordsworth Classics.

Doyle, A. C., Sir. 2010. *The Valley of Fear*. London: Bibliolis Books.

Dufour, M. 1991. "Le Corps éparpillé", in *Passé la frontière*. Quebec: L'Instant Même.

————. 1989. *Circuit fermé: nouvelles*. Quebec: L'Instant Même.

Esteban Erlés, P. 2010. *Azul ruso*. Madrid: Páginas de espuma.

————. 2008. "Habitante", in *Manderley en venta*. Zaragoza: Tropo Editores.

Faye, É. 1997. "Tandis que roule le train", in *Je suis le gardien du phare*. Paris: José Corti.

Fernández Cubas, C. 2008. "Mi hermana Elba", in *Todos los cuentos*. Barcelona: Tusquets.

———. 2008. "Los altillos de Brumal", in *Todos los cuentos*. Barcelona: Tusquets.

———. 2008. *El columpio*, in *Todos los cuentos*. Barcelona: Tusquets.

———. 2008. "En el hemisferio sur", in *Todos los cuentos*. Barcelona: Tusquets.

———. 2008. "Mundo", in *Todos los cuentos*. Barcelona: Tusquets.

———. 2008. "La noche de Jezabel", in *Todos los cuentos*. Barcelona: Tusquets.

———. 2008. "La ventana en el jardín", in *Todos los cuentos*. Barcelona: Tusquets.

Ferrer-Bermejo, J. 1982. "Dejen salir", in *Incidente en Atocha*. Madrid: Ediciones Alfaguara.

García Márquez, G. 2006. *One Hundred Years of Solitude*. London: Folio Society.

Gaudé, L. 2008. *La Porte des enfers*. Paris: Actes Sud.

Gautier, T. 1972. "Hashish Club", in *Hashis, Wine, Opium*. London: Calder and Boyars.

Ghelderode, M. de. 2001. "Le Jardin malade", in *Sortilèges*. Brussels: Labor.

Girard, J. P. 1999; 1992. *Espaces à occuper: nouvelles*. Quebec: L'Instant Même.

Shakespeare, W. 2012. *Hamlet*. Thatcham: Gardners Books Ltd.

Hill, J. 2005. "Voluntary Committal", in *20th Century Ghosts*. London: Gollancz.

Hoffmann, E. T. A. 1825. *Fantasiestücke*, in Callot's Manier. Leipzig: s.n.

———. 1825. *Nachtstücke*. Leipzig: s.n.

———. 1996. "The Deserted House", in *Fantasie—und Nachtstücke*. Düsseldorf; Zürich: Artemis & Winkle.

Homer. 1887. *Odyssey*. Oxford: Clarendon Press.

Ireland, I. A. 1983. "Climax for a Ghost Story", in: Manguel, A. (ed.) *Black Water: The Anthology of Fantastic Literature*. London: Picador.

Iwasaki, F. 2004. "El dominio", in *Ajuar funerario*. Madrid: Páginas de Espuma.

———. 2004. "El salón antiguo", in *Ajuar funerario*. Madrid: Páginas de Espuma.

———. 2004. "Hasta en la sopa", in *Ajuar funerario*. Madrid: Páginas de Espuma.

———. 2004. "La casa de muñecas", in *Ajuar funerario*. Madrid: Páginas de Espuma.

———. 2004. "La cueva", in *Ajuar funerario*. Madrid: Páginas de Espuma.

———. 2004. "La habitación maldita", in *Ajuar funerario*. Madrid: Páginas de Espuma.

———. 2004. "Monsieur le révenant", in *Ajuar funerario*. Madrid: Páginas de Espuma.

Jackson, S. 1999. *The Haunting of Hill House*. London: Robinson.

James, H. 2011. *The Turn of the Screw*. London: Penguin.

James, M. R. 2008. "The Haunted Dolls' House", in *The Haunted Dolls' House and Other Stories*. London: Penguin.

Joyce, J. 2012. "Eveline", in *Dubliners*. Richmond: Alma Classics.

Kafka, F. 2009. *Metamorphosis*. Edison, N.J.: Chartwell Books.

King, S. 2002. "1408", in *Everything's Eventual: 14 Dark Tales*. London: Hodder & Stoughton.

Leroux, G. 1920. *Le Mystère de la chambre jaune*. Paris: Editions Pierre Lafitte.

Lovecraft, H. P. 2005. "The Thing on the Doorstep", in S. T. Joshi (ed.) *The Dreams in the Witch House and Other Weird Stories*. London: Penguin Books.

———. 2005. "The Shunned House", in *The Dreams in the Witch House and Other Weird Stories*. London: Penguin.

———. 2005. "The Nameless City", in *Through the Gates of the Silver Key*. London: Penguin.

———. 1993. "The Unnamable", in *Crawling Chaos: Selected Works 1920–1935*. London: Creation.

———. 1993. *The Shadow over Innsmouth*. London: Penguin.

———. 1984. "The Music of Erich Zann", in *The Dunwich Horror and Others*. Sauk City: Arkham House.

Mandiargues, A. P. d. 1966. "Le Diamant", in *Feu de braise*. Paris: Grasset.

Martin, G. R. R. 1996. *A Game of Thrones: The Opening Chapters of Book One of A Song of Ice and Fire*. London: Voyager.

Matheson, R. 1977. *Hell House*. Toronto; London: Bantam.

Mathieu, C. 2002. *La Mort exquise*. Quebec: L'Instant Même.

Maupassant, G. de. 1997. "Who Knows?", in *The Best Short Stories*. Ware: Wordsworth Editions.

———. 1976. *Le Horla et autres contes cuels et fantastiques*. Paris: Éditions Garnier frères.

Merino, J. M. 2004. "La casa feliz", in *Cuentos de los días raros*. Madrid: Alfaguara.

———. 2002. "Ecosistema", in *Días imaginarios*. Barcelona: Seix Barral.

———. 2002. "Intimidad cibernética", in *Días imaginarios*. Barcelona: Seix Barral.

———. 2002. "Los viajeros perdidos", in *Días imaginarios*. Barcelona: Seix Barral.

———. 2001. *El viajero perdido*. Barcelona: RBA Coleccionables.

———. 1994. "El caso del traductor infiel", in *Cuentos del barrio del refugio*. Madrid: Alfaguara.

———. 1982. "La casa de los dos portales", in *Cuentos del reino secreto*. Madrid: Alfaguara.

———. 1982. "La noche más larga", in *Cuentos del reino secreto*. Madrid: Alfaguara.

———. 1982. "Nacimiento en el desván", in *Cuentos del reino secreto*. Madrid: Alfaguara.

———. 1982. "Valle del silencio", in *Cuentos del reino secreto*. Madrid: Alfaguara.

———. 1982. "El museo", in *Cuentos del reino secreto*. Madrid: Alfaguara.

Millás, J. J. 2010. *Lo que sé de los hombrecillos*. Barcelona: Seix Barral.

———. 2008. *Los objetos nos llaman*. Barcelona: Seix Barral.

———. 2001. "Oraciones metro a metro", in *Cuentos a la intemperie*. Madrid: SM.

———. 1998. "La casa vacía", in *Ella imagina*. Madrid: Santillana.

———. 1989. "El clavo del que uno se ahorca", in *Primavera de luto*. Madrid: Santillana.

———. 1989. "Trastornos de carácter", in *Primavera de luto*. Madrid: Santillana.

Monzó, Q. 1996. "La força centrípeda", in *Guadalajara*. New York & Rochester: Open Letter.

More, Thomas, Sir. 2010. *Utopia*. London: Bibliolis Books.

Nerval, G. d. 1971. *Aurélia*. Paris: Société d'édition d'enseignement supérieur.

O'Brien, F. 2007. *The Third Policeman*. London: Harper Perennial.

Olgoso, Á. 2013. *Las frutas de la luna*. Palencia: Menoscuarto.

———. 2009. "El proyecto", in *La máquina de languidecer*. Madrid: Páginas de Espuma.

———. 2009. "El purgatorio", in *La máquina de languidecer*. Madrid: Páginas de Espuma.

———. 2007. *Astrolabio*. Granada: Cuadernos del Vigía.

———. 2007. "Ingnición", in *Los demonios del lugar*. Córdoba: Almuzara.

———. 2007. "Los palafitos", in *Los demonios del lugar*. Córdoba: Almuzara.

———. 2003. *Cuentos de otro mundo*. Granada: Dauro.

Palma, Félix J. 1998. "Venco a la molinera", in *El vigilante de la salamandra*. Valencia: Pre-Textos.

Pellerin, G. 1991. *Principe d'extorsion: nouvelles*. Quebec: L'Instant Même.

———. 1987. *Ni le lieu ni l'heure: nouvelles*. Quebec: L'Instant Même.

Poe, E. A. 2004. "The Fall of the House of Usher", in *The Selected Writings of Edgar Allan Poe*. New York; London: W. W. Norton & Co.

———. 2004. "The Murders in the Rue Morgue", in *The Selected Writings of Edgar Allan Poe*. New York; London: W. W. Norton & Co.

———. 2004. "The Tale-Tell Heart", in *The Selected Writings of Edgar Allan Poe*. New York; London: W. W. Norton & Co.

Potocki, J. 1995. *The Manuscript Found in Saragossa*. London: Viking.

Radcliffe, A. W. 1992. *The Mysteries of Udolpho*. Oxford: Oxford U.P.

Roas, D. 2010. "Das Kapital", in *Distorsiones*. Madrid: Páginas de espuma.

———. 2010. "Duplicados", in *Distorsiones*. Madrid: Páginas de espuma.

———. 2010. "Excepciones", in *Distorsiones*. Madrid: Páginas de espuma.

———. 2010. "La casa ciega", in *Distorsiones*. Madrid: Páginas de espuma.

———. 2007. *Horrores cotidianos*. Palencia: Menoscuarto.

Schwob, M. 2008. "Un squelette", in *Un Coeur double*. Paris: Flammarion.

Shelley, M. W. 2008. *Frankenstein*. London: Penguin.

Siddons, A. R. 1979. *The House Next Door*. London: Collins.

Sternberg, J. 1998. "La Brume", in *Contes glacés*. Brussels: Labor.

———. 1998. "Les Traces", in *Contes glacés*. Brussels: Labor.

———. 1998. "L'Erreur", in *Contes glacés*. Brussels: Labor.

———. 1998. "L'Étage", in *Contes glacés*. Brussels: Labor.

———. 1998. "L'Étage", in *Contes glacés*. Brussels: Labor.

———. 1998. "La Sanction", in *Contes glacés*. Brussels: Labor.

———. 1998. "Le Tunnel", in *Contes glacés*. Brussels: Labor.

———. 1988. "La Banlieue", in *188 Contes à régler*. Paris: Denoël.

Stoker, B. 2003. *Dracula*. New York: Barnes & Noble.

Swift, J. 2010. *Gulliver's Travels*. London: Harper Press.

Thériault, M-J. 1978. *La Cérémonie: contes*. Montréal: La Presse.

Tolkien, J. R. R. 2011. *The Hobbit; The Lord of the Rings*. London: Harper Collins.

Vigalondo, N. 2009. *Marisa*. Produced by Nahikari Ipiña. [short film].

———. *The Door in the Wall, and Other Stories*. London: Grant Richards.

Walpole, H. 2010. *The Castle of Otranto*. London: Bibliolis Books.

Wells, H. G. 2006. "The Crystal Egg" in *The Crystal Egg and Other Tales*. Na: Alan Rodgers Books.

Yance, C. 1997. "Rien n'a de sens sinon intérieur", in: Grégoire, C. (ed.) *Le Fantastique même: une anthologie québécoise*. Quebec: L'Instant Même.

CRITICAL WORKS

Abuenque, P. 1962. *Le Problème de l'être chez Aristote*. Paris: PUF.

Aguirre, M. 1990. *The Closed Space: Horror Literature and Western Symbolism*. Manchester: Manchester University Press.

Aínsa, F. 2006. *Del topos al logos. Propuestas de geopoética*. Frankfurt am Main: Iberoamericana Vervuert.

Alazraki, J. 1983. *En busca del unicornio: los cuentos de Julio Cortázar; elementos para una poética de lo neofantástico.* Madrid: Gredos.

Alonso, S. 2000. "Introducción", in: Merino, José María. *Cuentos.* Madrid: Castalia.

Álvarez Méndez, N. 2002. *Espacios narrativos.* León: Universidad de León, Secretariado de Publicaciones y Medios Audiovisuales.

Andrade Boué, P., et al. 2010. *Espacios y tiempos de lo fantástico.* Bern: Peter Lang.

Andres-Suárez (ed.) 2008. "La era de la brevedad: el microrrelato hispánico", in *Internacional de Minificción.* Palencia: Menoscuarto.

Andres-Suárez, I.; Casas, A. (eds.) 2009. *Juan José Millás.* Cuadernos de Narrativa colection. Madrid: Arco/Libros.

———. 2007. *Cristina Fernández Cubas.* Cuadernos de Narrativa colection. Madrid: Arco/Libros.

———. 2005. *José María Merino.* Cuadernos de Narrativa colection. Madrid: Arco/Libros.

Andres-Suárez, I. 1997. "El cuento fantástico actual: la influencia de Julio Cortázar: Lo fantástico en José María Merino". *Lucanor,* 14. pp. 131–151.

Armitt, L. 1996. *Theorising the Fantastic.* London: Arnold.

Attebery, B. 1992. *Strategies of Fantasy.* Bloomington: Indiana University Press.

Augé, M. 2008. *Non-places. An Introduction to Supermodernity.* London: Verso.

———. 2000. *Fictions fin de siècle.* Paris: Fayard.

Bachelard, G. 1994. *The Poetics of Space.* Boston: Beacon Press.

Bakhtin, M. 2003. *Problems of Dostoevsky's Poetics.* Minneapolis: University of Minnesota Press.

———. 1981. "Forms of Time and of the Chronotope in the Novel". *The Dialogic Imagination.* Austin: Univ. Texas Press. pp. 84–258.

Bal, M. 2009. *Narratology: Introduction to the Theory of Narrative.* Toronto: University of Toronto Press.

———. 2006. *A Mieke Bal Reader.* Chicago; London: University of Chicago Press.

Ballard, J. G. 1962. "Which Way to Inner Space?", in *New World Science Fiction,* 40, pp. 116–118.

Baronian, J. (ed.) 1975. *La Belgique fantastique: avant et après Jean Ray.* Verviers: Gérard.

Barthes, R. 1968. "L'Effet de réel". *Communications,* 11, pp. 84–89.

Baudrillard, J. 1994. *Simulacra and Simulation.* Ann Arbor: University of Michigan Press.

Baxter, J. 2009. *J. G. Ballard's Surrealist Imagination: Spectacular Authorship.* Farnham: Ashgate.

Beilin, K. O. 2004. "Cristina Fernández Cubas: Me gusta que me inquieten", in: Beilin, K. O. (ed.) *Conversaciones con novelistas contemporáneos.* Madrid: Tamesis, pp. 127–147.

Belevan, H. 1977. *Antología del cuento fantástico peruano.* Lima: Universidad Nacional Mayor de San Marcos.

Bellemin-Noël, J. 2001. "Notas sobre lo fantástico", in: Roas, D (ed.) *Teorías de lo fantástico.* Madrid: Arco/Libros.

Berger, P. L.; Luckman, T. 1967. *The Social Construction of Reality. A Treatise in the Sociology of Knowledge.* London: Allen Lane, The Penguin Press.

Berthelot, F. 2005. *Bibliothèque de l'Entre-mondes.* Paris: Gallimard.

Berthin, C. 2010. *Gothic Hauntings: Melancholy Crypts and Textual Ghosts.* Basingstoke: Palgrave Macmillan.

Bessière, I. 1974. *Le Récit fantastique. La poétique de l'incertain.* Paris: Larousse Université.

Bhabha, H. K. 1994. *The Location of Culture.* London: Routledge.

Blanchot, M. 1982. *The Space of Literature.* Lincoln, Neb.; London: University of Nebraska Press.

Boa, E. 1996. *Kafka: Gender, Class and Race in the Letters and Fictions.* Oxford: Clarendon Press.

Bollnow, O. F. 2011. *Human Space.* London: Hyphen.

Bozzetto, R. 2005. *Passages des fantastiques: des imaginaires à l'inimaginable.* Aix-en-Provence: Publications de l'Université de Provence.

Bridgeman, T. 2007. "Time and Space", in: Herman, D. (ed.) *The Cambridge Companion to Narrative.* Cambridge: Cambridge University Press.

Brittnacher, H. R. 2006. "Gescheiterte Initiationen. Anthropologische Dimensionen der literarischen Phantastik", in: Ruthner, C., et al. (eds.) *Nach Todorov: Beiträge zu einer Definition des Phantastischen in der Literatur.* Tübingen: Francke, pp. 15–30.

Brod, M. (ed.) 1965. The Diaries of Franz Kafka 1910–1923. Harmondsworth: Penguin.

Brooke-Rose, C. 1981. *A Rhetoric of the Unreal: Studies in Narrative and Structure, especially of the Fantastic.* Cambridge: Cambridge University Press.

Burke, E. 2008. *A Philosophical Enquiry into the Sublime and Beautiful.* London: Routledge.

Caillois, R. 1975. *Obliques; precedé de Images, images.* Paris: Gallimard.

———. 1972. "Mimetisme et psychasthenie legendaire", in *Le Mythe et l'homme.* Paris: Gallimard.

Caland, F. C. 2003. "Partition, répartition et fonctions de l'espace dans la littérature fantastique", in Vion-Dury J., Grassin J-M., Westphal B. (eds.) *Littérature et espaces.* Limoges: Presses Universitaires de Limoges.

Campbell, J. 2008. *The Hero's Journey: The World of Joseph Campbell: Joseph Campbell on His Life and Work.* San Francisco: Harper & Row.

Campra, R. 2008. *Territorios de la ficción. Lo fantástico.* Sevilla: Renacimiento.

———. 2001. "Lo fantástico: una isotopía de la transgresión", in: Roas, D. (ed.) *Teorías de lo fantástico.* Madrid: Arco/Libros, pp. 153–192.

Candau, A. 1992. *La obra narrativa de José María Merino.* León: Diputación provincial de León.

Carpentier, A. 2007. *Ruptures: genres de la Nouvelle et du Fantastique.* Montreal: Le Quartanier.

Carringer, R. L. 1974. "Circumscription of Space and the Form of Poe's Arthur Gordon Pym". *PMLA,* 89 (3), pp. 506–516.

Carter, E., *et. al.* 2005. *Space and Place: Theories of Identity and Location.* London: Lawrence & Wishart.

Casas, A. 2010. "Transgresión lingüística y microrrelato fantástico" in 'Lo fantástico en España (1980–2010)'. *Ínsula: Revista De Letras y Ciencias Humanas,* 765, pp. 10–13.

———. 2009. "Una poética de lo fronterizo: *Ella imagina* de Juan José Millás" in: Andres-Suárez, I.; Casas, A. (eds.) *Juan José Millás.* Cuadernos de Narrativa colection. Madrid: Arco/Libros, pp. 203–215.

Casey, E. S. 1997. *The Fate of Place: A Philosophical History.* Berkeley; London: University of California Press.

Castells, M. 2010. *The Rise of the Network Society.* Oxford: Wiley-Blackwell.

Castex, P. G. 1951. *Le Conte fantastique en France de Nodier à Maupassant*. Paris: José Corti.

Castro, A. 2002. *El encuentro imposible: la conformación del fantástico ambiguo en la narrativa breve argentina (1862–1910)*. Göteborg: Acta Universitatis Gothoburgensis.

Castro Díez, A. 2000. "El cuento fantástico de Cristina Fernández Cubas", in: Villalba Álvarez, M. (ed.) *Mujeres novelistas en el panorama literario del siglo XX*. Cuenca: Ediciones de la Universidad de Castilla La Mancha, pp. 237–246.

Certeau, M. d. 1988. *The Practice of Everyday Life*. Berkeley, Calif.; London: University of California Press.

Ceserani, R. 1999. *Lo fantástico*. Madrid: Visor.

Chan Lee, C. 2005. *Metaficción y mundos posibles en la narrativa de José María Merino*. Valladolid: Universidad de Valladolid.

Ching, F. 1996. *Architecture: Form, Space and Order*. New York: Bloomer, Kent C.

Clute, J. and Grant, J. (eds.) 1999. *The Encyclopedia of Fantasy*. London: Orbit.

Conrad, J. 2010. "Geography and Some Explorers" in Ray Stevens, H.; Stape, J. H. (eds.) *Last Essays*. Cambridge: Cambridge University Press, pp. 3–17.

Cornwell, N. 1990. *The Literary Fantastic: From Gothic to Postmodernism*. London: Harvester Wheatsheaf.

Corroto, P. 2011. *"La realidad está llena de agujeros negros". Cristina Fernández Cubas. Publica 'Cosas que ya no existen'* [Online]. Available from: http://www.publico.es/culturas/359671/la-realidad-esta-llena-de-agujeros-negros [Accessed September 2014].

Costa, J., et al. 2008. *J. G. Ballard Autòpsia del nou mil.leni*. Barcelona: CCCB; Direcció de Comunicació de la Diputació de Barcelona.

Damasio, A. 2007. *En busca de Spinoza. Neurobiología de la emoción y los sentimientos*. Barcelona: Crítica.

Davies, P. C. W. 1996. *El espacio y el tiempo en el universo contemporáneo*. México: Fondo de Cultura Económica.

Davis, M. 1990. *City of Quartz: Excavating the Future in Los Angeles*. London: Verso.

Deleuze, G. and Guattari, F. 2004. *A Thousand Plateaus: Capitalism and Schizophrenia*. London: Continuum.

Delville, M. 1998. *J. G. Ballard*. Plymouth: Northcote House in association with the British Council.

Descartes, R. 2008. *Discourse on the Method: of Rightly Conducting the Reason and Seeking Truth in the Sciences*. New York: Cosimo.

DiSalle, R. 2006. *Understanding Space-Time: The Philosophical Development of Physics from Newton to Einstein*. Cambridge: Cambridge University Press.

Doležel, L. 1998. *Heterocosmica: Fiction and Possible Worlds*. Baltimore; London: Johns Hopkins University Press.

Durand, G. 1999. *The Anthropological Structures of the Imaginary*. Brisbane: Boombana.

Eamond, M. (ed.) 1987. *Anthologie de la nouvelle et du conte fantastiques québécois au XXe siècle*. Montreal: Fides.

Eckhard, P., et al. (eds.) 2010. *Landscapes of Postmodernity: Concepts and Paradigms of Critical Theory*. Berlin: LIT.

Eco, U. 1994. *Six Walks in the Fictional Woods*. Cambridge, Mass.; London: Harvard University Press.

———. 1979. *The Role of the Reader: Explorations in the Semiotics of Texts*. Bloomington; London: Indiana University Press.

Erdal Jordan, M. 1998. *La narrativa fantástica: evolución del género y su relación con las concepciones del lenguaje.* Madrid: Iberoamericana.
Feynman, R. P. 1995. *Six Easy Pieces: Essentials of physics explained by its most brilliant teacher.* Reading, Mass.; Wokingham: Helix Books.
Finné, J. 2006. *Panorama de la littérature fantastique américaine.* Liège: Editions du Céfal.
Ford, R. T. 1993. "Spaced Out in L.A." *Transition,* 61, pp. 82–112.
Foucault, M. 1999. *Religion and Culture.* Manchester: Manchester University Press.
———. 1986. "Of Other Spaces". *Diacritics,* 16 (1), pp. 22–27.
Fournier Kiss, C. 2007. *La Ville européenne dans la littérature fantastique du tournant du siècle, (1860–1915).* Lausanne: Age d'homme.
Francese, J. 1997. *Narrating Postmodern Time and Space.* Albany: State University of New York Press.
Frank, J. 1945. "Spatial Form in Modern Literature: An Essay in Three Parts". *The Sewanee Review,* 53 (4), pp. 643–653.
Freud, S. 2003. *The Uncanny.* London: Penguin.
Gaarder, J. 1994. *Sophie's World.* London: Phoenix.
Gama-Khalil, M. M. 2008. "A terceira margem do rio: a espacialidade narrativa como instigadora do fantástico", in: Gama-Khalil, M. M., et al. (eds.) *O ESPACO (EN)CENA.* São Carlos: Claraluz.
García, L., et al. 2010. "Dossier José B. Adolph", in *Tinta Expresa. Literatura Fantástica y Ciencia Ficción,* 4, Universidad Nacional Mayor de San Marcos.
García, P. 2013a. "La frase umbral: desliz al espacio fantástico", in Roas, D; García, P. (eds.). *Visiones de lo fantástico (aproximaciones teóricas).* Malaga: E.D.A, 2013, pp. 27–38.
———. 2013b. "The Fantastic Hole: Towards a Definition of the Fantastic Transgression as a Phenomenon of Space". *Brumal: Research Journal on the Fantastic.* Vol. 1, pp. 15–35.
———. 2013c. "El espacio como sujeto fantástico: el ejemplo de 'Los palafitos' (Ángel Olgoso, 2007)". *Pasavento. Revista de Estudios Hispánicos.* Vol. I, no. 1, pp. 113–124.
———. 2012. "The Fantastic of Place versus the Fantastic of Space". *Revista Letras&Letras.* Vol. 29, pp. 543–557.
Genette, G. 1992. *The Architext: An Introduction.* Berkeley; Oxford: University of California Press.
———. 1972. *Figures III.* Paris: Seuil.
Gennep, A. v. 1977. *The Rites of Passage.* London: Routledge and Kegan Paul.
Gomel, E. 2014. *Narrative Space and Time: Representing Impossible Topologies in Literature.* New York; London: Routledge.
Goodman, N. 1984. *Of Mind and Other Matters.* Cambridge, Mass.; London: Harvard University Press.
Greene, B. 1999. *The Elegant Universe: Superstrings, Hidden Dimensions, and the Quest for the Ultimate Theory.* London: Jonathan Cape.
Grivel, C. 1983. *Le Fantastique.* Mannheim: Mannheimer-Analytika.
Grossman, S. 2004. "Le fantastique contemporain du Quebec", in: *Revue IRIS. Centre de recherche sur l'imaginaire.* Grenoble: Université Stendhal, pp. 79–92.
———. 2000. "Le postmodernisme dans le fantastique québécois". *Quebec Studies,* 30, pp. 101–109.
Guillaud, L., Prince, N. (eds.) 2008. *L'Indicible dans les littératures fantastique et de science-fiction.* Paris: Houdiard.
Gullón, R. 1980. *Espacio y novela.* Barcelona: Bosch.

Hallet, W., Neumann, B. (eds.) 2009. *Raum und Bewegung in der Literatur: die Literaturwissenschaften und der Spatial Turn.* Bielefeld: Transcript.

Hamon, P. 1992. *Expositions: Literature and Architecture in Nineteenth-century France.* Berkeley; Oxford: University of California Press.

———. 1991. *La Description littéraire: anthologie de textes théoriques et critiques.* Paris: Macula.

———. 1972. "Qu'est-ce qu'une description?", *Poétique*, 12, pp. 465–485.

Harvey, D. 1990. *The Condition of Postmodernity: An Enquiry into the Origins of Cultural Change.* Oxford: Basil Blackwell.

Hassan, I. H. 1971. *The Dismemberment of Orpheus. Toward a Postmodern Literature.* New York: Oxford University Press.

Heidegger, M. 1971. "Building, Dwelling, Thinking", in: *Poetry, Language, Thought.* New York: Harper Colophon Books.

Herman, D. 2002. *Story Logic: Problems and Possibilities of Narrative.* Lincoln, Neb.; Chesham: University of Nebraska Press; Combined Academic.

Hofstadter, D. R. 1999. *Gödel, Escher, Bach: An Eternal Golden Braid.* New York: Basic Books.

Horstkotte, M. 2004. *The Postmodern Fantastic in Contemporary British Fiction.* Trier: Wissen shaftlicher Verlag Trier.

Hume, K. 1984. *Fantasy and Mimesis: Responses to Reality in Western Literature.* New York; London: Methuen.

Hutcheon, L. 1988. *A Poetics of Postmodernism: History, Theory, Fiction.* New York; London: Routledge.

Iser, W. 1978a. *The Act of Reading: A Theory of Aesthetic Response.* London: Routledge and Kegan Paul.

———. 1978b. *The Implied Reader: Patterns of Communication in Prose Fiction from Bunyan to Beckett.* Baltimore; London: Johns Hopkins University Press.

Jackson, R. 1981. *Fantasy: The Literature of Subversion.* London: Methuen.

Jakes, I. 1996. *Theoretical Approaches to Obsessive-Compulsive Disorder.* Cambridge; New York: Cambridge University Press.

Jameson, F. 1998. *Postmodernism, or, The Cultural Logic of Late Capitalism.* London: Verso.

Jammer, M. 1993. *Concepts of Space: the History of Theories of Space in Physics.* New York; London: Dover Publications; Constable.

Kaku, M. 2005. *Parallel Worlds.* New York: Doubleday.

———. 1994. *Hyperspace: A scientific odyssey through parallel universes, time warps, and the tenth dimension.* New York; Oxford: Oxford University Press.

Knickerbocker, D. 2003. *Juan José Millás. The Obsessive-Compulsive Aesthetic.* New York; Oxford: Peter Lang.

———. 2000. "Identidad y otredad en *Primavera de luto* de Juan José Millás." *Letras Peninsulares,* 13 (2), pp. 119–137.

Koolhas, R. 2002. "Junkspace". *Obsolescence,* 100, pp. 175–190.

Laflamme, S. 2009. *Récits fantastiques québécois contemporains.* Montreal: Beauchemin.

Lefebvre, H. 1998. *The Production of Space.* Oxford: Basil Blackwell.

Leibniz, G. W. von. 1965. *Monadology and Other Philosophical Essays.* Indianapolis: Bobbs-Merrill Company.

Lessing, G. E. 1836. *Laocoon: or the Limits of Poetry and Painting.* London: Ridgway & Sons.

Lockhart, D. B. 2004. *Latin American Science Fiction Writers: An A-to-Z guide.* Westport, Conn.; London: Greenwood Press.

Lord, M. 1995. *La logique de l'impossible. Aspects du discours fantastique québécois.* Québec: Nuit Blanche Editeur.

———. 1993b. "L'écriture fantastique au Quebec depuis 1980". *Présence Francophone,* (42), pp. 159–178.

Lovecraft, H. P. 2008. *Supernatural Horror in Literature and other Literary Essays.* LLC: Wildside Press.

———. 1984. *El horror en la literatura.* Madrid: Alianza Editorial.

Luckhurst, R. 1997. *The Angle Between Two Walls: The Fiction of J. G. Ballard.* Liverpool: Liverpool University Press.

Lyotard, J. 1984. *The Postmodern Condition: A Report on Knowledge.* Manchester: Manchester University Press.

Manguel, A. 1981. *The Dictionary of Imaginary Places.* London: Granada Publishing.

Margolin, U. 2005. "Character", in: Herman, D., et al. (eds.) *Routledge Encyclopedia of Narrative Theory.* London: Routledge.

Massey, D. B. 1994. *Space, Place and Gender.* Cambridge: Polity.

May, M. 2006. "Die Zeit aus den Fugen. Chronotopen der phantastischen Literatur", in: Ruthner, C., et al. (eds.) *Nach Todorov: Beiträge zu einer Definition des Phantastischen in der Literatur.* Tübingen: Francke.

McHale, B. 1987. *Postmodernist Fiction.* London: Methuen.

McKenzie, E. 1994. *Privatopia: Homeowner Associations and the Rise of Residential Private Government.* New Haven; London: Yale University Press.

Medina, S. 2006. *Figments of Space: Space as Metaphor in Jorge Luis Borges, with particular emphasis on 'Ficciones' and 'El Aleph'.* Ph.D. University of London.

Merleau-Ponty, M. 1962. *Phenomenology of Perception.* London: Routledge & Kegan Paul.

Moretti, F. 2005. *Graphs, Maps, Trees: Abstract Models for a Literary History.* London: Verso.

———. 1998. *Atlas of the European Novel.* London: Verso.

Mualem, S. 2012. *Borges and Plato: A Game with Shifting Mirrors.* Madrid; Frankfurt am Main: Iberoamericana; Vervuert.

Muñoz Rengel, J. J. (ed.) 2009. *Perturbaciones: Antología del relato fantástico español actual.* Madrid: Salto de Página.

Nietzsche, F. W. 2001. *The Gay Science.* Cambridge: Cambridge University Press.

Olalquiaga, C. 1992. *Megalopolis: Contemporary Cultural Sensibilities.* Minneapolis: University of Minnesota Press.

Olsen, L. 1987. *Ellipse of Uncertainty: an Introduction to Postmodern Fantasy.* New York; London: Greenwood.

Osborne, C. 1967. *Kafka.* Edinburgh; London: Oliver & Boyd.

Pallasmaa, J. 2005. *The Eyes of the Skin: Architecture and the Senses.* London: Academy Editions.

Pavel, T. G. 1986. *Fictional Worlds.* Cambridge, Mass.: Harvard University Press.

Paz, O. 1983. *El ogro filantrópico: historia y política (1971–1978).* Barcelona: Seix Barral.

Pimentel, L. A. 2001. *El espacio en la ficción: la representación del espacio en los textos narrativos.* México D.F.: Siglo XXI.

Poe, E. A. 2004. "The Philosophy of Composition", in *The Selected Writings of Edgar Allan Poe: Authoritative texts, backgrounds and contexts, criticism.* New York; London: W. W. Norton & Co.

————. 1846. "The Philosophy of Composition".

Poulet, G. 1961. *Les Métamorphoses du cercle*. Paris: Plon.

Prince, G. 1987. *A Dictionary of Narratology*. Lincoln: University of Nebraska Press.

————. 1982. *Narratology: The Form and Functioning of Narrative*. Berlin; New York: Mouton.

Prince, N. 2003. "Espace domestique, espace fantastique: pour une 'hétérotopologie' du fantastique fin-de-siècle", in: Grassin, J., et al. (eds.) *Littérature et espaces*. Limoges: Presses Universitaires de Limoges.

Rabkin, E. S., et al. (eds.) 1979. *Fantastic Worlds: Myths, Tales and Stories*. Oxford: Oxford University Press.

————. 1977. *The Fantastic in Literature*. Princeton; Guildford: Princeton University Press.

Rasmussen, S. E. 1959. *Experiencing Architecture*. London; Copenhagen: Chapman & Hall.

Reisz, S. 2001. "Las ficciones fantásticas y sus relaciones con otros tipos ficcionales", in Roas, D. (ed.) *Teorías de lo fantástico*. Madrid: Arco/Libros, pp. 193–222.

Richardson, B. 2012. *Borges and Space*. Oxford; New York: Peter Lang.

Ricoeur, P. 1983. *Time and Narrative*. Chicago: University of Chicago Press.

Roas, D. 2012. "Cronologías alteradas. La perversión fantástica del tiempo", in: García F.; Batalha M. C. (eds.) *Vertentes teóricas e ficcionais do insolito*. Rio de Janeiro: Caetes, pp. 106–113.

————. 2011. *Tras los límites de lo real: una definición de lo fantástico*. Madrid: Páginas de Espuma.

————. 2009. "El hombre que (casi) controlaba el mundo. Juan José Millás y lo fantástico", in: Andres-Suárez, I.; Casas, A. (eds.) *Juan José Millás*. Cuadernos de Narrativa colection. Madrid: Arco/Libros, pp. 217–225.

————. 2005. "La persistencia de lo cotidiano. Verosimilitud e incertidumbre fantástica en la narrativa breve de José María Merino", in: Andres-Suárez, I.; Casas, A. (eds.) *José María Merino*. Madrid: Arco/Libros, pp. 133–147.

————. 2001. "La amenaza de lo fantástico", in: Roas, D. (ed.) *Teorías de lo fantástico*. Madrid: Arco/Libros, pp. 7–44.

Roas, D. (ed.) 2003. *Cuentos fantásticos del siglo XIX. (España e Hispanoamérica)*. Madrid: Mare Nostrum.

Roas, D.; Casas, A. (eds.) 2008. *La realidad oculta: cuentos fantásticos españoles del siglo XX*. Palencia: Menoscuarto.

Rodríguez Hernández, T. 2010. "La conspiración fantástica: una aproximación lingüístico-cognitiva a la evolución del género". *Espéculo. Revista de estudios literarios*. Madrid: Universidad Complutense de Madrid.

Ronen, R. 1986. "Space in Fiction". *Poetics Today*, 7 (3), pp. 421–438.

Rotger, N. 2003. "La amenaza que la realidad esté agujereada", *Seminari Tecnologia i posthumanitat: l'artificialitat de l'ésser*. Barcelona: Universitat Autònoma de Barcelona.

Ruskin, J. 1905. *The Poetry of Architecture*. London: George Allen.

Rust, R. D. 1988. "Liminality in the *Turn of the Screw*". *Studies in Short Fiction*, 25 (4), pp. 441–445.

Ruthner, C. 2012. "Fantastic Liminality: A Theory Sketch", in Böger, A. and Schmeink, L. (eds.) *Collisions of Reality: Establishing Research on the Fantastic in Europe*. Berlin: De Gruyter.

Ryan, M. [Online]. Available from: "Space", in Hühn, Peter, et al. (eds.) *The Living Handbook of Narratology*. Hamburg: Hamburg University Press. Available from: http://www.lhn.uni-hamburg.de/article/space [Accessed 07 November 2014].

———. 2006. "From Parallel Universes to Possible Worlds: Ontological Pluralism in Physics, Narratology, and Narrative". *Poetics Today,* 27 (4), pp. 633–674.

———. 1993. "Cognitive Maps and the Construction of Narrative Space", in: Herman, D. (ed.) *Narrative Theory and the Cognitive Sciences.* Stanford, Calif.: CSLI.

———. 1991. *Possible Worlds, Artificial Intelligence and Narrative Theory.* Bloomington: Indiana University Press.

Rykwert, J. 1988. *The Idea of a Town: The Anthropology of Urban Form in Rome, Italy and the Ancient World.* New Jersey: Princeton University Press.

Saldarriaga Roa, A. 2002. *La arquitectura como experiencia.* Colombia: Villegas.

Schuhl, P. M. 1952. *L'imagination et le merveilleux. La pensée et l'action.* Paris: Flammarion.

Simmel, G. 1994. "Bridge and Door", "Brücke und Tür", in: *Das Individuum und die Freiheit. Essais.* Frankfurt am Main: Fischer Taschenbuch Verlag.

Smethurst, P. 2000. *The Postmodern Chronotope: Reading Space and Time in Contemporary Fiction.* Amsterdam: Rodopi.

Soja, E. W. 2000. *Postmetropolis: Critical Studies of Cities and Regions.* Oxford; Malden, Mass.: Blackwell.

———. 1996. *Thirdspace: Journeys to Los Angeles and Other Real-and-Imagined Places.* Oxford; Cambridge, Mass.: Blackwell.

———. 1989. *Postmodern Geographies: The Reassertion of Space in Critical Social Theory.* London: Verso.

Soubeyroux, J. 1993. "Le discours du roman sur l'espace. Approche méthodologique". *Lieux Dits, Cahiers Du GRIAS,* 1, pp. 11–24.

Tally, R. T. 2013. *Spatiality.* New York; London: Routledge.

Tcherepashenets, N. 2008. *Place and Displacement in the Narrative Worlds of Jorge Luis Borges and Julio Cortázar.* New York; Oxford: Peter Lang.

Tegmark, M. 2003. "Parallel Universes". *Scientific American,* pp. 40–51.

Todorov, T. 1975. *The Fantastic: A Structural Approach to a Literary Genre.* Ithaca: Cornell University Press.

Tschumi, B. 1996. *Architecture and Disjunction.* Cambridge, Mass.; London: MIT Press.

Tuan, Y. 1977. *Space and Place: The Perspective of Experience.* London: Edward Arnold.

Turner, V. W. 1969. *The Ritual Process: Structure and Anti-structure.* London: Routledge & K. Paul.

Vasset, P. 2007. *Un livre blanc.* Paris: Fayard.

Vattimo, G. 1988. *The End of Modernity: Nihilism and Hermeneutics in Post-Modern Culture.* Baltimore: John Hopkins University Press.

Vax, L. 1965. *La Séduction de l'étrange.* Paris: P.U.F.

———. 1960. *L'Art et la littérature fantastiques.* Paris: P.U.F.

Vernant, J. P. 1983. *Myth and Thought among the Greeks.* London: Routledge & Kegan Paul.

Vicente, H. 1999. *El vértigo horizontal.* Caracas, Venezuela: Centro de Estudios Latinoamericanos Rómulo Gallegos.

Vidler, A. 1992. *The Architectural Uncanny: Essays in the Modern Unhomely.* London; Cambridge, Mass.: MIT Press.

Villanueva, D. 1997. *Theories of Literary Realism.* Albany: State University of New York Press.

Villoro, J. 2003. "El vértigo horizontal. La ciudad de México como texto", in: Muñoz, S. (ed.) *Más allá de la ciudad letrada: crónicas y espacios urbanos.* Pittsburgh Biblioteca de América, Instituto Internacional de Literatura Iberoamericana. pp. 45–59.

Virilio, P. 1997. "The Overexposed City", in: Leach, N. (ed.) *Rethinking Architecture: A Reader in Cultural Theory.* London: Routledge, pp. 381–390.

———. 1991. *The Lost Dimension.* New York: Semiotext(e).

Warf, B. and Arias, S. (eds.) 2008. *The Spatial Turn: Interdisciplinary Perspectives.* London: Routledge.

Waugh, P. 1984. *Metafiction: The Theory and Practice of Self-Conscious Fiction.* London: Methuen.

Westphal, B. 2011a. *Geocriticism: Real and Fictional Spaces.* New York: Palgrave Macmillan.

———. 2011b. *Le Monde plausible: espace, lieu, carte.* Paris: Éditions de Minuit.

———. 2007. *La Géocritique. Réel, fiction, espace.* Paris: Éditions de Minuit.

Zoran, G. 1984. "Towards a Theory of Space in Narrative". *Poetics Today,* 'The Construction of Reality in Fiction', 5 (2), pp. 309–335.

Index